Teachers and Educational Change

SUNY series,
Restructuring and School Change

H. Dickson Corbett and Betty Lou Whitford, editors

Teachers and Educational Change

The Lived Experience of Secondary School Restructuring

James Nolan Jr. and Denise G. Meister

STATE UNIVERSITY OF NEW YORK PRESS

Published by
State University of New York Press, Albany

For information, address the State University of New York Press,
State University Plaza, Albany, NY 12246

Production by Kristin Milavec
Marketing by Michael Campochiaro

Library of Congress Cataloging-in-Publication Data

Nolan, James F., 1950–
   Teachers and educational change : the lived experience of secondary school
restructuring / James Nolan, Jr., and Denise G. Meister.
      p.   cm. — (SUNY series, restructuring and school change)
   Includes bibliographical references and index.
   ISBN 0-7914-4699-9 (alk. paper) — ISBN 0-7914-4700-6 (pbk. : alk. paper)
   1. High school teachers—United States—Case studies.   2. Educational change—United
States—Case studies.   3. Teacher participation in administration—United States—Case
studies.   4. School improvement programs—United States—Case studies.   I. Meister,
Denise G., 1951–   .   II. Title.   III. Series.

LB1777.2 .N64 2000
373.11'06—dc21   00-026563

10 9 8 7 6 5 4 3 2 1

We dedicate this book to Gary, John, Lew, Martha, Tanya, and the students of Team Apex. They permitted us to enter into their lives, and we became friends. They allowed us to watch their struggles and triumphs, and we tried to understand. They entrusted us to see how much they cared, and we were in awe.

Contents

Part III
Conclusion

Preface

The past decade has seen the publication of literally hundreds of books focused on the topic of educational change. These books run the gamut from step-by-step "how-to's" and reports of individual change efforts to complex analyses of educational policies and practices aimed at school restructuring and reform. Many of these texts portray change as simply a matter of finding the appropriate structures, mind-sets, strategies, and policies. In so doing, however, these texts neglect the human side of change. Others (Fullan, 1991; Evans, 1996; Hargreaves, 1997) present cogent theoretical analyses of the complexity of school restructuring and point out that in its most fundamental form school restructuring always comes down to a question of individual teacher change. Still others (Wasley, 1992; 1994; Lieberman, 1995) offer portraits or cases of selected individuals engaged in school restructuring efforts. Too few texts have offered in-depth stories of school change from the perspective of teachers who are simultaneously the subjects and objects of change (Fullan, 1991). The purpose of this book is to provide such a story.

The story focuses on the lived experience of five secondary teachers who were engaged in a school restructuring effort intended to reform secondary education at their high school by moving from subject-specific curriculum to interdisciplinary teaching, from individual departmental structures to team teaching, and from traditional 45-minute periods to intensive or block scheduling. The book represents the outcome of a year-long research study during which we spent considerable amounts of time "living" with these five teachers. Our goal was to capture and portray as vividly as possible the teachers' experiences during the restructuring implementation and their attempts to make sense of their experience. In doing so, we hope to flesh out and give life to many concepts that are used to analyze and explain school change and to allow the reader to vicariously experience life inside school change.

Because the story is real, it is also complex and multidimensional. In one sense it represents lost opportunities and failed initiatives; in another sense it represents classroom successes and feelings of accomplishments with students. In yet another sense the story depicts insensitivity, ill-thought-out change initiatives, and a very naive understanding of what support for reform means. In still another, the story depicts almost heroic efforts at making things work because of a deep commitment to what is best for students. It would be a mistake to read the text as simply a failed change effort. There were both successes and failures. We hope that the real value of the text lies in the reader's ability to understand how these five teachers experienced the restructuring effort. We intend to enable the reader to make connections between the change strategies that were employed and the resulting consequences for the teachers. We hope that our concrete depiction of this strategy-consequence connection will lead to the development of change strategies that are more fruitful, empowering, and teacher sensitive.

One of the most important understandings that we derived from our study was the interconnectedness of the themes that are depicted throughout the text. Though each of the themes depicted in the various chapters is powerful in its own right, a complete understanding demands that the reader see these themes as an interlocking and mutually reinforcing network of experiences, thoughts, and emotions that exerted a cumulative impact on the teachers. Though the themes are divided into separate chapters, they constitute one comprehensive, unified text of experience for the teachers.

The book is divided into three parts. Part I provides an introduction to the study. Chapter 1 provides an introduction to the setting and the five teachers. Chapter 2 provides a complete description of the research design and the theoretical framework undergirding it.

Part II describes the experience of restructuring as lived by these five teachers. Each chapter presents a different theme, but the themes are powerfully interconnected. The themes are uncertainty, intensification and limited time, lack of administrative leadership, subject loyalty versus team allegiance, and craft pride, caring, and moral purpose.

Part III of the text focuses on our understanding of change and how it is refined and challenged by this study. In particular we pay attention to seven major areas:

- the importance of teacher commitments to their students and their colleagues;

- the relationship between lack of teacher ownership of an initiative and resultant lack of understanding of the initiative;

- the complex, multifaceted nature of collegiality and collaboration;

- the potential role of evaluation in reducing the endemic uncertainty of change;

- the need for teacher teams to feel that they are connected to some larger vision;

- the exhausting nature of trying to balance subject integration and subject separation;

- and the double-edged nature of teacher caring for students in terms of educational change initiatives.

Part 1

Introduction

1

The Context

Whatever contributes to understanding also contributes to reconstruction.

—Willard Waller (1965)

Purpose of the Research

Analysts have noted a cyclical pattern of major reform movements. They erupt every decade or so, then recede to the background leaving the larger educational picture only slightly altered and producing nominal changes in educational practice (Murphy, 1990). A major reason for this problem is the neglect of the phenomenology of change. Failure to understand how people experience change in contrast to how it was intended is at the "heart of the spectacular lack of success of most social reforms" (Fullan, 1991). Bogdan and Biklen (1992) concur:

Change is complicated because beliefs, lifestyles, and behavior come into conflict. People who try to change education, be it in a particular classroom or for the whole system, seldom understand how people involved in the changes think. Consequently, they are unable to accurately anticipate how the participants will react. Since it is the people in the setting who must live with the change, it is their definitions of the situation that are crucial if change is going to work. (P. 200)

Fullan (1991) elucidates that people react to new experiences by attaching their own construction of reality to them regardless of the meaning others assign them. Thus, the implementation of educational change is never fully envisioned until the people in the particular situations attempt to spell them out in use:

In short, one of the basic reasons why planning fails is that planners or decision-makers of change are unaware of the situations that potential implementers are facing. They introduce change without providing the means to identify and confront the situational constraints and without attempting to understand the values, ideas, and experiences of those who are essential for implementing any changes. (P. 96)

Hargreaves and Fullan (1992) explain the critical role teachers play in the change process.

Teachers don't merely deliver the curriculum. They develop, define it and reinterpret it too. It is what teachers think, what teachers believe and what teachers do at the level of the classroom that ultimately shapes the kind of learning that young people get. . . . For teachers, what goes on inside the classroom is closely related to what goes on outside it. The quality, range and flexibility of teachers' classroom work are closely tied up with their professional growth—with the way that they develop as people and as professionals. (P. ix)

In response to calls for research that will enable educators to achieve a deeper understanding of the meaning of educational change for teachers, we designed the study reported in this text to describe and interpret how five secondary teachers, Gary, John, Lew, Martha, and Tanya, defined and made meaning of the change process that they were involved with. The following questions guided our study: What did these teachers experience? How did the teachers understand these experiences? How did their interaction with each other as a team contribute to their understanding of these experiences?

Institutional Setting

The research took place in a small, privately endowed residential school for boys and girls in the central portion of a mid-Atlantic state. Founded in 1909 by a business magnate and his wife and later fully endowed by them, the school provides education and care for students from disadvantaged families. Criteria used to judge disadvantaged children are as follows:

1. They are the "poorest"; that is, the family income is at or below the poverty level defined by the United States government.

2. They are "most alone"; that is, they have one or no parent, they have parents who are incarcerated or incapacitated or incapable of caring for them, or they have been abused or abandoned.

3. They are the "youngest"; that is, they are most apt to benefit through longevity in the program.

Following the Deed of Trust established by the founders, the school initially recruits students from the tristate area in the Mid-Atlantic, followed by recruitment of students across the United States. Currently, children from thirty-six states are represented in the school population. Committed to diversity in the racial, cultural, and gender makeup of the student body, the school includes minorities (56 percent), many of African and Hispanic descent. Females, who comprise 46.7 percent of the population, have been admitted since the 1977–78 school year. The high school, which houses grades nine through twelve, is made up of approximately five hundred students, fifty teachers, one assistant principal, one principal, and numerous support personnel. In addition to the senior high school, there is one elementary school, which houses preschool through fifth grades, and one middle school, which includes grades six through eight.

Adhering to the Deed of Trust, the school encourages early enrollment of children, beginning at age four, and does not accept children sixteen or older. An emphasis is placed on providing skills for job placement after graduation. In addition, the school contributes $5,000 per year for tuition and other expenses as an incentive for those students who wish to attend college.

Because of a concern by the Board of Directors and alumni that the school was moving away from the original intent of the founders' mission—to prepare students for the world of work—the school instituted a strategic plan to emphasize the vocational aspect of the school, as well as to continue preparing interested students for college study. The strategic plan called for a schedule that would give freshmen and sophomores opportunities to explore the following career pathways in the vocational education program: agricultural and environmental education, automotive systems, business and finance, communications technology, construction, health occupations, manufacturing/computer-aided drafting and design, and visual and performing arts. Freshmen were to spend the first semester rotating through all the career pathways in order to sample what each one offered in potential careers. For the second semester, freshmen were to select their three areas of interest for further exploration. Sophomores were to devote one 85-minute block of time every other day exclusively to the one career pathway of their choice.

In order to facilitate this initiative, the ninth- and tenth-grade teachers were informed in the fall of the previous year that they would be involved in a major restructuring program that would be put into effect the following school year. Three components comprised the restructuring: teaming, interdisciplinary teaching, and block scheduling. Both the freshmen and sophomore classes would be divided into two groups with approximately sixty-five students and four core subject teachers of English, mathematics, science, and social studies on each team. In order to accommodate the career cluster of the sophomores, a block schedule was created that divided the former eight-period day (with 45-minute periods) into two four-period days with periods lasting 85 minutes. The school also moved to a six-day schedule cycle. The teachers were to plan an interdisciplinary curriculum for the core subjects and were supposed to devote their planning period on odd numbered schedule days to interdisciplinary team meetings.

At the insistence of the foreign language teachers who feared their positions might be eliminated, administrators included a foreign language teacher as a fifth member on each of the four teams. The ninth- and tenth-grade teachers were told to form their own interdisciplinary teams and were given ten release days during the school year and one hundred paid hours during the summer hiatus to plan for the new curriculum.

We chose to study this particular setting because we believed—at the beginning of the study—that this setting represented a potential best-case scenario for successful restructuring. Several variables led us to this conclusion. First, the school had an enormous endowment that resulted in tremendous monetary resources. The school has the financial resources to do just about whatever it desires. Therefore, lack of funding would not frustrate implementation efforts. Second, this was a private school that was not subject to many state curriculum guidelines and constraints. Even though all of the teachers were properly certificated, the school was under no obligation to live up to state curriculum guidelines. Thus, the school was free to experiment with different types of curriculum and scheduling configurations. Third, this was a residential boarding school with minimal parental involvement in governance. Therefore, there would be no community or parental pressure groups to throw up obstacles to planned restructuring initiatives. Fourth, the small class size, averaging sixteen or seventeen students per class, allowed teachers greater flexibility and room for experimentation. Finally, the central office administrators informed us that the school had a site-based, shared decision-making model that had been used to make the decision to undertake the restructuring initiative. Thus, we believed that teachers had significant input into the decision-making process and were "on board." Though the context failed to live up to its advance billing, these were our reasons for selecting this particular school.

The Teachers

The five teachers in the study come from various backgrounds. Our purpose is to present background information that we believe will help the reader understand some of the actions, interactions, and reactions that occurred throughout the study. Although we did not probe into the detailed life history of the teachers, many times they mentioned their personal lives in relationship to an issue being discussed or during a reflective moment. Our hope is that incorporating this background affords the reader the opportunity to gain insight into the teachers and to add to the rich description of the context.

Lew

Lew, the social studies teacher and team leader, is an African-American (the only minority teacher on the team). In his early forties, he has been teaching freshmen at the school for eighteen years. Besides teaching, he coaches boys' varsity basketball. He arrives at school at 6:30 A.M. and stays until early evening, much later during basketball season. In addition to the ninth-grade teaming, he teaches a class called "Law and Youth," which he created for upperclassmen to examine legal issues that directly affect young people. His wife is a middle school teacher in the same school system, and he has a teenage daughter who attends a public school nearby.

He is a very popular teacher among students of all races and professes that he enjoys his interactions with his students more than any other aspect of his work. He grew up in the inner city and seems to be able to use his firsthand knowledge of tough neighborhoods to understand his students and relate to them. Students call him "hip." Current and former students can always be found in his room during their free time either assisting Lew in his clerical work or just talking with him. He is at ease talking about historical periods or rap music. When asked by a fellow teacher if he was familiar with a rapper whose name now eludes us, Lew quickly gave a short biography of the rapper and noted some song titles. When the teacher said jokingly that he was impressed, Lew responded, "What do you mean? Of course I know him. It's my job to know this stuff. We have to know what the kids are listening to. We have to know where they're coming from."

He balances well his position as teacher and adviser. He is very serious in terms of student learning and achievement and is quick to chide a student who is not meeting expectations that have been set. One particular vignette illustrates this side of Lew's personality. The day after report cards had been issued for the first time during the school year, Lew noticed that some of the students seemed disappointed that their grades were not higher. His hunch was that they felt betrayed by him. They thought he was a caring teacher who would give them high marks because he liked them. As usual, Lew preferred to address the issue head on rather than to skirt it. Lew expressed his feelings like this:

> I can see that some of you are disappointed by your grades. You thought that I would give you higher grades because I like you. Well, you should know that I might love you like a son or a daughter, but it won't make any difference when it comes to your grades. You'll get what you deserve. That's what you can expect from me, from employers and the world, what you deserve. No matter how much I like you or you like me, you have to earn your grades. (Field Notes)

This demeanor, however, does not offend the students, who are aware of his vulnerable side. For example, approximately two weeks before school was to begin for the school year, a recent graduate drowned in a swimming accident in her home state. Lew was instrumental in arranging a memorial service on campus at the start of the school year. A poster that Lew made with a picture of the girl in cap and gown, along with other pictures of her, still hangs on his wall with a caption in large letters, "We will always love you, LaToya."

Lew is a self-proclaimed perfectionist, always anticipating possible problems before they occur. For example, when the team of teachers chose to present their Jurassic Park unit at the regional Council of Teachers of Mathematics Conference, Lew insisted that they meet to practice their individual presentations even though the others felt it was not necessary. Lew also demanded that every detail be exposed and inspected before taking students on a field trip so that they would not be met with any "surprises."

Lew began interdisciplinary teaming with Tanya, the English teacher, three years prior to the mandate to expand the teaming to science, math, and foreign languages. When the mandate for freshman English and social studies teaming was made, Lew approached Tanya, a second-year English teacher, to team with him. Tanya agreed and the two decided to develop a curriculum following Lew's chronological presentation of history from pre–Civil War to the 1950s. Lew expressed success and happiness with the way he and Tanya had been teaming, stating that he was convinced the only way to team is to follow history chronologically, something he learned at a conference many years before.

By the time the study was completed, Lew had decided to give up the "Law and Youth" class in order to commit himself 100 percent to the ninth-grade teaming. He also resigned from basketball coaching in order to pursue a master's degree in American Studies. He did accept the position of coadviser of the senior class and taught remedial school during the summer.

Tanya

Tanya, the English teacher, is in her sixth year of teaching. Now in her late twenties, she came to the school directly from college graduation with her husband, who was pursuing a medical degree at a nearby teaching hospital. During her first two years, she taught literature to upperclassmen. Besides currently teaching freshman English, she coaches the cheerleaders and advises the school newspaper.

She seems very wise and experienced for her years and contributes this maturity to her teaming with Lew. She believes that Lew has taught her to worry about those things that she can control and to fight for those things she believes in, especially if it affects the students. She has stated that she is sure that other faculty and staff are probably surprised at how she has become more outspoken and self-assured since she first arrived. Tanya is a very outgoing individual who has congenial relationships with a large number of colleagues both within the English department and outside of it.

Tanya has found interdisciplinary teaming with Lew fairly easy even though she admits that she had to relinquish some content that she really enjoyed teaching. She believes that the discipline of English allows enough leeway to team with anyone using any theme or unit. She believes that she and Lew have worked very hard over the last several years to put together a quality model of English and social studies teaming and believes the other teachers will have to go through the first year of adjustment as she and Lew had done three years ago.

Tanya's relationship with the students, on the surface, seems more professional than personal. She focuses on student achievement and outcomes and does not seem to become so involved in their personal lives as some of the other teachers. Though she sometimes hides her caring from students, it is evident by watching Tanya that she cares about students deeply. She is the "behind-the-scenes" person who is responsible for all the details that must be completed for their projects and activities to be successful. She is the one, for example, who gets the food for the team parties and orders the supplies for the Ticket Incentive Center (TIC-it) program. She is the one who is willing to add an activity or delete one in order to meet time constraints or team objectives.

The students, too, affect her decisions. For example, she was considering resigning from the position of adviser for the school newspaper at the end of the school year because it was so time-consuming and she felt it was not a quality product in terms of its appearance (typesetting, printing, etc.). However, a senior sent her an e-mail message about how much he enjoyed the newspaper and thanked her for the time that she spent working with the students. This one e-mail message affected her greatly. She decided that if she was only influencing one person, it was enough for her to continue. In addition, she agreed to coadvise the senior class with Lew the next school year.

Of all the teachers, Tanya seems to have the best understanding of models of interdisciplinary teaching and teaming. She seems to be the one who questioned the most in terms of how they were teaming and if there were a better way. All her reflection and understanding may be because she was completing her master's degree in curriculum and instruction during the time of the study, and she utilized her studies to look at interdisciplinary teaming. She was aware of the multiple models of interdisciplinary curriculum that were available in the literature and often asked the administrators to clarify what they had in mind when they talked about moving to an interdisciplinary model.

Although Tanya had talked about beginning the American Studies master's program with Lew after she completed the other degree, she decided not to pursue it. She often talked to us about pursuing a doctoral degree in education at some point in her life, and she talked about her mother who was in the midst of completing a Ph.D. in counseling psychology. She knows that her teaching tenure at the school will probably be short lived because her husband, who is completing a fellowship in internal medicine, wants to move back home to the western part of the state.

John

John has been teaching science at the school for 14 years and chairing the Science Department for four years. In addition, John is chair of the Chemical Hygiene/Safety Committee and is responsible for educating all faculty in safety precautions. Prior to his teaching at this school, he taught in a public school in the central part of the state and also worked as a civilian for the United States Navy. He has always taught environmental science and used to teach a photography course, which he describes as a lab science. He was born and raised and still lives in a town about twenty miles from the school. In his midforties, he is single.

John had an interest in working with Lew and Tanya prior to the mandate of interdisciplinary teaming. He had approached Lew to work together with his "Law and Youth" class, specifically in terms of forensics when Lew was teaching criminal law. Because of time constraints, however, Lew and John never really actively pursued the teaming. John also knew Tanya because the two of them had worked together on some of the theater productions at the school. Because of this previous desire to work together and his role as freshman science teacher, John volunteered to join Lew and Tanya's team.

John maintains a professional rather than personal relationship with the students, and many students did not feel so close to him as they did to some of the other teachers. John has a very dry sense of humor. He often told students that he knew that they were aware that science was by far the most important subject that they could possibly study and that they would like to spend all day in science class. He also talked quite regularly and fondly about his imaginary dog, Einstein. Many students, failing to understand his dry humor, vowed that Einstein really did exist and asserted that John really did believe that they would like to spend all day in science. John's caring for the students seems to take a more academic, rational approach than a nurturing one; yet John has a very caring side to him that is more evident in one-to-one dealings than in a large group setting. He reminds one of the parent who may not openly demonstrate his affection for his children but is the most generous and caring in times of need.

We saw John personally make a handful of his students his "mission," and by the end of the year, they had established a great rapport with him. Although he preferred to keep his altruism private, he shared a moving story with us. In the early spring, we offered to take John to the airport after school. He was flying to St. Louis to attend the National Science Teachers' Association annual conference. When we entered John's room after school to get him, Adam, a student from the Apex team, and an eleventh-grade student were in his room. They were checking the weather in St. Louis on Netscape. Before John left, he asked the boys if they needed a soda or anything. In the car we remarked to John about the progress that he had made with Adam. We told him we remembered in the beginning of the year when John used to chide Adam that he needed more interests than music. John said Adam asked John if he could go to the school's open house (held on a weekend) even though his parents were not coming. John picked up Adam at his student home the day of open house, and they went to Burger King's drive through, one of John's usual stops for coffee on the way to school. He bought Adam a carton of orange juice, which cost one dollar. John made a joke to Adam about the cost, saying that he paid for the convenience of not getting out of the car. Adam, that same day, told Tanya that John spent all his money for a croissant and orange juice. Tanya joked that John had lots of money and Adam should order an expensive lunch if John offered to take him. We were not sure why John shared that story, but we were very touched by it.

During the study, John was completing course work for both a master's degree in education and a certificate for the secondary school principalship. He became very interested in "Systemic Change" and "Continuous Quality Improvement" throughout his course work and often talked in terms of the "big picture." He was also active with the National Science Teachers' Association and often spoke of his alignment with those who advocate for science standards. When an opening for supervising student teachers for a university in partnership with the school became available for the following school year, John took the position. Therefore, although he is still employed by the school and housed in the same building, he is no longer a member of the team.

Gary

Gary, who is in his early forties, has been teaching mathematics at the school for eleven years. Prior to this position, he taught junior high and senior high math for six years in public schools in this state and two years in a private school in the west. He has taught the following subjects: basic math, pre-algebra, Algebra I, Algebra II, trigonometry, geometry, and Algebra III. He also previously chaired the Math Department for two years and was responsible for instituting, writing, and implementing math competency tests that are still administered at the end of each grade in the high school to ascertain if a student is ready for the next level of math. He also coaches boys' varsity track in the spring. He holds a master's degree in education.

Gary was not a member of the team when it first formed. Instead, Marty, a math teacher with 30 years of experience, was placed on the team. Although Marty did not want to be on the team, he was certified in elementary education, not secondary mathematics, and did not feel comfortable teaching higher-level math courses. Thus, he was confined to teaching ninth-grade math. Because he needed to remain at the ninth-grade level, Marty was involuntarily placed on Team Apex. The result of this involuntary placement was unhappiness both on his part and that of the team. A summer of "behind-closed-door politicking" with the principal by Lew resulted in Marty's eventual removal from the team.

A few weeks prior to the start of the school year, Gary replaced Marty on the Apex team. Because of his late entrance onto the team, Gary was not involved in some of the initial deliberations that occurred. He was, however, familiar with the restructuring initiative from his teaching experience in Colorado, where he was part of an interdisciplinary team for one year in the middle school and was involved in block scheduling in the high school.

Gary did not really know the teachers on the team except for John, whom he knew from previously chairing departments together. Gary, however, seemed very easygoing in terms of trying to do what he could to accommodate a team that had already formulated themes prior to his involvement. He had technology skills that proved beneficial for some of the projects that were assigned. He is a no-nonsense kind of teacher whose calm manner seems respected by his students. His caring is most evident in the way he takes time to explain to students why they need to know something and to listen to their concerns and opinions. Students seem to really appreciate his calm, easygoing manner and his day-to-day consistency.

Gary had many incidents, both positive and negative, occur during the course of the study. He ran for department chair and lost by the vote of the high school principal, who had to break the tie vote. This was especially disappointing to him because he had been asked to run for the position by several of his colleagues. He also felt that the Math Department was not being attended to and allowed to move forward. Gary's eight-year-old daughter was diagnosed with diabetes, which is being controlled through insulin injection but still caused much worry and concern. His wife has just completed her studies for the degree of nurse practitioner, enabling the family to relocate if they want.

Martha

Martha, who is in her mid-forties, has been teaching Spanish and French for four years at this school. She has taught levels I and II of Spanish and all four levels of French. Prior to teaching here, she taught seven years in public schools in neighboring states and three years at a school for the blind in a metropolitan area. She also took a few years off before starting her current job to raise her children and earn a master's degree.

A large part of who Martha is involves her younger son who is autistic. Having had a very difficult time becoming pregnant, she was thrilled with the birth of her first son and surprised and thrilled with the birth of her second. She realized early that her second son had severe problems and finally found solace from a doctor in Oregon, who told her that she had to find a school with inclusion, that her son needed to be mainstreamed as soon as possible. One year prior to this meeting, on a lark, she had sent a résumé to the school where she now teaches. Ironically, two weeks after her trip to Oregon, the school called with a position. Martha knew of a nearby school district that was beginning an inclusion program. She and her husband decided that he had to quit his job, and they moved to the district that had begun full inclusion.

Martha's concern for the well being of children supersedes every other aspect of her work. We believe that she cares so genuinely for each and every student simply by her nature, but this nurturance is more intense because of her profound experience with her son. She is a high-energy teacher who may appear scattered to someone of a different nature. She is one of those people who see the glass half full, not half empty.

Martha and the other foreign language teachers advocated for their inclusion on teams that were originally designed to include the four core areas of English, math, science, and social studies. Her department feared that foreign languages might be dropped if they did not belong to a team, and this fear became the impetus for their push to join a team. Martha knew Tanya prior to the teaming and asked Tanya if she could join their team, which is what eventually occurred. Martha vacillated from the belief that interdisciplinary teaming would be easy to the belief that it would be difficult.

Martha plans to stay at this school for the remainder of her teaching career. She serves as a confidante for many students. At the end of the school year, she invited a student who had nowhere to stay after graduation to live with her and her family until college in the fall. She proceeded to help the girl receive a good financial aid package from the college of her choice, and her husband secured a part-time summer job for her where he works. When Martha retires, she and her husband plan to become houseparents at this same boarding school.

Team Apex

By the time school began in late August, these five teachers had become the core of the Apex team. Since they did not know each other well prior to the teaming, they spent much of their preparation time the previous school year and summer in team building activities. They discussed many possible names for their team and eventually chose Apex, using the acronym to represent what the team stood for: accountability, pride, exploration, and excellence.

They adopted the motto, The view from the top is worth the climb, and conducted a contest in the beginning of the school year for students to devise a symbol to represent Apex. The symbol that was chosen was the word Apex written to form a mountain peak.

All team students and teachers received T-shirts that included the following: the team name and the words the letters represented (accountability, pride, exploration, and excellence); the symbol; the motto; and the year of their graduation.

The teachers decided that the most expedient model for interdisciplinary teaming was the one that Lew and Tanya had devised for the English/social studies teaming. They also decided to deviate from this model in order to begin the year with the theme of Jurassic Park. This theme was initiated by John, the science teacher, who had attended a workshop on teaching Jurassic Park as an interdisciplinary unit at a science conference. Throughout the remainder of the year, the teachers integrated other units: Wild West, Immigration, World War I, World War II/Holocaust, and the Fifties.

We began "living" with the teachers on August 21, 1995, their first day back to school, which was an in-service day. Prior to that time, we had met with them twice before. The first time was on March 15, in order to discuss the research project with them. At this meeting they agreed to participate in the study, saying that they had stated from the beginning they wished they could somehow document their experience. They saw their participation in the research study as a good opportunity to have their experience recorded. The second time was on April 5, when one author joined them to visit a high school that was already involved in block scheduling.

When we met with them on August 21, we were struck by how they had blossomed from a tentative group of teachers into a confident team. At this time, we were introduced to Gary, who had replaced the original math teacher sometime over the summer. From talking to them, we got the sense that the majority of their teaching would not be interdisciplinary but would somehow relate to a central theme.

The first day of school with the students, August 22, began with a team meeting. The teachers met with the team in the auditorium following the typical "welcome back" program conducted by the administration. All five teachers, wearing Apex T-shirts, stood on the auditorium floor, eye level with the students. Lew, the team leader, welcomed the students to the high school and to the team. All the teachers talked briefly about their subject areas and how their disciplines related to the team. They spent the afternoon in abbreviated periods with each teacher individually. The teachers also had a team meeting to discuss their reactions to the day. Team Apex, conceived in the spring and developed over the summer was delivered this day, and the remainder of the year would be spent adjusting to its birth and monitoring and nurturing its growth.

School Setting

The school, built in 1934, is a huge, two-story brick building that sits high over a four-lane highway. It truly appears like a "castle on a hill" with its stature and old elegance. Upon entering the school from the main doors, one is in the middle of an impressive rotunda with high ceilings. Directly ahead lies the partly visible open staircase that leads to the second floor of the school. The hallways are wide, and the thick mahogany doors and built-in glass and wooden bookcases add a stately appearance. The classrooms are bright because the building retains the large window areas of old school structures. Realizing that most windows are downsized during the first phase of a building renovation, we were particularly struck by their height and width, as well as the large windowsills and old-fashioned pull-down shades.

All the Apex teachers, except for John, were in proximity to each other on the second floor. John remained on the first floor with the other science teachers since the rooms were equipped for laboratory experiments and the science teachers often shared equipment. The science room was very traditional. The back half of the classroom was set up with long tables for labs, as well as shelving around the two sides and back of the room. The front half of the room held armchair student desks, and the teacher's desk and lab table sat in the front of the room. There was little space to walk between the front of the teacher's desk and lab table and student desks. The front half of the room was tight so that there was more space for the lab section in the back of the room. There were also two very large closets in the classroom that were big enough to actually be offices. There was much evidence that a science teacher inhabited the room: there were rockets that former students had built and launched, charts of the elements, weather information, and two computers and a television.

Leaving John's room one walks a few short steps down the hall and takes a set of stairs up to the second floor where the rest of the teachers from Team Apex reside. Upon leaving the stairway one is immediately greeted by a huge banner proclaiming, Welcome to Team Apex. The hallway between the Team Apex rooms was constantly adorned by student work. Bulletin boards and display cases were used throughout the year to display student projects such as political cartoons, caricatures, poems, dinosaurs, graphs, and posters. Lew's room, which contained a water source, seemed like the size of two rooms. He placed his desk and six computer and individual study carousels on the right side near the back of the room. This side of the room also contained two regular-size closets. The student tables were in the middle of the room, set up to form a horseshoe. Approximately six students sat at one table. When Lew was unhappy with student behavior, he would move all the chairs into straight rows, and everyone would face front toward him. On the left side of the room were reference books, a stereo system, and the television. Lew's entire room was filled with motivational sayings, student work, historical facts, and team building messages. His penchant for collecting globes was obvious as they could be found in every size and shape throughout the entire classroom. He also displayed gifts and cards that had been given to him by students and other teachers.

Martha's and Gary's rooms were similar. They contained tables instead of individual student desks. Both were rectangular in shape. Martha's room was decorated with lots of Spanish and French posters, and she had a table-size puzzle of the Eiffel Tower and a Spanish villa set up at all times so that students could put the puzzles together when they were finished with their required work. Both Gary and Martha had their desks placed to the side of the room.

Tanya's room was a rectangle also, but it contained a side room that the team often used for meetings. There were also a refrigerator and microwave in there for the team teachers to use. The chalkboard in this side room still contained the timeline that the team created, during the summer, showing when the interdisciplinary units were to be taught. Tanya's desk and computer work area were set up behind all the student desks. Tanya taught in the front of the room, using a podium and a high stool. She kept a written monthly calendar on the side chalkboard so that students were aware of all their assignments and activities for the month. She displayed posters of famous writers, as well as posters that contained definitions of literary terms.

All the rooms had telephones, television, and at least one personal computer. All the teachers also had e-mail and seemed to use it as their preferred method of communicating with those outside the team. They also had access to the Internet both on their classroom computers and in the computer lab, which was also on the second floor. The computer lab was shared with the other ninth-grade team. On the first day of school, all the teachers had their rooms decorated for Jurassic Park. Each student locker had a dinosaur placed on it, and all the teachers had dinosaur decorations in their classrooms.

The school itself seemed very quiet. One reason was that there were no bells. The students were dismissed by the teacher and walked out of classrooms rather than dashing out at the sound of the bell. Also, because four of the five team teachers were in proximity, the students did not have far to walk to their next class. Thus, classes began very quickly, much sooner than the usual four-minute period that most schools allow for passing classes. The students also were given much freedom in terms of bathroom privileges and hall privileges. Perhaps with this freedom came a responsibility and maturity.

The only loud part of the school was the cafeteria. Although teachers, administrators, and students tended to eat at separate tables from each other, they mingled in a friendly, casual, but respectful manner that seemed to pervade the school. The cafeteria was a wide-open space with poor acoustics and could get rather loud at times. There was a microphone in there at all times so that announcements could be made.

The building itself was inviting and warm in its old stately way. It lacked the institutional "feel" of more recently built schools. Instead, the corridors and rooms seemed to bear the history and tradition of respect for knowledge and the promising future that education could bring. Perhaps this perceived belief played a major factor in creating an atmosphere of mutual respect and discipline. We felt comfortable there immediately.

2

Research Design

The real voyage of discovery consists not in seeking new landscapes
but in having new eyes.

—Marcel Proust (1981)

Overview

Patton (1990) explains why qualitative methods are ideally
suited to the task of describing program implementation.
He writes that it is important to know the extent to which
a program is effective after it is fully implemented, but to answer
that question it is important to learn the extent to which the program was actually implemented. An effective way to study program
implementation is to gather detailed, descriptive information about
what is occurring in the program; for example, what do the clients
in the program experience? Since program implementation is characterized by a process of adaptation to local conditions, needs, and

interests, the methods used to study implementation must be open-ended, discovery-oriented, and capable of describing developmental processes and program changes. Failure to monitor and describe the nature of implementation can render useless standardized, quantitative measures of program outcomes.

Aligned with Patton's beliefs, we designed a qualitative research case study to describe the meaning the teachers attached to the change process. Merriam (1988) defines a case study as "an examination of a specific phenomenon such as a program, an event, a person, a process, an institution, or a social group" (p. 9). She adds that the case study, in its attempts to uncover the interaction of significant factors characteristic of the phenomenon, seeks holistic description and explanation.

Lincoln and Guba (1985) cite the following advantages of utilizing a case study for the naturalistic researcher:

1. It is better suited for *emic* inquiry (a reconstruction of the participants' constructions).

2. It builds on the reader's tacit knowledge by presenting holistic, lifelike descriptions that permit the reader to experience the context vicariously.

3. It allows for the demonstration of the interplay between the researcher and the participants.

4. It provides the reader an opportunity to probe for trustworthiness.

5. It provides "thick description" requisite for judgments of transferability between the sending and receiving contexts.

6. It provides a grounded assessment of context by communicating contextual information that is grounded in the setting being studied.

By utilizing a case study design, we were able to develop a theoretical framework that assumed multiple realities exist and the world is a function of personal interaction and perception (Merriam, 1988).

Theoretical Framework

This study is based on the assumption that it is possible to discover how people formulate meanings in their lives. By focusing on the questions—"What did these teachers experience?" and "How did the teachers understand these experiences?"—we rooted our study in phenomenological inquiry, a form of interpretive inquiry that focuses on human perceptions, "particularly on the aesthetic qualities of human experience," placing attention on perception itself and the feelings that are immediately evoked (Willis, 1991, p. 173). Research in the phenomenological mode attempts to understand the meaning of events and interactions of ordinary people in particular situations (Bogdan & Biklen, 1992). Patton (1990) explains that interpretation is imperative to an understanding of experience and the experience includes the interpretation. Therefore, phenomenologists focus on how people put together the phenomena they experience in a way to make sense of the world, thereby developing a worldview.

By asking the question—"How did their interactions with each other as a team contribute to their understanding of these experiences?"—we also grounded our study in symbolic interactionism. Fullan (1993a) writes that people learn new patterns of behavior primarily through their interactions with others. Lincoln and Guba (1985) add that humans are always in relationships with one another, so it is impossible to study people without taking the relationships into account. Thus, change either does or does not occur depending on the basis of individual and collective responses to it, implying that shared meaning and shared cognition play significant roles in the change process.

Because of the nature of the changes being implemented, the interdependence of the participants became crucial to the study. In other words, the interplay of how the participants interpreted interdisciplinary teaching as both team members and individuals would affect how the changes were implemented. Bogdan and Biklen (1992) elucidate how human experience is connected to one's interpretation of it by using the example of a movie projector. The educational technologist sees the movie projector as a device to be used to enhance learning. A particular teacher, however, may see it as an object to entertain students. Thus, symbolic interactionism looks at how people create shared meanings through their interactions and how those shared meanings become reality (Marshall & Rossman, 1995; Patton, 1990).

Blumer (1969) writes that three premises are basic to symbolic interactionism. First, human beings act toward things on the basis of the meanings that those things have for them. Second, meanings arise out of the social interaction humans have with others. Third, meanings are managed and modified through an interpretative process used by people in dealing with the things they encounter.

By combining phenomenological inquiry and symbolic interactionism, we worked within the following theoretical framework. Wanting to describe how five teachers defined and made meaning of the change process in which they were involved, we focused on the essence of the shared experience. Meanings, however, arise out of the social interactions that humans have with each other. The interactions in this study were especially crucial since the five teachers had to communicate regularly in order to implement the restructuring initiative. Therefore, in order to describe the experience fully, we had to observe and record their interactions. However, since meanings are eventually arrived at alone by individuals, we needed each teacher to share his or her experience as an individual and then bracket, analyze, and compare the experiences in order to identify the essences of the phenomenon.

Here we describe the following components requisite to this qualitative inquiry: the selection of participants in the inquiry, the processes of data collection and data analysis, and the establishment of trustworthiness. As an initial step, we will make a statement with regard to our perspective by presenting a short history of the development of our interests and values as they are related to the subject of the research.

Researchers' Perspective

Lincoln and Guba (1995) have noted that, although objectivity is the goal of traditional research, it is largely an illusion. They further assert that trying to maintain objectivity while studying human interaction fails the researcher in two ways. First, it does not safeguard the data from the researcher; and second, it prevents the researcher from exploring the most relevant components of the data. Patton (1990) adds: "The ideals of absolute objectivity and value-free science are impossible to attain in practice and of questionable desirability in the first place because they ignore the intrinsically social nature and human purposes of research" (p. 55). Thus, he believes that a researcher's ability to remain neutral with regard to the phenomenon under study is the critical issue. Instead of trying to prove or to manipulate data to arrive at a particular perspective, the researcher has a commitment to understand the world as it is, to recognize the multiple perspectives and complexities as they emerge, and to balance the reporting of the data by including the negative case(s) along with the evidence.

Alberty (as cited in Patton, 1990) explains the researcher's role this way:

> As a documenter, my perspective of a program or a classroom is like my perspective of a landscape. The longer I am in it, the sharper defined become its features, its hills and valleys, forests and fields, and the folds of distance; the more colorful and yet deeply shaded and nuanced in tone it appears; the more my memory of how it looks in other weather, under other skies, and in other seasons, and my knowledge of its living parts, its minute detail, and its history deepen my viewing and valuing of it at any moment. This landscape has constancy in its basic configurations, but is also always changing as circumstances move it and as my perceptions gather. The perspective the documenter offers to others must evoke the constancy, coherence, and integrity of the landscape, and its possibilities for changing its appearance. Without such a perspective, an organization or integration that is both personal and informed by all that has been gathered by myself and by others in the setting—others could not share what I have seen—could not locate familiar landmarks and reflect on them as they exhibit new relationships to one another and to less familiar aspects. All that material, all those observations and records, would be a lifeless and undoubtedly dusty pile. (P. 499)

Our interests, values, and experience with the research problem were a source of motivation for this study. Having taught in the public schools for a number of years, we experienced change personally and witnessed the ways it affected our colleagues. We have also studied the change phenomenon. We have studied it from the perspective of teachers and their voice and from the perspective of educational administration and the school organization with its own culture and norms. Thus, we had a vested interest in the outcome; not in that we expected a certain outcome, but that the interest generated from these personal experiences kept us focused on the details of the inquiry.

From our experiences in the public schools, we are predisposed to the belief that teachers' needs and concerns must be addressed so that change can be implemented successfully. As teachers, we found that most innovations began as top-down mandates often made by district administrators with superficial or no input from the faculty. Because of this lack of collaboration, teachers often did not implement top-down mandates for various reasons. First, many teachers did not have the know-how or the self-motivation to learn how to implement the changes successfully. Second, many teachers resented the administration's disregard for their professional knowledge and insight. Third, veteran teachers believed that the innovations would be discontinued since no one was monitoring or assessing the implementation.

One of us experienced this type of change most vividly when the administration decided to detrack the high school where the author taught and chaired the English Department. Without any input from the teachers, parents, or students, the administrators told the teachers that all classes would be heterogeneously grouped the following school year. Department chairpersons asked for assistance so that teachers could gain skills and confidence in working with heterogeneous groups, yet no resources or time for professional development was provided. Each individual teacher dealt with the change in solitude. Some continued to teach the way they always did, not making any adjustments for the different ability levels. Many chose to teach "to the middle," and a very small percentage attended workshops and read journals to try to learn about instructional strategies, such as cooperative learning. Eventually, many departments found a way to reinstate tracking without labeling it as such. By changing the names of the courses that were offered, teachers were able to channel students back into their original ability groups in order to teach in the way they felt most confident and knowledgeable. This repeat cycle of failed change reinforced the teachers' belief that they only needed to ride the tide of administrative innovation until it fizzled.

We have seen successful implementation of change, however, when teachers were involved in all stages of the innovation. For example, one author was a founding member of the student assistance team at a high school. Although the selection of teachers for the team was made by administrators, teachers had the right to decline the position. The team trained together in an intensive week-long program that was committed to forming strong bonds among team members. Team members then returned to the high school and spent months writing policy and procedures, discussing each aspect in detail. By the time the team was prepared to begin serving the student population, every person on the team had a complete understanding of the procedures, as well as strong ownership in the program.

In addition, our many years as classroom teachers allowed us to utilize our tacit knowledge in this study in three distinct ways. First, it gave us a quick understanding of the teacher culture and the nuances that comprise teachers' work. We did not have to spend a large amount of time in the setting just to understand the vernacular or routine as we would if we had studied an organization unfamiliar to us, such as a hospital or corporation. Second, it allowed us to become quickly entrusted to the teachers since they realized that we had an understanding of their work. Since they sensed that we understood their "shorthand" and vernacular, we became more credible and respected. Third, it helped us organize this book so it would make sense and could relate items in a more meaningful way.

Through an intensive review of the literature regarding the change process, we have ascertained that our feelings are common among teachers who have experienced change by both top-down mandate and collaboration. The literature helped us understand why implementing change is so difficult.

We realized, too, that we needed to constantly balance our viewpoints with the perceptions of the teachers in the study. We accomplished this by keeping the research questions at the forefront, by keeping journals that reflected personal feelings, and by having each other to validate findings and perceptions. In addition, member checks with the participants helped us ascertain that we had separated our views from the teachers' perceptions.

Selection of Participants

We gained access to the site of the study because of an educational partnership between the university where we teach and this particular boarding school. Because of the extensive degree of change that the teachers would be experiencing—teaming, interdisciplinary teaching, and block scheduling—we believed that studying the teachers as they implemented these changes would give insight into the perceptions that teachers have about the implementation of change.

Purposive sampling of teachers is central. The purpose of this sampling was to describe and illustrate what was typical to those unfamiliar with the program—not to generalize about the experiences of all participants (Patton, 1990). According to Erlander, Harris, Skipper, and Allen (1993): "Purposive and directed sampling through human instrumentation increases the range of data exposed and maximizes the researcher's ability to identify emerging themes that take adequate account of contextual conditions and cultural norms" (p. 82). Patton (1990) refers to this as *information-rich cases*, which allow the researcher to learn about issues that are of central importance to the *purpose* of the research.

The sampling design we used was critical case, which Patton (1990) defines as one that can make a point quite dramatically or is, for some reason, particularly important in the scheme of things. He adds that a clue to the existence of a critical case is a statement to the effect that, "if it can't happen here, it can't happen anywhere" or vice versa (p. 174). Patton also discusses that, although studying one critical case does not technically permit broad generalizations to all possible cases, *logical generalizations* can often be made from the weight of evidence produced in studying a single, critical case. He uses an example in physics. In his study of gravity, Galileo wanted to find out if the weight of an object affected the rate of speed at which it would fall. Rather than supplying random objects of different weight in order to generalize, Galileo selected a critical case—the feather. He knew that if a feather fell at the same rate in a vacuum as some other heavier object, he could *logically generalize* from this one critical case to all objects. These findings were useful and *credible* (p. 175).

The school in the study had this critical element. Since it was a private boarding school, there was no outside pressure from parents or community to impede the initiative. Also, since the school had a wealthy endowment, financial resources, a major issue in most restructuring efforts, were not an issue. Additionally, since the school was private, it was not subject to state curriculum guidelines in terms of planned courses. Therefore, the school was in a much better position than most public schools to completely revamp its approach to curriculum. Three potential major stumbling blocks, then, were eliminated and allowed the teachers to concentrate solely on implementing change without outside constraints.

Two other features added to the critical case. One was the teaming aspect. Research demonstrates that successful change is more likely to occur when teachers are involved in collaborative settings (Fullan, 1991; Hargreaves, 1994; Maeroff, 1993). The other component was the small class size. The five teachers were in charge of sixty-five students, with each class averaging thirteen students. The small size would facilitate the restructuring project in terms of numbers, making it easier for the teachers to spend more time with individual students and to plan projects and activities that lent themselves to interdisciplinary group work. In other words, the teachers could be involved in collaborative settings with their students as well as with each other. Therefore, the teaming concept of the restructuring initiative and the small class size lent themselves again to the adage, If it can't happen here, it can't happen anywhere.

From an outside look, this school had the components to implement the restructuring initiative—financial resources, no outside pressure groups, few curriculum restraints, small class size, and teaming that would promote collaboration. Under these circumstances, we believed that we would be able to describe implementation issues that were germane to the phenomenon itself.

In this study the participants were selected with the help of key informants—the assistant superintendent and restructuring project director. Our involvement with the teachers began in March. Earlier that spring, one of the researchers had been told of the restructuring project by the school's assistant superintendent. The restructuring initiative was described as eventually including the entire high school but beginning with the ninth and tenth grades. We told the assistant superintendent of our interest in school change and restructuring and inquired whether there would be any possibility of studying the restructuring process from the point of view of the teachers involved. The reason for selecting this particular school setting was our belief that this context constituted a critical case (as previously discussed). The assistant superintendent was receptive to our inquiry and suggested that he make some internal inquiries and get back to us.

A few weeks later, the assistant superintendent phoned to say that he had informed the restructuring project director of our interest in studying the project and that the director of the project was receptive to our involvement. He also told us to work directly through the restructuring project director, not through the building principal, since the principal would not be the administrative leader of the project. We phoned the restructuring project director and discussed our interest in the study with him. He was very interested in having us study the initiative and promised to set up meetings for us with the various ninth- and tenth-grade interdisciplinary teams so that we could find a team of teachers who would be interested in working with us on the study. He called back a few weeks later to give us a date for meetings with the two ninth-grade teams and advised us that meetings with the tenth-grade teams would be arranged at a later date.

We arrived at the school on a chilly morning in mid–March expecting to meet with the two ninth-grade teams. When we arrived in the main office, we were informed by the project director that only one team was able to meet with us that day. He escorted us to a classroom where we meet Martha. She told us that the team was actually meeting at Tanya's house and told us to get back in our cars and follow her there. After a windy, somewhat convoluted, fifteen-minute drive, we arrived at Tanya's home and introduced ourselves to the five teachers. We explained that our goal was not to evaluate the project but rather to try to understand the restructuring experience from their point of view and to portray it for others to understand as well. We described what our roles would be and also what they would be expected to do. We also apprised them of our plans for protecting their confidentiality. We then answered a few questions and asked if they had any interest in working with us. To our pleasant surprise, the teachers were enthusiastic about having us study them. They said that they had been wondering how to go about documenting the experience and were delighted that we could play that role. They also informed us that they were a bit lost and felt that we might be of some help to them. They had been given ten days of release time to begin planning an interdisciplinary curriculum as well as money to obtain staff development. They described themselves, however, as being at a loss in terms of where to obtain appropriate professional development and where to go for help. They were hoping maybe we could make suggestions. While trying to make clear that our role was to study the process and not to act as facilitators, we did provide a few suggestions about where they might go for help. This dilemma, of attempting to preserve our roles as researchers while at the same time providing help, input, and guidance when the teachers asked for it, was in play throughout the entire study. Our conversation was abruptly ended when the phone rang. Tanya, visibly upset, hung up the receiver and informed the team that the principal was very angry that they had left the building without permission and demanded that they return immediately. The team apologized to us, explained that they had permission to leave the school from the project director, and returned to school immediately. Before leaving, they reiterated their interest in working with us.

During the next month we made repeated phone calls to the project director to attempt to set up meetings with the other ninth- and tenth-grade teams. Finally, we phoned the assistant superintendent to seek his intervention. He informed us that the project director was no longer with the school and that the leadership for the project had been turned over to the high school principal. As it turned out, it became impossible for a variety of reasons to arrange meetings with the other ninth-grade team or the tenth-grade teams. Thus, through attrition, the lone remaining team, the team we had already met, became the focus of the study. We did not see this as an issue, however. We felt the sampling fit the following four criteria requisite for an information-rich case: the purpose of the study, the resources available, the questions being asked, and the constraints being faced (Patton, 1990). We had already met with the teachers and had begun to develop a rapport with them. In addition, they had expressed a desire to participate in the study because they wanted their story documented and told. Thus, we knew they were willing participants, a critical factor in establishing trust during the study and credibility through member checks. Lincoln and Guba (1985) write that meaningful human research without the full understanding and cooperation of the participants is impossible.

Data Collection

The primary purpose of gathering data in naturalistic inquiry is to construct reality in ways that are consistent and compatible with the constructions of a particular setting's inhabitants (Erlander et al., 1991). Thus, the way for us to know what others were experiencing was to find methods of data collection that allowed us to devise procedures and strategies to consider experiences from the participants' perspectives. Therefore, we chose fieldwork as the research instrument.

Erickson (1986, p. 121) writes that the intensive fieldwork requisite to naturalistic inquiry is the best method of research when the following questions must be answered:

1. What is happening, specifically, in social action that takes place in this particular setting?

2. What do these actions mean to those involved in them at the moment the actions take place?

3. How are the people in the immediate setting consistently present to each other as environments for one another's meaningful actions?

4. How is what is happening in this setting as a whole related to happenings at other system levels outside and inside the setting?

5. How do the ways everyday life in this setting is organized compare with other ways of organizing social life in a wide range of settings in other places and at other times?

The answers to these five questions, Erickson continues, are imperative to educational research. The first reason concerns the "invisibility" of everyday life. Erickson explains that we do not realize the patterns of our everyday actions because it is so familiar to us. Citing the anthropologist Clyde Kluckhohn, Erickson uses the aphorism, "The fish would be the last creature to discover water" (p. 121). The second reason is the need for "specific understanding" through documenting the concrete details of practice. Specific details are paramount in order to understand the actions taking place, especially if we are trying to understand the participants' points of view. The third reason is the necessity to consider the "local meaning" that events have for the people involved. Surface similarities can be misleading in educational research. Therefore, when a research issue considers the local meaning of the participants, fieldwork is an appropriate method. The fourth reason is the need for "comparative understanding" of different social settings, explaining that teachers' actions in the classroom and building level are influenced by what transpires in the wider spheres of social organization and cultural patterning. The final reason is the need for "comparative understanding" beyond the immediate circumstances of the local setting, such as examining differences in institutional contexts as an example.

Because the purpose of gathering and analyzing data is to construct a "comprehensive, holistic portrayal" of the social and cultural dimensions of a particular context, each case, site or event must be treated as a unique entity with its own particular meaning (Patton, 1990). We relied on in-depth interviewing, participation, and observation in the setting, document review and field notes, which are the fundamental methods that qualitative researchers rely on for gathering information (Marshall & Rossman, 1995).

In-Depth Interviewing

The purpose of an in-depth interview is to understand the experience of other people and the meaning that they make of that experience (Seidman, 1991). An interview is a useful way to obtain large amounts of data quickly, but the pertinence of the information can only be ascertained if the researcher has constructed meaningful, thought-provoking questions (Erlander et al., 1993; Marshall & Rossman, 1995). Following Seidman's model (1991), we utilized a three-interview series conducted with each participant.

The first set of interviews was conducted in September and focused on the teacher's professional background, the decision-making process leading up to the restructuring decision and the goals of the restructuring effort. The second set of interviews, conducted in January, focused on the implementation process to that point, including successes, failures, problems, and unresolved issues. The third and final set of interviews, conducted during the first week of June, asked the teachers to look back on the process and reflect on it.

Seidman (1991) explains that the third interview may be the most important but it cannot be productive if the foundation for it has not been established in the first two interviews. He expounds:

> Even though it is in the third interview that we focus on the participants' understanding of their experience, through all three interviews participants are making meaning. . . .When we ask participants to reconstruct details of their experience, they are selecting events from their past and in so doing imparting meaning to them. (P. 12)

The in-depth interviews gave us the opportunity to travel back and forth in time. They allowed us to probe into issues that we saw emerging and gave the teachers the opportunity to clarify the meaning they were creating. The interviews also gave us the opportunity to establish credibility. By interviewing each of the five teachers separately, we were able to connect their experiences and check the comments of one teacher against those of the others. Finally, the interviews gave the teachers the opportunity to reflect on their experience and facilitated their understanding of the restructuring initiative and the nature of their work.

Participant Observation

Lincoln and Guba (1985) assert that the advantage of tacit knowledge and the ability to be infinitely adaptable make the human investigator ideal in situations in which the design is emergent because the human "can sense out salient factors, think of ways to follow up on them, and make continuous changes, all while actively engaged in the inquiry itself" (p. 107). In order for the human instrument to use all these abilities to the fullest possible extent, frequent, continuing and meaningful interactions between the investigator and the respondents or other objects of investigation must exist.

In this study we became observers as participants. We spent two or three days a week in the field the first semester and one day a week the second semester. Although the research focused on the teachers' perceptions of implementing change, we observed them teach, participate in team meetings and interact with others. This immersion allowed us to "hear, see, and begin to experience reality as the participants do" (Marshall & Rossman, 1995, p. 79). Although interviews allowed us to travel "back and forth" in time, observation permitted us to discover the "here-and-now interworkings" of the environment via the use of the five human senses (Erlander et al., 1993, p. 94).

By being participants, we believe that the students, as well as everyone else involved in the restructuring, became familiar and comfortable with us. Although this method might have narrowed the data that we collected (Merriam, 1988), in conjunction with the in-depth interviewing previously discussed, we were able to question the data that were unclear or incomplete.

Following the advice of Lincoln and Guba (1985), observations were less structured in the beginning stages of inquiry in order to permit us to expand our knowledge and to develop a sense of what was salient. We realized the challenge of combining participation and observation in order to become capable of understanding the restructuring endeavor as insiders while describing the program for outsiders (Patton, 1990). We found the balance by heeding the advice of Bogdan and Biklen (1992, p. 90) and asking the following question: "Our primary purpose in being here is to collect data. How does what we are doing relate to that goal?"

In retrospect, we are confident that the study would not have been so rich without the participant observation. Our physical presence on site helped us better understand the context within which the restructuring was taking place. It also allowed us to be discovery oriented and inductive in approach (Patton, 1990). By being in the field, we were able to observe the teachers' behavior in their natural surroundings. Without that picture, we would have had to rely only on the participants' words, not their actions. Our presence allowed us to learn things about the participants that they might have been unwilling to discuss in an interview (Patton, 1990). By being in the field, the immediate came to the forefront and became critical data in understanding how the teachers perceived the change process. Finally, our presence allowed us to check findings and probe on an ongoing basis rather than wait until a predetermined time to discuss what transpired and might not have had the same relevance or impact as it did when it occurred.

Document Analysis

As purported by Marshall and Rossman (1995), we supplemented interviewing and participant observation with the analysis of documents produced in the course of everyday events. The term *document* refers to the broad range of written and symbolic records, including historical or journalistic accounts, works of art, photographs, memos, brochures, meeting agendas, notes, and speeches from teachers and others (Erlander et al., 1993). Document analysis was a flexible yet systematic process that allowed our hunches and tentative hypotheses to serve as guides in the discovery of valuable data (Merriam, 1988).

We collected the following documents: minutes from team meetings and curriculum planning sessions; memos to and from team teachers and administrators; e-mail from team teachers; lesson plans and activity guides; photographs of students, projects, and class trips; students' work and reflections; and a draft copy of the school's five-year strategic plan.

Field Notes

After collecting data on site, we recorded notes of what transpired. Patton (1990) writes that field notes should contain everything that the researcher has observed and believes is worth noting. He continues that field notes must contain rich description by including the following aspects: recording the date, the place, those in attendance, a description of the physical setting, the social interactions that occurred, and the activities that have taken place.

Our field notes also included a reflective part that demonstrated a more personal account of the time spent on site. The emphasis was on speculation, feelings, problems, ideas, hunches, impressions, and prejudices. This part also included plans for future research and clarified and corrected mistakes or misunderstandings (Bogdan & Biklen, 1992). Each researcher completed field notes independently and then e-mailed the field notes to the other researcher each week.

Data Analysis

Each of the authors completed the data analysis independently followed by a series of meetings to arrive at a joint interpretation of the data. What follows here is a description of the data interpretation process that we followed. Data analysis is the researcher's process of systematically searching and arranging interview transcripts, field notes and other materials to increase one's understanding of those data and to present the discoveries to others (Bogdan & Biklen, 1992). Strauss and Corbin (1990) add that analysis of the data represents the operations by which data are broken down, conceptualized, and put back together in new ways.

The human instrument allows data to be collected and analyzed in an interactive process (Erlander et al., 1993). This technique mirrors the way that humans solve their daily problems. As soon as data are obtained, tentative meanings are applied to them. When new data are obtained, meaning is revised. Erlander et al. (1993) expound:

Traditional restrictions to ensure objectivity seem to be directed at neutralizing the differences in observational and analytical abilities among researchers by making them largely nonoperational. The naturalistic researcher attempts to develop and maximize them in situations that provide feedback on their efficacy. (P. 39)

Alberty (as cited in Patton, 1990) explains how documentation and analysis are intertwined:

Documentation is based on observation, which is always an individual response both to the phenomena observed and to the broad purposes of observation. In documentation, observation occurs both at the primary level of seeing and recording phenomena and at the secondary levels of reobserving the phenomena through a volume of records and directly, at later moments. Because documentation has as its purpose to offer these observations for reflections and evaluation in such a way as to keep alive and open the potential of the setting, it is essential that observations at both primary and secondary levels be interpreted by those who have made them. The usefulness of the observations to others depends on the documenter rendering them as finely as he or she is able, with as many points of correspondence to both the phenomena and the context of interpretation as possible. Such a rendering will be an interpretation that preserves the phenomena and so does not exclude but rather invites other perspectives. (P. 505)

The data in this study included verbatim transcripts, field notes, documents, and reflexive writings. In order to reduce the data and manipulate them to discover categories, we utilized a combination of Strauss and Corbin's coding procedures and Lincoln and Guba's constant comparison method, which we now present.

Preliminary Readings

After each interview, we listened to the tapes on our drive back and forth from the research site. We also listened to the tapes again when we made corrections for the transcriber. Over the course of the study, we continued to read the interview transcripts and field notes in order to make each subsequent interview protocol contain questions that were specific and probing in light of the previous interview and to hone in on specific situations in our observations and informal conversations with the teachers.

During these readings, we also tried to begin to understand the story from the participants' perspectives and to bracket (Moustakas, 1994) our preconceived ideas and perceptions. We began to analyze in a more in-depth, systematic fashion at the end of the research study.

Organizing the Data

We began by making four sets of all the data: one for safekeeping, one for highlighting and writing ideas, and two for cutting. We color coded the interview transcripts—blue for the first, green for the second, and yellow for the third—in order to refer quickly to the implementation stage the teachers were experiencing at the time of the data collection. We color coded the field notes pink, the documents purple, and our reflections in fluorescent yellow. We then numbered each page consecutively, starting with the interviews. We put the interview data in one notebook and the field notes, documents, and reflections in another.

Open Coding

Our first step of the analysis was to unitize the data, called "open coding" by Strauss and Corbin (1990). We followed Lincoln and Guba (1985), who write that a unit must meet two criteria. First, it must reveal information that is relative to the study and stimulate the researcher to think beyond the particular bit of information. Second, the unit should be the "smallest piece of information about something that can stand by itself—that is, it must be interpretable in the absence of any additional information other than a broad understanding of the context in which the inquiry is carried out" (p. 345).

We began by reading the interview transcripts two times to refamiliarize ourselves with the data. We then read the transcripts a third time, bracketing sentences and paragraphs and placing code or "idea" words in the right margin. Following Strauss and Corbin (1990), during these readings, we asked questions to start identifying concepts and developing them in terms of their properties (traits or attributes that are characteristic or essential to a quality) and dimensions (the location of these properties on a continuum).

During our fourth reading, we began to cut apart the units and put them into categories of ideas, using labels we devised for quick reference. Many of these labels were generated through our reading and understanding of the literature on change or by words or phrases that the teachers repeated. We coded a unit for a provisional category by comparing it with previous units. If it "looked/felt like" (Lincoln & Guba, 1985) a previously coded unit, we put it in that category. If not, we started a new category of ideas. We kept these cut units in shoe boxes, separated by provisional categories of ideas. In situations where the data could possibly fit into two categories, we chose the category of idea that was more prominent. At first, making the decision between two categories was difficult, but it became easier as we worked through each unit of the data. For reference purposes, we also numbered each unit consecutively on the back so that we could quickly locate a unit if necessary. We also noted if the particular unit contained a good quote by placing *Q* on the card and also by recording the interviewee's name, interview number, page number, and line number on a separate sheet of paper.

An interview unit looked like this:

Everything. Overwork. To do the same job that I've always done I couldn't do it this year and that was hard on me. Stress came from being overworked, *20*

from feeling the pull toward school rather than my own family and just day-to-day dealings trying to save programs like the French this winter and what they put us through with the French III and IV. That was all hard.

M, V3, 182   *Inten. Q*

M, V3, 182 refers to the third interview (*V3*) with Martha *(M),* which is located on page 182 of the transcribed data. "Inten." refers to the idea category of intensification, and *Q* means that we might use it as a quote. The "20" on the right side of the unit refers to the twentieth line of transcript on that page. In addition, the number 92 on the back of the unit (unseen on the example) means it is the ninety-second unit categorized.

After we completed open coding of the interviews, we followed the same procedure for the field notes, documents, and reflexive writings. Besides recording the date and page number, we included the following information on the field note units that we cut apart and put into boxes: the date and page number, *TM* for team meeting, *PO* for participant observation during a class period of either observing or talking to the teacher, *L* for lunch, and *C* for general conversation with one of the teachers.

Below is an example of a field note unit:

Lew told me that he and Tanya must have their classes back to back next year. He is frustrated because he cannot get the Wild West museum completed.

Subject Area   FN, PO, *11/2, 393*

"Subject Area" refers to the category of idea. *FN* refers to field note; *PO* refers to participant observation, in this case a conversation with the teacher while we were observing his class; 11/2 refers to the date; 393 refers to the page number of the data. In addition, the number 368, which is on the back of the card (unseen on the example), means that this unit is the three hundred sixty-eighth unit that we categorized.

During this open coding, we also kept two notebooks. In the first notebook, we kept some notes on symbolic interactionism and phenomenological inquiry in order to have them at our finger tips for quick reference. We also recorded how we coded so that we would be able to explain it, step by step, as well as present it for an audit check to demonstrate trustworthiness, which will be explained later in this chapter.

Our second notebook contained two sections. The first was a "theme" book, which really was a book of ideas. In this section, we recorded categories and themes as we saw them emerge. We also used this section to brainstorm category terms, using a thesaurus and rereading some of the literature on change. The second section of this notebook included "memoing" in which we tried to make sense of the units that we had devised. Much of this memoing dealt with why certain incidents occurred and why teachers reacted the way they did to these incidents. We seemed to have an unquenchable thirst for understanding the "why" of what transpired. We felt, however, it was necessary to try to step into the participants' shoes, so to speak, to know what they were feeling. Many times this transfer felt comfortable. Other times, however, particularly when we did not have the same inclination as the teacher, it became more difficult. Thus, memoing helped us to uncover properties of the category, which Lincoln and Guba (1985) write is requisite in order to make it possible to formulate a rule for the assignment of incidents to categories.

The third section of the notebook included our perspectives as we thought they might be emerging as we analyzed the data. We recorded these perspectives when they surfaced so that we were able to sort through them at the end of all the coding. We felt this was another way to ascertain trustworthiness.

Open coding heightened our awareness of the importance and power of semantics. At the end of the open coding process, we had developed twenty-three categories of ideas. They were as follows: curriculum issues, for kids' sake, intrinsic rewards, team obstacles, commitment to team, intensification, time, fears, concerns, relationships, uncertainty, losses, gains, conflict, lack of administrative support, top-down mandate, lack of communication, team formation, goals of restructuring, lack of professional development, balkanization, professional jealousy, and subject-area loyalty.

Axial Coding

After unitizing, "playing" with words in the thesaurus and dictionary, brainstorming, and rereading the literature on change, we were now ready to axial code, which means to put the data back together in new ways by "making connections between a category and its subcategories" (Strauss & Corbin, 1990). Following the suggestions of Strauss and Corbin (1990), we engaged in the following analysis: the terms and conditions that gave rise to the phenomenon, the context in which the phenomenon was embedded, the strategies used to manage and respond to the phenomenon, and the consequence of using those strategies.

We conducted this part of the coding by rereading each cut unit and recording its contents in a type of shorthand of key words or phrases on a sheet of paper, which we kept in a loose leaf notebook for easy manipulation and reference. On this paper we also included the unit number from the back for easy reference.

We were now able to categorize the units in light of the properties generated through open coding. If a unit looked like or felt like the previous one, we put it in the box with the previous one and recorded it on the same sheet of paper as the previous one. If not, we put it in a new box and listed its contents on a new sheet of paper. We put the units that no longer seemed to fit into a specific category in a miscellaneous pile, as suggested by Merriam (1988). This process helped us further focus on the content of each category (Lincoln & Guba, 1985). It was almost like starting the data analysis anew except that we were now intimately involved in the data so that we felt more confident in our coding. As we continued this process, old categories disappeared, and new ones emerged.

At the end of this coding, we had a total of four hundred units in eleven categories, as well as approximately twenty-five uncategorized units in the miscellaneous box. When a unit of data fit into more than one category, we put it into the category where it made the most significant contribution. We put only one unit into two categories because we did not want to destroy the value of categorization (Erlander et al., 1993).

Selective Coding

Selective coding naturally evolved from the axial coding. This final process involved taking all the units that were now categorized in the loose leaf notebook and reviewing all the properties of each unit again. We reread and studied them again, focusing specifically on the categories or themes that had emerged. Through asking the same questions that we asked in axial coding with an even more rigorous approach, we were able to broaden a category by noting possible relationships between major categories along the lines of properties and dimensions. Thus, some of the eleven categories of ideas were subsumed into subcategories of a category.

At this time we checked that the categories were internally consistent with each other but externally distinct from one another. We also followed Patton's (1990) method of prioritizing themes according to salience, credibility, uniqueness and heuristic value. For example, many aspects of the implementation were so impeding that, in reality, the literature would suggest that these teachers would not have genuinely tried to implement the restructuring project. These teachers, however, never stopped doing the best they could under the circumstances. This *uniqueness* to the study becomes an important quality, one we explicate under the theme "Craft Pride."

In order to make a final check of our analysis, we went through each unit one more time, first looking at the unit in the loose leaf notebook, then finding the actual unit on the card. If the unit still met the conditions that were cited above, we entered the unit information on the computer, which was to be used in writing the presentation of the findings. We also noted the word *quote* in bold, capital letters if we believed the unit contained a valuable quote to be included in the book.

Establishing Trustworthiness

All research, both quantitative and qualitative, is concerned with producing valid and reliable knowledge in an ethical manner (Merriam, 1988). The basic issue in relationship to trustworthiness is the following: How can the researcher persuade the audience that the findings of the inquiry are worth taking note of, worth taking account of? What arguments can be made, what criteria invoked, what questions asked, that would be persuasive of this issue (Lincoln & Guba, 1985)?

Qualitative data do not profess to be replicable. Instead, the researcher purposely avoids controlling the conditions and concentrates on noting the complexity of situational contexts and interrelationships as they occur (Marshall & Rossman, 1995). Therefore, trustworthiness is established in naturalistic inquiry by using techniques that "provide truth value through credibility, applicability through transferability, consistency through dependability, and neutrality through confirmability" (Erlander et al., 1993, p. 132).

Marshall and Rossman (1995) write that all research must respond to canons that stand as criteria against which the trustworthiness of the study can be evaluated. These canons can be phrased by asking four questions (Lincoln & Guba, 1985).

First, how credible are the particular findings of the study, and by what criteria can they be judged? *Credibility* means the degree of confidence that the study represents the experiences, perceptions, and stories of the actors being studied. Patton (1990) explains that a credible research strategy requires the researcher to adopt a stance of neutrality regarding the phenomenon under study. This means that the researcher does not set out to prove a particular perspective or manipulate the data to arrive at predisposed truths. Instead, the researcher is committed to understanding the world as it is, to remain true to its complexities and multiple perspectives as they emerge, and to be balanced in reporting the evidence, both confirming and disconfirming. Marshall and Rossman (1995) add that the goal of credibility is to demonstrate that the inquiry has been conducted in such a manner as to ensure that the subject was accurately identified and described. They expound:

> The strength of the qualitative study that aims to explore a problem or describe a setting, a process, a social group, or a pattern of interaction will be its validity. An in-depth description showing the complexities of variables and interactions will be so embedded with data derived from the setting that it cannot help but be valid. Within the parameters of that setting, population, and theoretical framework, the research will be valid. A qualitative researcher should therefore adequately state those parameters, thereby placing boundaries around the study. (P. 143)

Second, how transferable and applicable are these findings to another setting or group of people? *Transferability* is the burden of demonstrating the applicability of one set of findings to another context. This burden, Lincoln and Guba (1985) explain, rests more with the reader who would make the transfer rather than with the original researcher. This construct occurs when the reader wants to apply the findings about the population of interest to a second population of interest believed or presumed sufficiently similar to the first to warrant that application (Marshall & Rossman, 1995). Merriam (1988) adds that the researcher in a case study does not want to know what is generally true of the many, but instead, wants to understand the particular in depth.

Lincoln and Guba (1985) explain how establishing transferability by a researcher in a qualitative study differs from establishing validity in a quantitative study:

> While the conventionalist expects (and is expected) to make relatively precise statements about external validity (expressed, for example, in the form of statistical confidence limits), the naturalist can only set out working hypotheses together with a description of the time and context in which they were found to hold. Whether they hold in some other context, or even in the same context at some other time, is an empirical issue,

the resolution of which depends upon the degree of similarity between sending and receiving (or earlier and later) contexts. Thus, the naturalist cannot specify the external validity of an inquiry; he or she can provide only the thick description necessary to enable someone interested in making a transfer to reach a conclusion about whether transfer can be contemplated as a possibility. (P. 316)

Erlander et al. (1993) add that the naturalistic researcher does not maintain that knowledge gained from one context will not have relevance for other contexts or for the same context in another time frame. Instead, they believe that transferability across contexts may occur because of shared characteristics. Rather than attempting to select isolated variables that are equivalent across contexts, the naturalistic researcher tries to describe in detail the interrelationships and intricacies of the context being studied. The result is a thick description that cannot be replicated but enables observers in other contexts to make tentative judgments about applicability of certain observations for their contexts and to form working hypotheses to guide empirical inquiry in those contexts.

The third question to judge trustworthiness is, how is it assured that the findings be replicated if the study were conducted in the same setting with the same participants? *Dependability* is the researcher's attempt to account for changing conditions in the phenomenon chosen for the study and changes in the design that are created by increasingly refined understanding of the setting (Marshall & Rossman, 1995).

The difference in terms of quantitative and qualitative research is as follows:

Positivist notions of reliability assume an unchanging universe where inquiry could, quite logically, be replicated. This assumption of an unchanging social world is in direct contrast to the qualitative interpretive assumption that the social world is always being constructed, and the concept of replication is itself problematic. (Marshall & Rossman, 1995, p. 145)

Lincoln and Guba (1985) explain that qualitative researchers realize the possibility of "instrumental" unreliability; that is, humans do become fatigued and careless. However, these same researchers are not willing to have charged off to their "unreliability" changes that occur because of changes in the entity being studied or because of changes in the emergent design as insights grow and working hypotheses appear. Therefore, these researchers see reliability as part of a larger set of factors that are associated with observed changes. The researchers, therefore, looking for dependability, seek means for taking into account factors of instability and factors of phenomenal or design-induced change.

Fourth, how is it assured that the findings are reflective of the participants and the inquiry itself rather than a creation of the researcher's biases or prejudices? *Confirmability* captures the traditional concept of objectivity (Marshall & Rossman, 1995). Lincoln and Guba (1985) emphasize the need to ask if the findings of the study could be confirmed by another. They explain that the researcher views confirmability as the move away from the objectivity of the researcher to the data themselves as confirmable. Therefore, the naturalistic researcher does not try to ensure that observations are free from contamination by the researcher but to trust in the confirmability of the data themselves (Erlander et al., 1993).

The following section describes the naturalistic techniques that we employed to establish credibility, transferability, dependability, and confirmability.

Prolonged Engagement

Erlander et al. (1993) explain the significance of prolonged engagement when conducting a case study as follows:

> Prolonged engagement provides a foundation for *credibility* by enabling the researcher to learn the culture of an organization or other social setting over an extended period of time that tempers distortions introduced by particular events or by the newness of researchers and respondents to each other's presence. Prolonged engagement also helps the researcher build trust and develop a rapport with respondents. (P. 133)

Lincoln and Guba (1985) add that the purpose of prolonged engagement is to render the researcher open to multiple influences—the
"mutual shapers and contextual factors"—that impinge on the
phenomenon being studied (p. 304).

We spent about sixty days on site over a nine-month period
during the school year. From August 21 until the Christmas break,
we spent two or three days per week on site. After Christmas, we
spent one day per week until the end of April. During our time on
site, we observed classes and team meetings, which were held every
other day, and ate lunch with the teachers. We also attended all of
their three field trips.

We believe this prolonged engagement allowed the teachers
and us to become well acquainted. Even though we felt welcomed
from the first time that we met the teachers, we found their trust
grew as our time with them continued. The teachers often asked us
to cover their classes or to give opinions about a student's behavior
or an activity they planned. Part of this trust probably emanated
from our understanding of the teacher culture, which comes from
our own classroom teaching experience. We think our teaching
experience might have been evident to them from the beginning,
since we were able to respond to their feelings and understand the
nuances of their work. Knowing the teaching culture saved time
that would otherwise have to be spent learning the vernacular,
decorum, and protocol of the profession. We also believe that they
trusted our professionalism, so they felt comfortable voicing their
concerns about other team members and problems with the restructuring implementation, knowing that their comments would
be kept confidential.

We realized the danger of "going native." Lincoln and Guba
(1985) warn that the longer the researcher is in the field, the more
accepted he or she becomes, the more appreciative of local culture,
the greater the likelihood that professional judgment will be
influenced. There were times when it was difficult to remove our
strong feelings for particular teachers in particular situations. We
were capable, however, of remaining observers rather than participants by reminding ourselves of the reason for being on site and by
not voicing comments that were not pertinent to the study. Through
the member check conducted with the teachers, which will be discussed later in this section, we are confident that we captured the
teachers' stories.

Persistent Observation

Through our prolonged engagement on site, we were also able to assure *credibility* by conducting persistent observation, defined as accentuating "that presence by actively seeking out sources of data identified by the researcher's own emergent design" (Erlander et al., 1993, p. 136).

The initial time planned to spend on site for this study was four months. However, already in October, we realized that four months would not be sufficient time to understand the teachers' perceptions about implementing the restructuring project. By extending the time in the field, we avoided premature closure. For example, one of the major issues with which we grappled was trying to understand why three of the teachers (science, math, and foreign language) continued to work so diligently on an implementation model that was not designed to fit their subject areas. If we had not engaged in persistent observation over a prolonged period of time, we would have reported the premature closure that they continued because they were unfamiliar with interdisciplinary curriculum and were floundering as all novices do. However, through probing, questioning, and watching the teachers' interactions, we were able to ascertain that the difficulty created was not only from the newness of the innovation, but also largely from the tension created between wanting to stay loyal to their subject discipline and to stay committed to the team. This finding, which became a theme of the study, was difficult for the teachers to articulate because of their own inability to name it or recognize/admit it in the early stages of implementation.

Triangulation

Lincoln and Guba (1985) write that triangulation is directed at the judgment of the accuracy of specific data items. They add that each piece of information in a study should be expanded by at least one other source, such as a second interview or a second method. We engaged in triangulation, which leads to *credibility* and *confirmability,* by using multiple sources of data and methods, as well as conducting three in-depth interviews.

Data sources included the following: interviews, participant observation, documents, and reflexive journals. Every unit that was enumerated in the coding process could be found throughout the various methods of data collection. Although we began the analysis for units with the interviewing data, we could not describe the results so richly or feel so confident with the analysis without the field notes, documents, and journal entries to validate the category ideas that eventually emerged into themes. The time spent on site as a participant observer was invaluable in terms of understanding the teachers' perceptions firsthand. Interviewing alone would have rendered, at most, a vicarious experience. Instead, we came closer to realizing the phenomenon ourselves.

Seidman (1991) writes that the three-interview structure incorporates features that enhance the accomplishment of internal validity (*credibility*). By conducting three interviews over a period of nine months (final interview was conducted during the first week of June, one month after the final participant observation), we were able to clarify, probe and tease out new categories that we saw emerging, to place participants' comments and actions in context, to probe areas that surfaced anew or needed to be reexamined, and to allow the teachers to make sense of their experience to themselves as well as to us. This latter advantage alone is a critical factor in establishing internal validity or *credibility* (Seidman, 1991). Finally, by asking all five teachers the same questions in the three interviews, we were able to understand how the teachers were making sense of their experience, which was the purpose of the research.

Referential Adequacy Materials

Referential adequacy materials, which we have labeled "documents" throughout the study, support *credibility* by providing "context-rich, holistic materials that provide background meaning to support data analysis, interpretations, and audit" (Erlander et al., 1993, p. 139). The documents that were collected included the following: minutes from team meetings and curriculum planning sessions; memos to and from the teachers and the administrators; e-mail from the teachers; lesson plans and activity guides; photographs of students, projects and class trips; students' work and reflections; and a draft copy of the school's five-year strategic plan.

Member Checking

Member checking, which Lincoln and Guba (1985) believe is the most important technique in establishing *credibility,* allows the teachers in the study to test categories, interpretations, and conclusions. Unless the researcher has reasons to doubt the integrity of the participants, the member check is a reasonably valid way to establish the meaningfulness of the findings and interpretation.

Erlander et al. (1993) add that credibility must be established with the individuals and groups who have supplied the data for the inquiry:

> It [credibility] is assessed by determining whether the description developed through inquiry in a particular setting "rings true" for those persons who are members of that setting. Because these persons represent different constructed realities, a credible outcome is one that adequately represents both the areas in which these realities converge and the points on which they diverge. A credible inquiry generally has the effect on its readers of a mosaic image, often imprecise in terms of defining boundaries and specific relationships but very rich in providing depth of meaning and richness of understanding.
>
> Because the major concern in establishing credibility is interpreting the constructed realities that exist in the context being studied and because these realities exist in the minds of people in the context, attention must be directed to gaining a comprehensive intensive interpretation of these realities that will be affirmed by the people in the context. (P. 30)

Member checking, then, differs from triangulation in this way. Triangulation is a process carried out with respect to *data*—items of information derived from one source checked against another source. Member checking, however, is a process carried out with respect to *constructions* (Lincoln & Guba, 1985).

We conducted informal member checks throughout the duration of the study. Because of the participant observation over a prolonged period of time, we were able to have teachers clarify or expound on something they previously said or did. Also, through utilizing the three in-depth interviews, we could verify interpretations from data

collected in earlier interviews. We did this by summarizing perceptions that emerged from the previous interviews and asking the
teachers if these perceptions were accurate, and if so, if they still
held true.

We conducted two formal member checks, one in March when
we were nearing the end of the data collection process and one in
October after we had analyzed all the data. We approached both
meetings with some trepidation. Following the advice of Lincoln
and Guba (1985), we reminded them prior to the meetings of the
purpose of the research study and the method that was used. We
also told them that we needed feedback from them on three levels:
judgment of the overall credibility, statements about major concerns or issues that they might have, and statements about factual
or interpretive errors that they detected. Since they often were
looking for a validation of their program, we reminded them that
our study was not an evaluation of their implementation procedures. This factor was difficult for them to understand even though
it was made clear to them throughout the course of the study.

All five team members attended both meetings even though the
science teacher was no longer a part of the team in October. At the
meetings we gave them a detailed explanation of our theoretical
framework, which showed how five teachers united and decided to
use the interdisciplinary model that was already being utilized by
the social studies and English teachers, and how their interactions
with each other and their own self-reflection led to their perceptions about the change process they had undergone. We reviewed
the themes and subthemes with them, using specific examples and
quotes to demonstrate the themes.

John expressed a concern with a theme we had labeled, "Lack
of Administrative Support" during the final member check in October. He was afraid that the theme label implied that the administration did not support them financially. We asked if changing the
word "support" to "leadership" would be more fitting. Even though
the other teachers took no exception with the word "support," John
felt more comfortable with it, and so did we. Therefore, we changed
the theme name to "Lack of Administrative Leadership."

All five teachers agreed that we had captured the essence of
their experience. The social studies teacher put it most succinctly
and pointedly when he said, "This is a mirror image of what we
went through. I have no qualms with it."

Reflexive Journal

The reflexive journal supports not only the *credibility* of the study but also the *dependability, confirmability,* and *transferability* (Erlander et al., 1993). Lincoln and Guba (1985) view the reflexive journal as a way to record information pertaining to method and self-reflection:

> With respect to self, the reflexive journal might be thought of as providing the same kind of data about the human instrument that is often provided by the paper-and-pencil or brass instruments used in conventional studies. With respect to method, the journal provides information about methodological decisions made and the reasons for making them—information also of great import to the auditor. (P. 327)

The purpose of our reflexive journals was threefold. One, it helped us remember specific feelings we had concerning events that occurred. Two, it helped us sort out why certain incidents were transpiring and if our own perceptions could be misleading us. Three, it helped us formulate ideas and generate questions.

Most of our entries were posted to the field notes that we wrote. Some were recorded on tape recorders as we drove home from the site. Some were written longhand. It seems as if the journals did not necessarily make everything clear, but it did seem to bring us to a deeper level of understanding or questioning as we conducted the study.

Thick Description

Thick description provides for transferability by describing in "multiple low-level abstractions the data base from which *transferability* judgments may be made by potential appliers" (Erlander et al., 1993, p. 145). Lincoln and Guba (1985, p. 125) add, "The description must specify everything that a reader may need to know in order to understand the findings (findings are *not* part of the thick description, although they must be interpreted in the terms of the factors thickly described)." Finally, Patton (1990) writes that discipline and rigor of qualitative research analysis depends on presenting solid, descriptive data in such a way that readers can understand and draw their own interpretation.

Through our prolonged engagement on site, we are able to describe fully the setting and the participants. We have tried to capture the feeling of what it was like to actually be in the particular context. Thick description made it easier for the readers to experience the change phenomenon vicariously through the participants' experiences and to draw inferences concerning the match of this particular case to their own context.

Merriam (1988) writes that external validity (*transferability*) is the most difficult to ascertain in qualitative research, but also adds that it may be just as difficult in quantitative research:

> The question of generalizability, however, has beset case study investigators for some time. Part of the difficulty lies in thinking of generalizability in the same way as do investigators using experimental or correlational designs. In these situations, ability to generalize to other settings or people is ensured through a priori conditions such as assumptions or equivalency between the sample and population from which it was drawn, control of sample size, random sampling, and so on. Even in these circumstances, generalizations are made within specified levels of confidence. (P. 173)

Through rich description, we are not searching for abstract universals but for concrete universals arrived at by studying a specific case in detail (Erickson, 1986). The general can be found in the particular. Erickson (1986) makes this point with regard to teaching:

> When we see a particular instance of a teacher teaching, some aspects of what occurs are absolutely generic, that is, they apply cross-culturally and across human history to all teaching situations. This would be true despite tremendous variation in those situations—teaching that occurs outside school, teaching in other societies, teaching in which the teacher is much younger than the learners, teaching in Urdu, in Finnish, or in a mathematical language, teaching narrowly construed cognitive skills, or broadly construed social attitudes and beliefs . . .
>
> Each instance of a classroom is seen as its own unique system, which nonetheless displays universal properties of teach-

ing. These properties are manifested in the concrete, however, not in the abstract. (P. 130)

Kennedy states, "The researcher need not be concerned with generalizing—it should be left to those 'who wish to apply the findings to their own situations'" (Merriam 1988, p. 177). Given this statement, we, as researchers, are concerned with presenting enough detail about the study—the phenomenon, the context, the research design, and the research process—so that the readers can make their own informed generalizations and apply the information to their particular situations (Lincoln & Guba, 1985; Merriam, 1988).

Audit Trail

The audit trail leads to *dependability* and *confirmability* by allowing an auditor to determine the trustworthiness of the study (Erlander et al., 1993). Following the advice of Lincoln and Guba (1985), we kept the following materials: raw data of interviews, field notes, and documents; data reduction and analysis procedures, including the unit cards, the categories established in the loose leaf notebook, the final categories on the computer printouts, the small notebooks that contain notes on themes, ideas for themes, and procedures of data analysis; and materials relating to intentions and dispositions, such as journal entries and memoing.

Given this explanation of the research study and an introduction to the school setting, we are now able to turn to the experience of restructuring for these five teachers. As noted in the preface, the chapters in the text are linear and separated from each other. In reality, however, the themes are intertwined and mutually reinforcing. They constitute a powerful web of experiences, thoughts, and emotions.

Part 2

The Restructuring Experience

3

Uncertainty

> Ultimately the transformation of subjective realities is the essence
> of change.
>
> —M. Fullan (1991)

Overview

One of the most pervasive themes throughout the nine-month study was uncertainty, which was articulated from the inception of the restructuring project to the last interview that we conducted with the teachers. Lortie (1975, p. 136) writes: "The teacher's craft is masked by the absence of unclear models for emulation, unclear lines of influence, multiple and controversial criteria, ambiguity about assessment timing, and instability in the product." Rosenholtz (as cited in Hargreaves, 1994) agrees, describing uncertainty as the lack of unclear agreement, common definition, or collective confidence in shared teaching technologies.

Maeroff (1993) adds that it is common for teachers to struggle with the following questions when they embark on a new innovation:

1. Why are we changing?

2. What are we worried about losing or leaving behind?

3. What are we most uncertain about?

4. What do we have to unlearn?

5. What are we committing ourselves to?

He concludes from his research that all these questions formulate teacher uncertainty—about the curriculum, about the way to assess, and about the best way to use time.

In addition, imposed change can create loss of purpose and direction, undermining teachers' framework of reality. This situation is especially true if the imposed change affects the things that the teachers value most. Sikes (1992) explains:

> This is not to say that teachers' values are necessarily "right" or for the greatest good of the greatest number of people. Nevertheless, whatever the case, their perceptions and experiences will be influenced by the extent to which there is congruence between their aims, purposes, values and those pertaining in the systems where they are employed. (P. 41)

These endemic uncertainties of teaching and implementing change were exaggerated during this study because of three distinct issues surrounding the restructuring project: the administration imposed the changes without including teacher input; the school had a history of adopting trends and then abandoning them without warning; and no written curriculum existed for discipline-based or interdisciplinary teaching.

Lack of Teacher Input into Decision Making

The teachers never knew or understood the goals of the restructuring project. All the teachers articulated possible goals of the restructuring project with each one giving a different goal. These are the goals that the teachers thought might have prompted the decision to undertake the restructuring project: to raise college board scores, to teach the students life skills, to show students the application to theories they learn, to model teaching blocks of time from higher education, to be trendy, to assist students in the transition from school to work, to offer more courses, and to improve education. One teacher actually seemed perplexed by the question and added "Is that the right answer?" to the end of her goal statement as if perhaps there were a right answer and she hoped she knew it.

The only teacher who seemed to be remotely knowledgeable about one phase of the restructuring, the block scheduling, was John, who believed his position as chair of the Science Department resulted in his inclusion on visits to schools that were engaged in block scheduling. He explained that the members of the Science Department advocated for block scheduling because it would provide them with ample time for conducting laboratory projects in tandem with lecture. He did not know, however, how the interdisciplinary teaming fit into the block scheduling scheme or how it became a part of the initiative.

The same uncertainty prevailed when the teachers were asked to explain how the teams were formed. All were able to articulate that the freshman and sophomore classes were to be teamed and that the teachers were to join teams voluntarily or be placed on a team by the administration. This administrative decree of joining voluntarily or forcibly became a catch-22 for many of the teachers. They did not know each other's teaching beliefs and values. They hardly knew each other personally, yet they felt they would rather join a team than be placed on one. Martha explained the final result for the formation of Apex:

> That is how we teamed. It was through the back door. We didn't know each other. The other team [of ninth grade teachers], all five of them knew each other. So, we had a little slow start in the beginning. (Interview 1)

Tanya and Lew, the English and social studies teachers who were already teaming, were forced to expand their team if they wanted to continue teaching freshmen. They had to protect what they had spent three years building by finding volunteers to join their team and hope these new members would adapt to their program. The risk was that if the new team members rejected their approach, it would invalidate what they had been doing in the name of inter-disciplinary teaming for the past three years. This risk was com-plicated by the fact that the other ninth-grade English and social studies teachers, who had also been teaming for the last three years, were also looking for three new members to join their team. Since both of these dyads had different philosophies of education and teaching styles, a competition to form the best team was ini-tiated, something that escalated throughout the course of the imple-mentation and will be discussed in detail in chapter 5.

Martha, as well as the other foreign language teachers, faced the dilemma of not originally being part of the teaming process. The department feared that these new teams, depicting the core subjects as English, math, science, and social studies, were the beginning of the elimination of foreign language completely from the school program. This conclusion was a result of the lack of communication between the administration and the faculty in terms of the goals of the restructuring project and the school's past history of change. Martha explained that the Foreign Lan-guage Department became suspicious of losing a teacher the pre-vious year when the administration, on the mandate of the Board of Trustees, put an emphasis on agricultural science and technol-ogy. They were convinced that no foreign language teacher was furloughed only because one foreign language teacher accepted a supervisory position in the school. They were also convinced their concerns were well founded, too, since this woman's teaching position was not filled.

Because of this fear and uncertainty, the Foreign Language Department asked the administration to allow them to join teams. Although their addition to the team added an extra scheduling burden, the administration agreed. When asked how Martha then found a team, she re-created the sense of urgency and uncertainty that she felt:

> They announced it and within thirty seconds the other team [ninth grade] was picked. I went across to A [another foreign language teacher] and said, "A, what's going on?" She said, "All I know is I'm on a team." A was afraid that the Foreign Language Department would be ignored in the whole process, so she was ecstatic to have S and J come to her and say, "Will you be on our team?" She said yes right away cause she was

really happy they weren't discarding foreign languages as a valuable part of ninth grade. Our team, I went running around deciding who I could work with because I wanted to team, and I think I was ahead . . . I know W did not and D also did some legwork. She went to a tenth grade group. We didn't know which grades were going to have foreign language teachers. I went and talked to R [tenth-grade team member], and I said I could be on your team. . . . He said yes. . . . I never once had gone to Lew because I didn't know him that well, but I bounced it off Tanya and she said yes, fine. Then we found out it [interdisciplinary teaming] was only going to be in ninth grade. I sent forth this proposal at a Foreign Language Department meeting that said that we had to have two foreign language teachers on each team. There was no other way it was going to work and that we were all in agreement, and the principal came into a meeting and said no way. It was going to be one teacher per team per discipline, and of course he already had to back off and let B be with A, but we really could have used D on our team to pick up the slack. (Interview 1)

Lew supports Martha's story of how she became a member of the team but puts a different perspective on the subject:

I really don't know when Martha got on our team. Tanya said to me, "Did you hear we have a new team member?" and I said, "Who?" She said, "Martha came to me and said she is on our team. So I said, "Oh, really? Why?" Because I didn't even know the foreign languages were going to be involved. That's how the lack of communication is around here. We didn't even know that foreign language was a part of it, which we're still not so happy about, but not with Martha, but with the fact that foreign language brings another variable into the picture that allows our kids not to be our kids because they have to take Spanish, German, or French that determines where they may or may not go [in terms of forming the student teams]. (Interview 1)

John's inclusion on the team was, by his own admission, with a little prodding from the administration. John explains his addition to the team as follows:

I was walking down the hallway one time, and the principal said to me, "Well, what's it going to be?" I didn't know what he was talking about. I said, "What do you mean, what's it going to be?" [The principal said,] "Well these people signed up to be on a team. Are you going to be on a team, or aren't you going to be on a team?" It was supposedly a voluntary thing, but being that in the past two years I have taught mostly freshman classes, I felt like I would stick with freshmen, and being that most of the other science teachers already had their schedules and already were set in with their curriculum and what they were teaching, I wasn't going to hop out of this and go to something else, so I just, more or less, kind of fell into it. (Interview 1)

Gary recalled that he originally wanted to be a member of the team, but the math position had already been filled by a veteran teacher who had an elementary education teaching certificate and did not want to teach any levels of math above ninth grade. This veteran teacher, however, was unhappy with the teaming situation, and the administration, at the prodding of the other Apex teachers, allowed him to withdraw from the team and still teach basic levels of math. Gary then joined the team and thinks that the formation was "somewhat voluntary."

One thing the teachers did agree on was that the faculty members never had the opportunity to vote if they wanted the initiative or not, nor did they have the opportunity for any real discussion or debate about the merits of the restructuring initiative. By having no input into the decision-making process, the teachers felt confused and hurt. Lew captured the teachers' feelings. When asked if the teachers had any input into the decision to restructure, Lew said, "Not at all, not at all, and you will find that to be the case in, like I said, most of the things that are passed down to us, and that is what keeps a lot of dissension, and that is what keeps a lot of indifference, to tell you the truth" (Interview 1).

Lew's comments parallel the admonitions of Bolman and Deal (1991), Fullan (1991), and Sikes (1992) who write that teachers lose their sense of meaning and their confidence in knowing what to do when change is imposed. Lew reflected:

A lot of decisions are made for us and kind of thrust upon us and it is kind of interesting because I guarantee you right now most of the faculty don't have any idea what we are doing or what we are trying to do and that is sad, too. It is almost like we are an island to ourselves. We just kind of got pushed off to the side. We do what it is that we're trying to do, and then my concern is, who is really checking to see if we are really on target or if there is a target. I don't know. (Interview 1)

Even at the end of the school year, when the teachers were approached to make scheduling recommendations for the next year, their advice was ignored, making them feel their opinions and expertise were meaningless. According to Barth (1990) teachers make decisions hundreds of times a day; yet they are excluded from important decisions that directly affect them, which produces feelings of inefficacy and isolation that erode the profession. The one scheduling request dealt with their desire to have sufficient individual planning time during each six-day schedule cycle. The teachers felt that they had lost planning time because of teaming. Every teacher in the school who was not teaming had one individual planning period each school day. Since the Apex teachers were teaming, they had to devote their individual planning period every other day to teaming, which left them with only three individual planning periods per six-day cycle to prepare for their own individual classes or departments or other duties. The administration acknowledged that they already knew this problem existed but did not know how to remedy it. When the team devised a solution, the administration agreed to it, but reneged one month later when they realized the extra planning time added a burden to the noncore subject areas. The team felt that they were ignored and that the administration could have dealt with the inequity other ways, such as having other teachers facilitate the student activity periods that were held at the end of even-numbered days of the schedule cycle.

The second scheduling request dealt with the grouping of the freshmen as sophomores the following year. The teachers believed that the students from the two ninth-grade teams should be mixed together to form tenth-grade teams instead of being kept together as intact teams for both ninth and tenth grades. They felt it was important for the students to mix with other students and wanted to lessen the possibility of homogeneous grouping, not by ability but in terms of the learning experiences the students would be having. The teachers realized that the students in the two ninth-grade teams were experiencing different teaching styles and content and that it was imperative to mix the students in tenth grade so that they all had a variety of learning opportunities. The administration seemed to agree at first, but ended up keeping the teams intact for the following school year. The teachers were convinced this was done for reasons of convenience and that, once again, their professional expertise did not count.

This continued neglect of the teachers' voices throughout the implementation of the restructuring program magnified the teachers' uncertainty in both the purpose of the restructuring and their effectiveness in carrying it out. This constant uncertainty offers support for Sikes's claim that, regardless of the factors that motivate change, teachers infer from imposed change that their teaching is not appropriate or adequate (1992). This inference, especially when compounded with a mandate that has no clearly articulated goals, adds to the doubt that teachers have when trying to ascertain if they are effectively teaching their students. The paradox is that teachers, who are marginal participants in the overall discussions about restructuring, are the key figures in whether that restructuring makes a difference for the students (Webb, Corbett, & Wilson, 1993). How the restructuring affects the students directly relates to how the teachers view the changes and translate the ideas into classroom practice.

History of Adopting Trends

The Apex teachers perceived that they were part of a culture which had a long history of initiating change without asking for teacher input, without communicating goals, without planning any kind of assessment, and then abandoning the innovation in a similar fashion. This history of adopting and dropping innovations led to teacher skepticism and more uncertainty. Three distinct features highlighted the importance this tradition had on the teachers' feelings and concerns: the trend to jump on and off the bandwagon of innovations, the lack of evaluation of any programs, and the tendency to incorporate too many changes at one time.

The school's tendency to adopt multiple innovations simultaneously seemed to have roots in the restructuring of the entire system that took place six years prior to our study. At that time, the president resigned, and high-level administrators, such as the heads of finance, residential life, food service, and admissions, were fired. Even though the new president vowed there would be no more dismissals, people were wary. This fear resulted in the teachers' and the houseparents' forming unions to protect their positions from being eliminated arbitrarily. During the six-year period since that time, new administrators seemed to come and go, each initiating a program and leaving either before its actual implementation or during the early stages of implementation. The departure of the restructuring project director mentioned in chapter 2 is a prime example.

Some of the teachers said they felt they had a voice in education prior to this change in administration and also stated that the old administration took a more active interest in the teachers and the students. They said the former administrators used to visit their building, observe their classes, and talk to them about their concerns. Now things seemed to happen whimsically, such as the hiring of 26 new faculty two years prior to this study so that the school could put more emphasis on academics and college preparation. This emphasis on college preparation angered the alumni, who stated that the Deed of Trust was being broken because the mission of the school is to prepare students in technical skills and trades for the work world after high school.

This alumni concern led to a court mandate that the school return to its career focus. With this new mandate came talk of career clusters and hands-on learning. Many newly hired academic subject-area teachers feared they would lose their jobs. This vicious cycle continued. At the end of the nine-month study, two of the administrators who initiated the restructuring had resigned, and the vocational director had been moved to another position after receiving a poor performance review. The vocational teachers had written three different curriculum guides over the past three years under this administrator's direction.

The teachers were able to recite a litany of innovations that had come and gone over the past six years. Tanya captured the past history of change in a simile: "Things do change like lightning around here. You can blink and something is different" (Interview 1). She continued to explain that she and Lew did not even take the mandate to form five-person interdisciplinary teams seriously at first, ignoring the request to form teams:

The other team actively recruited. Lew and I thought this might pass as other things have passed. We were going to do outcomes and they [the administrators] passed on them for four years and then they came back to them. And we are going to do peer observation and evaluation. It happened and kind of faded. So we thought—maybe I did at least—if we ignore it, they will ignore it, and they did until it was the deadline and it was, well, get a team. So at that point we got a team. (Interview 1)

John cited that the school had gone through so many changes over the last couple of years that did not seem to have any rhyme or reason. Martha added that all the teachers were so wary of this new initiative that they asked the administration to make a four- or five-year commitment to it and then evaluate it for its effectiveness. Gary felt that the pattern was to start some programs and then drop them a year or two later without evaluating their worth.

Tanya described her need for time to implement an innovation and feel successful with the results, using her teaming experience with Lew as an example:

The second year started to make sense that we could actually bring the curriculums together, and we started to do that with some of the projects that we had begun, and, ironically, by the third year we were happy. We now saw where it totally made sense that English and social studies had a total connection and that we could teach throughout the curriculum using the two disciplines. But then, as always around here, they came in with another idea and said now let's expand it to the five interdisciplinary groups and that created a different problem in itself. (Interview 1)

Numerous changes that transpired at the beginning of this endeavor added to the ambiguity. John explained:

We kept changing. We weren't sure what we would have to work with, and then we were told one thing about computers and then another thing about computers. It all worked out, but had we up front been told, this is what it would be and we could've planned from there, and these are the people on the team and these are the people you will work with, we could've planned from there, and not have people be changed and not have the perimeters being changed. (Interview 1)

Gary added that the tenth-grade teams, which had taken time in the spring to prepare for the interdisciplinary teaming, were told that the schedule would not allow it and their teaming had to be abandoned:

The tenth grade teams last year went through all their planning time in the spring, and then when it came around to do the schedules, then the administrators decided it wasn't going to work schedule wise. I would have been frustrated putting all that time in and then finding out that you can't do some things you want to do. (Interview 1)

Lew seemed to capture the frustration and concern of the team in his response to the question of why his biggest fear was that the whole initiative would be dropped:

In these eighteen years I probably have taught social studies ten different ways, going from remedial section to an honor section to the interdisciplinary. It was like a mixture of things that I have done throughout the years because they [the administrators] always come up with a new way, and I have always been—I guess I have always been willing to take a challenge. When they throw out the challenge, hey, I'll try that, you know, and then I'll do that. But every time I start to get it moving, they say we have to do away with that. You know, we have gone from hetero to homo to hetero [geneous grouping]. We do all the different things and we are constantly changing, and I guess the sad thing is that we never assess or evaluate to say, well, was that worth keeping or why are we throwing it out, and I have a problem with that. I know there are no plans to evaluate what we are doing because I have always asked about that, and there is no answer for that. (Interview 1)

This tendency to jump off and on the bandwagon of innovations kept the teachers in a constant state of uncertainty in terms of the continuance of the project. This fear of abandonment, which was voiced by all the teachers, was epitomized by Lew:

I just hope the rug is not pulled out from under us like it has been over the years because what we already said, Tanya and I both said, if we are both working here down the road, regardless of what they [the administrators] do, we won't change. Our curriculums will stay as they are. (Interview 1)

Adding to the skepticism from this history of adopting trends was a lack of evaluation of any programs whenever a new mandate appeared. Gary voiced his frustration with the lack of evaluation as follows:

That's the same thing that has happened in the past. We've started some programs and a year or two later we dropped them and never really evaluated were they worthwhile, did they do any good, or any of that. It's kind of a pattern around here. (Interview 2)

Tanya explained:

And even with the teaming, we never tested our results. I would think that in most schools, after you did a teaming with history and English and you were thinking of joint interdisciplinary in ninth grade, there would be a data collector that you could use, that they [administrators] would've even consulted with someone to come in and test this. Let's see how your kids are affected. Let's take a look and let's have a control group. No, no, we'll just do it. (Interview 1)

The teachers lamented that no process to evaluate the restructuring initiatives had been put into place. They saw the lack of evaluation as a strong indication that the administration was really much more interested in the appearance of change than in actually making significant changes.

Lack of a Written Curriculum

The lack of any written curriculum for grades nine through twelve seemed to play a minor role in the beginning of the implementation but became a major factor as the teachers tried to implement the interdisciplinary curriculum. When asked to show or discuss their written courses of study, each teacher stated that none existed in his or her subject area. Instead, the teachers talked about different aspects of curriculum planning in which they had engaged on a schoolwide basis or about some specific steps they had taken in their departments to assess student achievement. In terms of schoolwide curriculum planning, the teachers talked about setting benchmarks, devising 13 outcomes, and creating checklists to show mastery of skills.

The most helpful curriculum writing they engaged in, however, was "mapping," which each department created to show what content or concepts must be covered in a certain grade level. They also knew that the administration established curriculum coordinators or strand leaders and segmented the school into four different areas. These leaders, especially the core subject leader, however, did not seem to be effective. Tanya explained:

> They created, I believe it was two years ago, curriculum coordinators or strand leaders, and they segmented the school into four different areas. One was health, one was technology, one was music and performing arts, and the other was the humanities area. I think it was originally humanities, fine and performing arts, and then they separated those two and gave the man in humanities everything curriculum-wise, and that is his job. He has been responsible for everything other than math and science at the high school level. I think he might even have math and science now, which is an impossible job. You just cannot know that much about everyone's curriculum. He was a teacher. I don't think they sent him out for all kinds of training. I don't think you could get that kind of training in a couple of months anyway. (Interview 1)

Gary, who had taught in numerous other schools, expressed surprise and amazement when he first came to the school and was told no written curriculum existed. He explained the Math Department's curriculum planning as follows:

> When I first came and I asked to see a copy of the curriculum, basically there wasn't a whole lot to see. I was told, well in algebra you cover this and this and this, and nobody even . . . really that first year—I was amazed—nobody ever

really checked up to see what was going on. Over time we developed this thing called "map," which was basically drawn up by the people in the departments, and in the Math Department in particular, we took Algebra I and we decided, well this is what we want to cover in Algebra I; this is what we want to cover in geometry; this is what we want to do in Algebra II. So we had certain benchmarks that we had set up that we wanted to attain in each of those courses, but since we've kind of gotten away from the "map" of the past few years, again, we're back to like just really nothing, and in a way, in the Math Department, at least the textbook does have some factor in it because we do go by usually the topics that are in there now. What we've gone on to do the past few years is we've developed our competency test in mathematics so that we do have certain competencies in Algebra I, Algebra II, pre-algebra that need to be met on those levels, and that is kind of what we've been trying to make sure they perform those certain tasks at certain levels so they can use them later on. But again we're still kind of using the "map" guidelines even from there. (Interview 2)

Without any written curriculum, the teachers were unable to place individual subject area frameworks on the table to begin deliberations for interdisciplinary teaming. Instead, the teachers wrote on the chalkboard the content that they covered from September until June. They spoke in broad terms, such as an historical period for social studies, a novel or literary unit for English, a theory for science, and the content from a chapter of the textbook for foreign language and math.

Since none of their broad content issues seemed to relate to each other and the teachers had no models of interdisciplinary teaming to follow, they chose to continue with the model that Lew and Tanya had already put in place. This model centered around the historical periods that Lew taught. When Tanya and Lew started this model three years prior to the study, Tanya felt comfortable with the focus on historical periods. Since Lew taught American history and Tanya taught American literature, there was little tension trying to integrate the two subjects. All Tanya did in some instances was to change the month she taught a literary work or period. Other times, she opted to replace a literary work with another more fitting one. In any event, Tanya felt she was still able to teach the concepts and skills that she needed to teach, such as literary terms, writing and mechanics since she was not bound by a content curriculum. She explained:

> We had a map system when I first came, and you have so many objectives and ways to meet these, but you had to teach these key concepts, and I still keep those in the back of my head. Certain literary terms that I make sure I get to because it is at this grade level that they should [know them], and I know what I have from my student teaching—what the curriculum was there—so I have created with Lew the curriculum based on his curriculum. We put ours together. But an English curriculum does not exist. I think as long as you are teaching the writing process and some English skills in ninth grade it is not do- or-die year. If I don't teach them something, they will get it. (Interview 1)

The other teachers, however, did not fit so easily into the historical scheme, especially since their subject areas were so content specific. John taught earth science, Gary taught algebra and geometry, and Martha taught Spanish I and II and French II. The content specificity in these subjects did not allow the replacement of one content-specific unit for another. For example, Tanya, the English teacher, could replace one novel with another to fit the historical theme of the Holocaust and still teach poetry devices and expository writing, all within the reference of American writers. John, the science teacher, however, could not replace atomic molecular theory with genetic engineering and still have the students understand that all material is comprised of atoms. Gary, the math teacher, could not replace an algebraic formula with statistics about the number of children killed in the Holocaust and then move to the next algebraic concept. The same is true in foreign language study. Martha could not skip conjugating verbs to talk about Spain's and France's roles in World War II. Yes, John, Gary and Martha could add to their curriculum, but they could not replace subject-specific curriculum content the way that Tanya could.

Although the specificity of the subject area made it obvious that their curriculums as they originally existed could not be integrated, no one was really willing to articulate that because of the lack of a written curriculum. Since there were no written departmental curriculums to support them, all the teachers felt that they would be seen as not supportive of the team if they raised such objections. Since the teachers' curriculums were only "in their heads" rather than in a written form, the teachers did not have the materials available to help them understand or deliberate as to the best way to approach showing the connections between the subjects. Without a written curriculum in place, the teachers could not stand behind a schoolwide curriculum that validated what they were teaching in their individual subject areas.

In October, the teachers brought this issue to the central office administrator asking that he answer the following four questions:

1. How should we develop the interdisciplinary curriculum— maps? themes? benchmarks?

2. May we have some vertical articulation of curriculum?

3. May we have more staff development and more input since we are the driving force of the implementation?

4. Will we have continued support, such as remuneration for team planning time over the summer?

This administrator told the teachers that he would address their concerns at the next in-service day. When that day arrived, however, the teachers said that he spent less than five minutes on curriculum right before their break when no one wanted to ask questions and detain others from their lunch.

In addition, the lack of written curriculum added to the teachers' uncertainty concerning the interdisciplinary curriculum model that they were creating. In their team minutes from a meeting during the spring before implementation, the teachers noted that a critical planning step to interdisciplinary teaching was to have a schoolwide study of the curriculum and what was being taught. As the year of implementation progressed, the teachers began to question their ability to engage in interdisciplinary teaming the way they had originally decided. Also, the lack of a written curriculum kept them from believing that their model was "correct" vis-a-vis models they had seen presented at workshops in the spring and the model that the other ninth-grade team had devised. Gary articulated this uncertainty:

I think that is a big factor as far as what we need to look at curriculum-wise because we have to decide, are we going to follow a curriculum by departments or are we going to be really creative and come up with a curriculum for ninth grade and then follow through with it for tenth grade, and maybe, I mean, we've been talking about setting benchmarks and doing those kinds of things. No one seems to have made those kind of decisions, and that's why I kind of feel we are floundering cause we have so many things in the air yet. (Interview 2)

Even when the teachers from both ninth grade teams met with the principal near the end of the school year, the lack of written curriculum remained at the forefront. When the principal asked the two teams to comprise a mutual list of written objectives, Lew stated that objectives could not be written if a curriculum did not exist. The principal agreed and said that curriculum writing would have top priority the next school year, especially since they had to write curriculum to meet the self-study component of an upcoming accreditation visit.

The two ninth-grade teams' decisions to utilize two different models of interdisciplinary teaming added to the uncertainty. Apex's choice was driven by specific content, whereas the other team allowed the students to drive the content. The models were so diverse that they could not be assimilated into one model. Lew expounded:

We have been busting our behind to try to make sure that we are staying within the curriculum because everybody in our group is concerned about content, and so as a result we are going to try to work it and make the curriculum work for us within the concept of teaming, whereas I think the other group is saying we are going to make the teaming concept more important and the curriculum takes a second place and whatever we can bring in is okay, and I just don't know if that is right. So that is where we are. It has always been that way around here, where we have what we call a lack of communication, and it is just a problem because it allows us to have autonomy, but that is not always good for the outcome. (Interview 1)

All this uncertainty left the teachers "ripe" for curriculum deliberation. Gary and John talked about rewriting the math and science curriculums so that the different subjects of math and science would be integrated themselves. Gary had taught integrated math in a Colorado private school and realized that was key to why that interdisciplinary teaming worked. He also remembered that no social studies teacher was employed at the school. Instead, the science, math, and English teachers incorporated social studies in their curriculums. John stated, too, that integrated science would allow him to teach genetics within the guidelines of his subject area.

All the mounting uncertainty led to an awareness that a written curriculum was imperative before all the subject disciplines could be integrated effectively. The teachers realized, however, that a written curriculum, discipline based or interdisciplinary, would probably not materialize because of the lack of administrative leadership and the intensified workload and limited time of the teachers. These two reasons, which also emerged as themes, perpetuated the uncertainty and caused a vicious cycle of trying to implement the innovation yet feeling it could not work as it currently existed.

4

Intensification and
Limited Time

One doesn't discover new lands without consenting to lose sight of
the shore for a very long time.

—André Gide (1927)

Overview

T he second theme that permeated the entire year-long implementation process was the issue of intensification of work
and limited time to complete it. Intensification is defined as
"a bureaucratically driven escalation of pressures, expectations and
controls concerning what teachers do and how much they should do
within the school day" (Apple, as cited in Hargreaves, 1994, p. 108).
Apple and Jungck (1992, pp. 25–26) refer to intensification as a
"chronic sense of overload," from the trivial to the complex, and
summarize the results of such demands as follows:

1. reduced time for relaxation at work and risk of isolation;

2. lack of time to better one's craft and keep abreast of current issues in one's field;

3. dependence on externally produced materials and expertise, which jeopardize teachers' self-trust and pride;

4. reductions in the quality of service because corners are cut to save time; and

5. devaluation of concerns of caring, connectedness, nurturing, and fostering growth.

The intensification of work and time limitations that the teachers experienced were related to four issues: an increased workload, less preparation time, isolation from others, and personal guilt and stress.

Increased Workload

By committing themselves to interdisciplinary teaming and block scheduling, the teachers found themselves in the midst of an increased workload. This increase occurred through demands that were imposed by the implementation process, the administration, and the teachers themselves.

Interdisciplinary teaming itself implies increased workload. Since the teachers had ten planning days during the spring of the previous school year and 100 planning hours over the summer, they felt confident when they began the school year with a unit on Jurassic Park. The time that they had to plan and implement the unit matches Jacobs's (1989a) findings, which show that teachers estimate 164 hours of time is needed to develop and implement a complex interdisciplinary unit. This amount of time includes brainstorming, developing and sequencing activities, finding resources and materials, setting up speakers and field trips, researching subject matter, teaching the unit, and monitoring student and teacher progress. As the year continued, however, the teachers did not have the same amount of time to plan and implement the other units plus attend to their other work and duties.

Huberman and Miles (1984) write that intensification plays a major role during the early implementation stage, adding that teachers feel they have too many simultaneous tasks to perform in the time available, causing them to feel overloaded and energy depleted. Also, because the teachers chose to follow historical themes for interdisciplinary teaming, the three new team teachers had to read novels and prepare new lessons that were not a part of their previous curriculums. All the teachers had to plan for the Jurassic Park unit and to read Ruth Hartz's book on her survival as a young Jewish girl during the Holocaust for the Holocaust unit. However, Gary, John, and Martha also had to plan for the Wild West, Immigration, World War I, and the Fifties, all units which did not fit naturally into their curriculums.

Gary described how the need to incorporate the themes and the lack of time intensified the workload:

> I mean the Internet, what I've been learning on the Internet has been wonderful, and I feel like if I take the time and go and play with that and try to find out what's there to incorporate in what's going on, I lose my time that I do have, and time is like the precious thing I think right now because, I mean, we do have all these wonderful things, but you have to have the time to incorporate them. I mean, I was just playing around on the Internet the one day, and I found a thing about Ellis Island. I think it was certainly worthwhile, but if I didn't just take the time that particular day, I never would've known it was there. (Interview 2)

In addition to the interdisciplinary teaming, the block scheduling also made new demands on the teachers' time. Used to teaching in a 45-minute period, the teachers had to adjust to an 85-minute period of time. The teachers felt that they had to adapt to this time schedule by adding more hands-on activities, which, in turn, generated more work to be graded. They felt physically drained by the end of the day since they had to "perform" for such a long period of time before a break between classes. When asked to explain what made the year stressful, Martha, the foreign language teacher, explained the experience as follows:

> Well, having no time to get any paperwork done at school and yet having to do more paperwork because of the hour and a half class, so whereas before I was in a 45-minute period I

was more verbal with the kids. Now I was forced—I could not maintain an hour and a half of verbal communication for an hour and a half three times a day, so I would do it for 45-minutes and then turn to a project. Well those projects have to be corrected, although I must say I threw a lot in the trash. I could not keep up with my work. . . . The teaming, for all intents and purposes, I had five preps with a French II on the team and a French II off the team. Even the final exams had to be two separate finals. So new team courses, trying to find materials like going to find Ruth Hartz [Holocaust survivor and speaker] to make the program successful. (Interview 3)

The administrative demands were related to responsibilities the teams were given but did not necessarily want because it took away from their teaching time. One example of this was the administration's request for the teachers to formulate their own schedules for the following school year. Although the teachers had requested that they be allowed to divide the incoming freshmen into four sections, they did not want to have to devise a teaching schedule for themselves. They believed that they did not have the expertise to schedule or the understanding of how to do it. All they wanted was some input into the scheduling process and, instead, were saddled with the project itself. When they finally did devise a schedule that gave them the extra planning time they wanted, the administration reneged because that schedule conflicted with other subjects that the freshmen had to take. In this situation the teachers felt frustrated because they spent so much time trying to devise a schedule and then their recommendation was ignored.

The teachers also felt strapped by having to schedule and administer standardized tests to their students. These standardized tests were administered by the school each year to assess student progress. The teachers believed the scheduling of the exam should have been an administrative task. The task was intensified because some of the students took core subjects outside the team. For example, those students who were weak math students left the team for a pre-algebra class with a nonteam math teacher. Also, some nonteam students took classes on the Apex team. For example, Gary had some students in geometry who were sophomores who had to repeat the class; and Martha had some upperclassmen in her French classes. Because of this mix with nonteam students, the teachers spent much time discerning when and where tests would be administered. Also, in order to accommodate the even-odd, six-day cycle, which permitted each teacher to see individual classes and students only every other day, the teachers administered the tests in small sections over a one-week period. Thus, scheduling the exams in increments prolonged the test taking and disrupted the regular class day.

Another source of frustration was a portfolio class, which met approximately twice a month. Each teacher had a group of freshmen from their team who needed help putting together a portfolio, which would be presented to a committee at the end of the senior year. Most teachers in the school started with a group of students and kept that same group of students until they graduated. John had liked this idea because he felt the students became more independent over the years and could work alone on putting together the portfolio. The other team teachers, however, had decided that they wanted to work with their own students and, therefore, had elected to work only with freshmen. John really disliked working with the freshmen, especially since he had 19 in his portfolio class and knew that the other science teachers had fewer. Martha even offered to take half of John's students, but he declined her offer. All the teachers, however, did feel the portfolio class was one more responsibility that they did not have time to implement effectively.

The teachers imposed some of the increased workload on themselves. Because they wanted to offer many opportunities to their students, they scheduled field trips and incentive events that took much time and effort to coordinate. Field trips meant making telephone calls for buses, box lunches, and site reservations; coordinating schedules so that athletes arrived back at school earlier for practice or games; preparing school assignments for those students ineligible to attend; and completing forms for the school, houseparents, and site. Incentive programs meant giving up evenings. Instead of spending time with family or completing school work or relaxing at night, the teachers chose to provide pizza parties quarterly for students who achieved good grades. Incentive programs meant designing certificates for award ceremonies and buying items for the TIC-it program, an incentive plan that allowed students to buy items with coupons they obtained for good grades and citizenship.

Another factor that increased the workload was simply the mind's awareness of the initiative that they were implementing. The teachers felt as if they were constantly thinking about the way they could team better. Perhaps Lew as team leader was able to capture this feeling best. When asked how he would compare the workload this year to previous years, Lew responded:

> It's a lot more, it's far more ... because the whole time that I'm doing my, at least planning for my classes, I'm always thinking of trying to be more innovative or trying to be more team oriented. I'm always thinking. Like I said, sometimes I'm thinking for myself and sometimes I'm thinking for my team. I'm always trying to figure out ways to do. I know they [other teachers on the team] are going to ask a question but how, how else can this be done. So it really is a lot more work even if it's no more than just a thought process or just things that I'm trying to develop on paper with lessons and things of that nature. I'm always thinking far ahead. I've developed plans to teach this same course a lot of different ways over nineteen years, but each year I think I find myself doing it differently, which I think has helped me because it never fits into the plan I had the year before. Yes, I guess that is the right way to do it anyhow. But this year it's almost like everything's out the window—it's like starting over again. It's like I'm a first-year teacher again for two reasons—the intensive scheduling and then for the total team process. So, I think, yes, it is far more work. (Interview 2)

One other issue that increased the workload for some of the teachers was their desire to protect their subject area. The two people most affected by this phenomenon were Martha and John. The Foreign Language Department's concerns that foreign languages could be eliminated from the curriculum remained at the forefront of their minds. Thus, they did not want to eliminate any of their course offerings, such as German or upper levels of Spanish and French. This desire to offer all the languages and levels added a burden to their desire to become full-time teachers on a team.

They tried to resolve this issue by asking the administration to hire two more foreign language teachers. The administration's response was to take foreign language off the teams or to eliminate

German as a foreign language option for freshmen. The foreign language teachers did not want to leave the teams, again fearing they may lose their positions. Nor did they did want to eliminate German for freshmen for two reasons. First, it would deny those students who already started taking German in the middle school the opportunity to continue their studies uninterrupted. Second, by having students substitute German with Spanish and French, they would probably not return to German studies their sophomore year, which could possibly eliminate German from the school curriculum. This dilemma added to Martha's workload. It kept her wanting to remain as loyal to the department as to the team, and she eventually realized that she could not continue at her pace:

> Do you know what I did to my department head today? She sat and read all this stuff to me that she thought was important, and I just looked at her and said, "I can't do any of this." I said, "I'm doing the foreign language program for—University this summer, I'm running both National Exams and she wants competency tests for the kids coming up from the middle school, and I had started that last year, and I wrote up one whole competency test all by myself, and I looked at her and I said, "Are you getting any help from anybody in this department on any of these topics?" And she said no. Then I said, "I can't give you any either." I said that I'm doing everything I can. (Interview 2)

John, too, felt the extra load from trying to fill his position as Chemical Hygiene/Safety Committee coordinator for the district and Science Department chair. John articulated his frustration this way:

> I think I wear a lot of different hats here at the school, and this year I think you realize I have a lot of different things going on, and the one thing that it affected as far as I am concerned is my effectiveness as Science Department chair because so much time was spent on teaming that I wasn't able to do a lot of things that I do with the Science Department. We've had very few meetings this year, we've gotten very little accomplished this year as far as our department is concerned, and I believe that we have to articulate, where does the department fit in and where does the team fit in, and I believe that we have been negligent on that. (Interview 3)

Loss of Preparation Time

Teachers value their preparation time. By committing themselves to interdisciplinary teaming, the teachers gave up preparation time, which added to the intensification and time limitations. The teachers were committed to meeting as a team every odd-numbered day of the six-day cycle. Because of this team meeting, the teachers only had three individual planning periods per six-day cycle to complete their own work. Since all of them were involved in activities outside the team, they had to use this limited preparation time to meet with other colleagues and to complete their class work, their team obligations or other duties. The teachers did not use their team planning time to write interdisciplinary curriculum. Instead, as Hargreaves found in his study, the teachers' time together focused on short-term, practical issues that affected all of them as team members. For example, instead of utilizing a planning period to work together on a unit, the teachers reported on their individual progress in incorporating their subject area into the unit. They also dealt with logistical issues and behavior problems with children, all important immediate concerns.

In addition, their team planning period met during the third period, which included a half hour lunchtime. Thus, the teachers often met as a team until there was only 20 minutes left for lunch. This situation eliminated their ability to complete a few small tasks during the lunch period. The most teachers could accomplish in that 20 minutes was to eat lunch, check their mail, and set up the room for the next class.

Also, homeroom period was eliminated with the block scheduling initiative. Instead, 20 minutes was added to the first-period class for taking attendance, watching Channel 1, and listening to announcements. John explained how all these factors affected time:

> We used to have a homeroom period. So you would come into school and you would have 10 minutes or whatever, and then you would have your homeroom period for 20 minutes. It might've been 18 but around that. So during your homeroom period you would kind of get yourself together. So I could take—my homeroom would do a lot of things for me. You would end up with a freshman homeroom, and then the next year you would have that homeroom as a sophomore, junior,

and then senior. The year I had the senior homeroom they would come in every day, turn on the weather station, get the satellite to give us what was going on and take care of a lot of things in the room, just to do something and that type of thing. So that gave you time there where if I had to run and copy something, if I wanted to go down and get a cup of coffee, I could do that. Now if I had a freshman homeroom, it would be a little different, but you see what I mean. And so you have that time there that you could use productively and at the same time you could kind of just relax. Then after that they head onto their classes, so you have 5 minutes then. And then last year as department chair, I had a free period as department chair. I had a regular free period. So I think that last year I taught four classes, and I had three free periods a day. This year I teach, I only have a free period once every other day . . . and then the other thing is that we used to have study halls, and I used to have students who I had before who would come in to help me, and I always had some good students who would come in and, more or less, be like classroom assistants, and they would be able to set up while I was tearing down and that type of thing, and I didn't have to be over them telling every detail what to do. . . . Things that needed to be copied, they could take and setup the materials for lab activities, microscopes put them away, clean them up, that type of thing. Now I have to do all that myself, and I just find that I am inundated and just can't get it done, and it's really affecting my classes because the kids used to complain all we ever do in here is activities. So, you see, you just can't get a balance there. (Interview 2)

In that same interview John verbalized how all the intensification led to his being less effective in the classroom:

I don't know, it's a funny situation, and I just wish that things would slow down. I wish they [the administrators] would address the fact that we don't have planning time. The one thing I really need is time to sit in here to plan my lessons and my activities, and that's the one thing that I've always been good at before, and when my students came in, it was like a little science lab, but it's not that way this year. It's more chaos and actually more lecturing this year, and I thought I'd do less. I never lectured much before, and I am now because I can't do my activities because I can't get them set up in time, and if I wait to set them up, then I just waste time. I don't know. I think that maybe when I finish graduate school and get my principal's certificate I'll be better off, too. That takes a lot of time. (Interview 2)

These feelings reflect Huberman and Miles's (1984) research study that found, in the early stages of implementation, teachers were self-preoccupied, relegating student learning to a lower level of concern. The teachers in their study complained of day-to-day coping, continuous cycles of trial and error, the inability to get through daily or weekly plans, and the sacrifice of other core activities. Also, apprehension, confusion, and distress—which resulted from feelings of professional inadequacy—as well as flaws in the innovation and exhaustion were reported.

The lack of individual planning time had a catch-22. The teachers did not want to forfeit the team planning time. They saw the meeting time as crucial to their ability to team successfully. However, they did not believe it was fair that they were being penalized three planning periods because they were teaming. They did discuss possible ways to acquire more time the next school year.

One suggestion was to hire aides to take their activity period, but the majority of the teachers did not want to give up their students to someone outside the team, something Maeroff (1993) writes complicates reallocating time. He explains that teachers want to be seen as performing their duties when not in the presence of students, yet teachers want to retain their day-to-day control over classroom reality. Lew recorded their frustration of insufficient time in the team minutes, which were forwarded to the administrators. The teachers were aware that the tenth-grade teams did not have a common meeting time and, therefore, were unable to do any interdisciplinary work.

Panaritis (1995) believes that time is an essential ingredient not only in the planning of an interdisciplinary curriculum, but also in the understanding of each individual teacher's pedagogy (organization and classroom management techniques, teaching style, methods, interests, and strengths) and of the elements that affect each teacher's curriculum (graduation requirements, state mandates, major concepts, textbooks, and homework). The teachers seemed to sense that the team planning time was crucial to their coherence and understanding of each other's work.

Separation from Other Colleagues

The teachers felt separated from other colleagues in the school. Besides the increased workload and time limitations, they felt that the block scheduling and the teaming took away time to spend with others and just relax. Hargreaves (1994) labels this kind of time the sociopolitical dimension of time, which refers to the ways in which the particular forms of time become administratively dominant, which is a main element in the control of teachers' work and the curriculum implementation process.

Goffman (1959) explains that teachers relax in "back regions." Front regions, on the one hand, refer to the teacher onstage, in front of students or others in some kind of professional capacity. Back regions, on the other hand, are those areas where teachers can relax; they are backstage, unwinding or fraternizing with their peers. Without this kind of backstage time, the teachers became more alienated from their nonteaming colleagues.

Gary explained how and why his loss of backstage time resulted in isolation from other colleagues:

> I feel I barely get to see anybody else at school because the one day I have three classes and I have team planning time, which we use almost every day, and the other day I have one planning period and the rest of them I have either classes or the team projects' time, and I feel the only time I see anybody is when I go to lunch, and that's kind of a sad thing there, too, because there used to be some other teachers that I would be able to do some work with and I feel that I've lost that. (Interview 2)

John explained his frustration, too, because of the loss of backstage time in terms of time to relax:

> I believe the intensive scheduling has really limited the amount of time that teachers have, and in doing that I don't get to see a lot of the teachers that, you know, like I used to have a cup

of coffee with them, five, ten minutes just to relax. I don't have time to do that. I can't even get a cup of coffee with our schedule the way it is. I usually bring it from the outside when I come in the morning. I don't have time to relax all day, and I think that part of that is teaming and I think that part of it is scheduling. I believe that is something we really need to address. We just need in the course of the day time to prop our feet up, get a newspaper, cup of coffee, and relax. (Interview 2)

The team teachers' proximity to each other isolated them from the other teachers, too. All the teachers except John changed classrooms to team, which removed them from their fellow department members and, in many cases, from colleagues whom they taught next to for years. Thus, their interactions with other colleagues were stifled. They did not have the option to poke their heads out of their rooms during the passing of classes or drop by someone else's room to maintain a congenial or collegial relationship. This isolation magnified the separation of the team from the rest of the school and may have created what Maeroff (1993) labels "elitism." Citing Henry Levin, director of the Accelerated Schools program, Maeroff writes that a problem with teaming is that the whole faculty can see the team as "insiders who had a boondoggle."

The Apex teachers felt that they were viewed as wanting to be left alone and felt that their friends resented the team. Hargreaves (1994) writes that "selfish, precious prima donnas" is often the label attached to those who separate themselves from the company of others when they are engaged in the processes of creation that give teaching its interest and life. Lew perceived that perhaps they were being labeled "prima donnas":

The perceptions I pick up sometimes—I don't know if they think we are prima donnas or we are trying to be, or are we doing something that is a threat to them—you know, I sometimes pick up a vibe of that sort. It's nothing anyone said directly, but it's always like a little joke here or there about the team this or how's teaming going. So that little dig or that little rub that I'm not sure if it's a positive or a negative at times, so I just don't concern myself with it. (Interview 2)

Tanya remembered that almost the entire faculty drove three hours to attend her wedding a few years before but now her relationship with many faculty members had changed. She felt resentment and jealousy because of the teaming:

[Good friend] bothered me a little bit this year, a little bit, that was kind of a low feeling for me because she, I think, was jealous that I was on the team and it took away from what we could do, and even with our schedules she is all concerned that next year we might have an extra planning period more than anyone else. We'll have one more and that's not fair. She said that's just not fair. I said well we do things, it's not as though I'm down in the workout room working out. I really think we need a planning period. We got into an argument. We have not argued this year up until this point—of course with her being out for six weeks [child-rearing leave] it really helped. I missed her but I didn't because I was so busy that I didn't even notice. Were it last year I probably would have missed her more. But she said you might think you need extra planning periods, but I don't see you needing an extra planning period. I don't see anybody on your team needing an extra planning period. That's just not fair. At that point I said to her, just get over it and we never—so I think she is representative of the faculty seeing us as this cute little team and if we get more anything, they're going to be the first ones to say that's not fair. They hate when we wear our [team] shirts. People hate that. And we get comments still from people like [name of a teacher colleague], who was very close to me, and snide remarks, this is the team table [at lunch], and they will go sit somewhere else. They'll sit by themselves before they would sit with us. So we kind of made ourselves into a clique, which we shouldn't have done. We probably should have deliberately, looking back, spaced ourselves and not acted like—that's sad because why should you have to do that? (Interview 3)

An irony to this isolation existed. Although the teachers were physically separated from their colleagues, their presence as a team was more obvious. Since team meetings preceded lunch for three days of the six-day cycle, at least three days a week the teachers went to lunch together. Their arrival at lunch as a team heightened the other teachers' awareness of their presence. Even when they arrived at lunch a few minutes earlier than the other teachers (an option they could choose because of the team meeting first), they were seen as a core because they were seated together. On special occasions, such as field trips, all team students and teachers wore their Apex T-shirts. Also, because of the uniqueness to some of the projects (which will be discussed in chapter 7) that they undertook, they received lots of media attention, both television and newspaper, which was prompted by the school's Public Relations' Department, not the teachers themselves. Finally, in order to show student work, the teachers enlisted every available display case, which, again, made them ubiquitous.

This omnipresence led to two opposing results. Besides the feelings of professional jealousy and resentment from their peers, the other teachers saw Apex as a team of "fun and games." During the Jurassic Park unit, the students had dinosaur cutouts on their lockers. During the Wild West, they had cowboy hats. All the display cases and media attention focused on projects of authentic assessment, which lent itself to criticism by those who preferred using standard assessment tools and teaching techniques. The second result, however, was that other teachers, aware of what the team was teaching, often supplied them with articles or pictures or just tidbits of information that they could use. Prior to their teaming, no one knew or cared what they were doing as individuals. As a team, their work was public.

Probably the most frustrating aspect was being separated from their department members. John was concerned that his inability to chair the Science Department as effectively as before could lead to a fragmentation of the science curriculum. He believed that departments needed to be stronger than before if teaming was to continue. He rationalized his belief this way:

> What I see happening is the department chair is going to be much stronger if we are going to offer services in science, math, history, and English. If you're going to have curriculum that's going to spiral, I think that they are going to have to have more of a leadership role in what they do and what transpires and what happens. (Interview 3)

Even Lew, who felt that members in the Social Studies Department were always cohesive, now sensed they were separating themselves from him:

I think we are one of the more closely knit departments of the whole school. We didn't have any back fighting or knit picking or any of those kinds of things, political problems. We were all just kind of like the laid back group that kind of got along, go to lunch and do things like that. But I think what is happening by me being pulled out, I think, it almost is perceived that I am almost like out. I'm more of an outsider now than I was before, and even becoming a team leader puts me in that kind of situation because it is almost like I have a department that I am actually trying to control as opposed to being part of their department, and it's almost like every time when there is going to be a meeting or something that I get the call, are you available, as opposed to saying, hey, we are having a meeting, you should be there. So, I do see a difference, but I don't think anybody [in the department] has taken a negative. That's just how our department is. But I think everybody is recognizing that there is a big major difference right now, and I don't necessarily like that because of our relationship that we had, and that goes back to the intensive scheduling, too. I really think that has totally isolated and secluded everyone into their own area because of the way it is set up. There is very little time to interact anymore, and that is probably with the kids as well. The only time to interact is during lunch, and by me not being a real lunch person, I don't always see other adults at all that often at this point in time. (Interview 2)

Lew ended up in a confrontation with P, a veteran social studies teacher, which directly related to teaming. When the team teachers decided to move into proximity with each other, Lew's room on the other side of the building became available. No one wanted the room, and Lew suggested it to P, who was having problems with a leak in the roof in his room. P decided, however, that he did not want to change classrooms.

Lew then secured that room for the team in order to build a Wild West living museum, a hands-on project that would culminate in opening the museum to the entire school after it was completed. The museum included a saloon, a bank, a farmhouse, a tent, and a railroad track and train. In addition, students made up skits and historical briefs about the Wild West. Unfortunately, because of time constraints, the team was unable to complete the museum. The teachers then decided to allow the next year's team to work on it and left it three-quarters completed.

Right before the Christmas break, however, P asked Lew to remove the museum because his roof was leaking again and he wanted to change rooms. Lew explained to the teacher that he could not move the museum, that two months of hard work was involved. One of the researchers happened to be in the room with Lew that day when P came to discuss the issue with Lew. When P left, Lew was very upset. Lew told us that this incident would become another issue that the administration would want him to settle himself. He iterated that no one understood or appreciated what they were doing.

Lew did talk to the administrators, and P's roof was fixed over the holiday break. The dilemma was solved but Lew was hurt that someone thought it was so unimportant and so easy to remove something that they worked on for so long. This same teacher resigned unexpectedly on a Friday in the spring after he did not receive a position in the Human Resources Department. Although Lew felt bad that P left, he was relieved that he would not have to deal with him and the room again, something he felt guilty about but acknowledged.

Gary, too, felt major repercussions from being separated from his department. He explained:

> It's kind of difficult right now even contacting the other members of the Math Department because everybody seems to be doing so many different things. We don't have the time to get together and share ideas as much as we used to. That's something that we have been asking about being able to do on in-service days and so forth, but we haven't had any success with that yet. The other thing is that since there are two ninth-grade teams, we are basically trying to cover the same material in our courses, but the team work seems to be totally different. So, we're not exactly as coordinated maybe as we have in the past as far as what we're presenting, although I think that by the end of the year we will have the same things

presented in algebra and geometry. But the extra things that we do are a little different, which is probably the same thing that happened in the past when we did other projects, too. But I do feel that we've lost some of the continuity we used to have. I felt our Math Department, in particular the past few years, we've had some young people come in, and we've had a very good relationship with the department and the teams kind of have taken away from that, I think. (Interview 2)

In the early spring of the study, Gary decided to run for department chair, a position he held a few years before. Department chairs were elected every two years by the members of the department. Several math teachers had approached Gary to run, and he was assured that he had the support to win. Gary did run and he tied, 4-4, with his opponent. Another election was held, and the vote remained the same. The principal broke the tie by voting for the other math teacher. This close election, along with fighting over the schedule for the next year, left the department divided. Gary feared some math courses would have to be dropped and a teacher furloughed.

Another issue which contributed to the teachers' sense of alienation from other members of the staff was the ongoing conflict with the other ninth-grade team. This conflict, which had its origin in the original social studies/English two-person interdisciplinary teams, escalated throughout the implementation process for a variety of reasons. This interteam conflict is discussed in detail in chapter 5.

Personal Guilt and Stress

The intensification, time limitations and separation were compounded by teacher guilt and stress, which, in turn complicated the implementation process. Werner (as cited in Hargreaves, 1994), who has studied the importance of time for the process of curriculum implementation, reports that administrators and innovators are the guardians of "objective" or rational time. He adds that teachers do not experience time the same way, that they experience time within the context of their own classroom structures. His findings show that teachers feel guilt and frustration because they cannot implement a new program so quickly and so efficiently as the administrative timeline dictates. Teachers see these imposed requirements as impossible mandates that ignore the teachers' existing pressures and demands, as well as the guidance requisite to integrating innovations with existing practices and routines. It is at this time when teachers' requests for more planning time or relaxed innovation timelines are apt to be strongest.

This is the time, too, that teacher guilt surfaces. Using Alan Davies work as his resource, Hargreaves (1994) divides teacher guilt into two categories. The first, *persecutory guilt,* derives from doing something that is forbidden by an external authority or failing to do something that is mandated by others. In teaching, this kind of guilt comes from accountability demands and bureaucratic controls. Examples include teachers' believing they must cover the required content instead of creating more stimulating lessons or overtly but superficially complying with innovations that are unwanted or doubted or impractical.

The second, *depressive guilt,* which begins in the early years of life, occurs in situations where individuals feel they have ignored or betrayed the people or values whom they represent. Teachers feel this guilt when they do not believe they are meeting the needs of their students. Thus, in the context of teaching, caring for students is as important as doing what is right, two issues that become blocked when teachers meet impossible constraints.

Martha explained how the time demands and intensified work eliminated her ability to nurture students in her home, an activity she felt was important:

> I admit to doing more for kids my first two years here. Last year I was too busy. I didn't take kids home on weekends. Now I want to get back to that this year. . . . If a kid was crying, I took him home for the weekend. You know, let him live in a family bed and let him eat a family meal. A lot of teachers do that. If you get too busy—I spent the whole weekend doing school work Saturday night and Sunday morning. I can't bring a kid home when I'm doing that. That is one of my goals—to take a needy kid home. (Interview 1)

The teachers also experienced depressive guilt when they felt they were letting down their fellow team members. With the increased work and loss of preparation time, John felt guilty for not volunteering to perform team tasks. He explained:

Sometimes I wasn't able to do things that I would've liked to have done. I don't feel that I was as effective as what I would've liked to have been and wasn't as supportive in some areas as what I would've liked to have been. But I think that's something that the team didn't seem to have any problems with, and they seemed to work around it. For example, the TIC-it program. I wasn't able to go and buy stuff, and I wasn't able to do a lot of the extra things that needed to be done, and I just feel that if you want to be part of a team, you should support that team and work with the team. A lot of times I wasn't able to do some of the things, so the other people carried the ball. They didn't complain about it or anything, but it did annoy me. (Interview 3)

Hargreaves (1994) writes that the pressing demands of accountability and intensification can occupy so much of the teachers' schedules that little time is left for the informal moments to show care and concern, which many teachers believe is their major purpose. The teachers felt that the intensive scheduling and teaming excluded them from interacting with former students. They also believed that they needed to see all the freshmen every day rather than every other day in order to maintain the desired rapport and work ethic. Lew, who was used to interacting outside the classroom setting with his present and former students throughout the course of a day, expressed both depressive and persecutory guilt:

There are now times when I see certain kids, you know a kid that we have had over the years, I'll say, hey, how have you been, I haven't seen you almost for the whole year. That is one of the drawbacks of the situation set up like it is. Time is so regimented that there is not much more you can do. And then the free time . . . that's why even with lunch I don't really want to waste that time because I may just grab something real quick that I have with me so that I can keep working and moving in the way that I have to stay on top of everything. (Interview 2)

The Apex teachers felt the time constraints tighten as the year progressed. Gary used the metaphor of riding a carousel to describe the experience:

Its been like continuously riding a carousel. . . . It just seems, you know, that you just keep going and going and going, trying to do more and more and more and you don't seem to have any down time, and I know there are things I have left go that I should be doing and there are things that I wanted to do that I never got around to do and didn't have time, and maybe this is my problem with time management or something like that, but I still don't ever feel like there is enough time. (Interview 2)

These time constraints turned to feelings of guilt when teachers were not able to support their fellow team teachers in the same capacity as the others. John explained:

We have to do all these things together all the time, and it really gets strained, and it's really tough to coordinate these things. You have to make phone calls, you have to make arrangements, you have to fill out forms and stuff, and you know, it eats up your time. That is the one thing I feel really bad about because I know the party last night, a little thing, but Tanya got the pizza, Lew got the Coke and stuff, we used Lew's room. They had time to do it. You know, they could make the calls, they could . . . I didn't have the time to set up even a trip to the museum in Philadelphia. I was all for that. I had several museums. But to make the calls and that sort of thing, even though I have a phone in my room, I didn't have the time to do it, but Gary did. He has the time to do it, so he did, and that's really good, but then I feel like I'm not doing my part in teaming, and it all boils down, I think, to what I teach and the preparation that I have for what I teach, and also I think my duties as a department chair, which I have really put on the back burner, and other duties that I have around the school, like the chemical hygiene coordinator, so the rest of the team members don't see that. I get the impression sometimes that they think I should be doing more. I kind of feel like, sometimes I feel like, you know, the third wheel or something like that. (Interview 2)

All the teachers, except John, stated that they used all their personal days by early spring in order to have some time to relax, to get away from the school setting. Martha actually experienced a physical ailment that she directly related to the school year. When asked how her students did on the Foreign Language National Exam, Martha replied:

> Their scores were all worse. All of them, even my French III's who should not even be affected were affected because they [the administrators] made me teach three hour-and-a-half long courses a day this year and there is no break and I had no prep because the kids were always in my room. . . . Next year's schedule is much better. So they are working on those problems because they know they were killing me. I started on a thyroid condition two months ago, and they are darn lucky I finished the school year. Yeah, I never got better from the stress of the winter and into the spring, and that helped when I went in and told [the principal and assistant principal] what this year did to me. They saw it themselves. I had big lumps right here in my neck. I said, "The lump is right here in my neck." I said, "Look, you guys can't do this to me next year." If they think they have a teacher who will do it, they will use us. (Interview 3)

John realized the toll the intensification was taking on every one of the team members. During an interview the day after the second-quarter pizza party, John reflected on how he thought everyone was feeling:

> I kind of feel right now this time of year for some reason I feel burned out. I think Gary today expressed the fact that he really feels that he might be burned out, and I kind of even had the impression last night at the party that Tanya didn't have the zip and zing that she usually has. I don't know how long Lew can keep going the way he does. I don't know if he can continue with basketball and everything else that he has. I don't know how he can keep doing it. And I just think that we have to slow the pace a little bit, sit back a little bit, reflect on what we have done and where we are and where we want to go and then just take our time and work toward getting there and not be in a rush to go someplace where we might not want to be. (Interview 2)

5

Lack of Administrative Leadership

Skill and confidence are an unconquerable army.
—George Herbert (1651)

Overview

The teachers felt a lack of day-to-day administrative leadership from the inception of the restructuring project. Although they received financial resources and release time during the spring and summer prior to the implementation, they felt that there was no administrative leadership to facilitate their endeavors. This lack of support from both building and central administration added to the difficulty of trying to implement a restructuring mandate that had unclear goals and magnified the teachers' uncertainty.

Four of the teachers, on separate occasions, stated that they felt "on their own," and they all expressed the perception that the administration did not seem to care if they succeeded or failed. Three of them articulated that perhaps the administration wanted them to fail so that they could say they tried but it did not work. John was able to summarize the teachers' feelings in this way:

> You doubt your ability when you are doing something new. And don't get me wrong, the administration really has made a lot of gestures as far as giving us some time off and bringing substitutes in and paying us to work over the summer. They really have done a lot of things that surprised me, but I kind of feel that it's not so much the material things. I kind of think that it's, more or less, my need, it really is, to know where we should go and what we should be doing so that we feel confident where we are going. It's almost like being out there on a limb, doing your own thing. (Interview 2)

Although we understood why the teachers read the lack of administrative support on a day to day basis as an indication that the administrators did not care about the success or failure of the project, we read the hands-off administrative style differently. We believed that the administrators were trying to give the teachers some breathing space and latitude and also that they themselves really lacked the technical knowledge about interdisciplinary teaming that would have allowed them to be helpful to the teachers.

The administrators seemed to understand the needs of the teachers in terms of supplying the "concrete" items to facilitate the project. For example, Ackerman (1989) writes that time, budget, and schedule are critical components to implement interdisciplinary teaching. Time is needed to plan lessons and activities, to write new assessment tools, and to communicate and coordinate with colleagues. Budget must be available to support curriculum development, staffing, and acquisition of materials. Schedules must be devised to allow common planning time for teachers and to make teachers accessible to students. The teachers felt that many of these concrete items were supplied. However, they felt that they needed leadership in terms of writing curriculum and understanding interdisciplinary curriculum to facilitate the initiative. This lack of leadership was troubling and added to the uncertainty and intensity of their work.

Apple and Jungck (1992) warn that even if schools set rhetorical goals to appease outside groups, some teachers may be committed to these goals, believing they are worth meeting and spending the additional time to implement them. These teachers will exhaust themselves, working even harder in an already intensified world to overcome obstacles. At the same time, however, this increased work will create an impossible situation for teachers to meet goals.

The possibility existed that the administration did propose this restructuring project to appease the Board of Directors and alumni, who, as previously discussed, were unhappy with the school's move toward an academic slant. If so, the mandate might have been made for appearance, not substance. Gary iterated these feelings:

> I don't feel the support that we've had in the past on certain projects. I think it started last year when this was all in the planning stage. . . . In some aspects I think they want us to do these things, but I don't think they really care whether it works or not as long as they can say, hey, we're doing team teaching and all this other stuff. There doesn't seem to be a lot of follow through. . . . No one has really come in and really observed how things are going. Another one of those things where, well, yes, you're going to do this, and we can say we're doing it, but I don't know that it really has as far as their [administrators'] support on it, I think we are limited. (Interview 2)

John validated Gary's feelings:

> It's like, you know, well, we gave them all this money, we gave them, . . . if they don't produce, well, you know, and sometimes I wonder if maybe in the back of their minds they don't want us to fail, but sometimes I think maybe they do. Then they can say, well, we tried that and it didn't work. (Interview 2)

Another issue was "goal displacement," a term coined by Robert Merton (1957, as cited in Hargreaves, 1994). Goal displacement occurs when people become so fascinated by the means by which goals are pursued that the original goals are forgotten or neglected.

Since the teachers never engaged in a schoolwide discussion regarding the goals of the restructuring project, they were never sure
of the goals. The ideas they articulated as possible goals (see chapter 3) were never at the forefront anyway because they were too
preoccupied with the change process. Hargreaves (1994, p. 23)
explains: "As efforts are channeled into implementation, the reasons for making the change in the first place fade quickly into the
background. As a result, people who are affected by change often
wonder what the change is for."

The lack of administrative leadership was detrimental to the
project and thwarted the teachers' feelings of efficacy. Three distinct issues added to these feelings of being on their own: lack of
schoolwide professional development, lack of guidance and feedback, and unresolved conflict between the two ninth-grade teams.

Lack of Schoolwide Professional Development

After the teachers formed teams the spring semester prior to the
implementation, they were given ten days of release time from
their normal teaching duties during that semester and one hundred paid hours of work during that summer to plan an interdisciplinary curriculum and attend any workshops that would help
them to plan. The teachers appreciated the time and money, but
they did not know to whom or where to turn for the training. The
central office and building administrators did not provide the teachers with any help in finding possible training workshops or even
school visitation sites. Contacts with other teachers inside or outside their own building provided the only links to possible staff
development activities. During the first meeting between the researchers and teachers in March, one of the first questions that
teachers asked us was whether we were aware of any good staff
development opportunities for them. Eventually they did visit one
high school about sixty miles away, which they heard was involved
in block scheduling, curriculum integration, and teaming through
a relative of one of the Apex teachers who was an elementary
teacher in the district where the site visit occurred. We went with
the teachers on this site visit.

When we arrived at the visitation school (April 5, four months
before the implementation was to begin), we met with the high

school administrators who talked about the "nuts and bolts" of the restructuring, such as how time was blocked and how students were grouped. The administrators noted that they were fairly sure that there was no interdisciplinary curriculum in place in any of the classes, but they assured us that the teachers would be able to talk in-depth about teaming and integrating, if it did exist, when we met with them. When we did observe classes and talk to teachers, they did not see themselves as teaming or integrating, and the students themselves were unable to articulate why they were grouped the way they were or how the block scheduling affected their learning. The Apex teachers were so unenlightened by this visitation that they chose to leave early and eat lunch at a restaurant. Tanya summed up the visit with these words: "If the kids don't know they're doing it, they're not doing it" (Field Notes, April 5).

The second professional development activity they attended together was a team-building workshop in May. They felt that this conference helped them understand the team building process more clearly but did not answer any questions about interdisciplinary curriculum. The team then asked to attend the Association for Supervision and Curriculum Development's annual conference since interdisciplinary curriculum was a featured strand. Since the conference was in California, making expenses high, the administration allowed one teacher from each of the two-ninth-grade teams to attend. Martha represented Apex and felt it was an invaluable experience. However, since the other teachers did not attend the conference, they did not feel any ownership in what Martha learned. Therefore, what she experienced was never really studied in terms of how the Apex teachers could formulate themes or units.

Interdisciplinary curriculum was not the only area of neglect. No faculty members received professional development in teaching strategies to use in block scheduling. The teachers knew by the previous December that they would be engaging in block scheduling the following year. Therefore, they asked the administrators to set up training during several in-service days scheduled in April, but their request was ignored. Tanya continued:

> The [in-service] days came and went. I don't think we did much of anything those days. I think they were department interbuilding work. So we missed an opportunity there. At the

end of last year, we were saying, we are doing this and we don't know what we are doing, we need help, we need some training. Across e-mail, probably a week before school was out, there came a little message, there will be an opportunity for training on intensive scheduling in August. People are going, okay. It was August 1, 2, 3. Why would you do that at that point? So I am sure they didn't have a big crowd for that if it ever happened at all. (Interview 1)

Martha explained how they tried to educate themselves plus write an interdisciplinary curriculum without any professional development provided by the administration:

We went everywhere we could and read everything we could and tried to just learn what it was, and the three of us stepped back and let Tanya and Lew sort of guide us with curriculum. We didn't know enough to sit down and say, these are the important things for ninth graders. We trusted Tanya and Lew to have those ideas, and that is going to be fine with me. . . . I see some areas where we should be working with the kids, hygiene and stuff like that, but we'll talk about that next summer, bringing that in next year. Se we started with the history basis. We went to [high school they visited], we rented a video from ASCD, . . . I don't know what else we did. We got literature and read and studied and felt we were on the right track then. (Interview 1)

Lew and Tanya were probably the least surprised by the lack of professional development because they experienced the same when they started teaming years ago. Lew explained how he and Tanya forged their curriculum:

The first year was really interesting because we really had no idea what we were doing. [Administrator no longer with school], as I said, was supposedly in charge, and he told us, he sat us down, the four of us, myself, Tanya and [two other ninth-grade English and social studies teachers] and he said this was definitely a major emphasis for the school and he would be there every step of the way and we had an unlimited budget and we could do all these fantastic things just like we are hearing now, and then all of a sudden the next year, we couldn't buy books and we couldn't get certain materials. Then they said, well maybe get that out of your department budget, and then the department said, we didn't budget for these kinds of things, and there was a big discrepancy on how we would get our materials, and when we went back to [the administrator], he seemed to not know what we were talking about, and so it got really screwy from the very beginning. You know, we started to see then that we were kind of on our own, and then after the year went on, we really didn't see any guidance whatsoever or any kind of feedback or any input or any concern from anyone, and that really got us off to a real strange start. So Tanya and I kind of just bumped our way around, and we didn't do a whole lot together as opposed to just little projects, things we thought might be good or we kind of talked. We really were getting to know ourselves was what it came down to . . .

I guess the biggest problem is again, you know, we are out here and we felt like we were out on a limb with getting started, and as you saw when you first latched on to us, we were given time but no real guidance or direction. So we are trying to put together what we find very difficult to do without the training and the proper guidance. (Interview 1)

This lack of professional development not only left the teachers feeling stranded, but also confused about the possible methods to integrate curriculum. A constant question no one could answer was, "Are we doing it right?" The administrators did not have any model for the teams to investigate or emulate. Even the experts on interdisciplinary curriculum purport different methods. These diverse models in the field made the need for schoolwide in-service even more critical.

If nothing else, the teachers needed a shared language so that they could define what they were trying to do and reach an agreement as to the best model for their students. For example, Jacobs (1995; 1989b) explains six options for content design. Her options range from discipline-based integration, such as whole language to complete integration, where subject-area divisions no longer exist. In-between are designs of parallel teaching, multidisciplinary teaching, and interdisciplinary teaching. Drake (1993) adds a model called transdisciplinary or real world, which places emphasis on relevance and meaning through a life-centered approach, making content intrinsically unimportant. In this model, student interests, not predetermined guidelines, determine the content. Beane (1997), however, suggests that popular curriculum consultants such as Hayes-Jacobs and Drake have neglected the historical basis of curriculum integration as a form of democratic pedagogy. He insists that true curriculum integration demands that teachers and students work together to plan curriculum jointly around relevant life issues and questions.

This lack of professional development to discuss curriculum, to examine models of interdisciplinary curriculum, and to address students' needs made it impossible to create a common ninth-grade interdisciplinary curriculum for both teams to implement. It also created more uncertainty since both ninth-grade teams chose different models of interdisciplinary teaming. Apex chose to stay content-specific and present content through historical themes. The other team selected Drake's model that deemphasizes discipline specific content and places more emphasis on student choice. Thus, the two models of interdisciplinary teaming exacerbated the fact that no written curriculum existed and left the teachers concerned that the students were losing a common pool of knowledge.

We witnessed one meeting between a central office administrator and the Apex teachers where this confusion in language was readily apparent. The administrator kept using the term *curriculum integration*, by which he meant Beane's concept while the teachers used curriculum integration á la Hayes-Jacobs to mean any form of crossing subject boundaries. Not recognizing that their common labels really symbolized different conceptions, the teachers and the administrator left the meeting thinking they were headed in the same direction when they were worlds apart. This lack of agreement became clearer a few days later in a written communication from the central office administrator. Lew summed up the frustration this dilemma created:

> They throw us into the fire and then figure out ways of putting it out later. You know, say, okay, now how do we go about doing this? And that's the other way, that's backwards, and

then after we actually may figure it out and start to work a process, they may scrap it without listening if it was the right process, and that is really where our problem is, I think, more than anything else at the school, is that we don't have—no one does the research prior to doing the project is what it comes down to. That is what we tell our kids that they can't do. I mean, we talk about this [Wild West] museum that we want to build. We say, see I'm going off now, but we say that if we taught our classes the way that we are administered by the administration, we would fail. All of our kids would fail, there wouldn't even be a question. So that almost scares us to say they are setting us up to fail because we are not being given the proper process of implementing any of the things that they want us to implement. It's almost like saying, go do it, then go get training, then if we don't like it, we'll scrap it, and our question is, well, how do you know if you like it because you haven't evaluated it. It is a strange setup. (Interview 1)

Lack of Guidance and Feedback

The Apex teachers felt they had no guidance or feedback during the implementation process. Even when they did approach the administration for feedback, they felt that they were ignored. For example, when the teachers sent the central administrator questions to be answered regarding the curriculum and model of interdisciplinary teaming to follow (as discussed in chapter 3), the teachers received a five-minute report on an in-service day right before lunch. Lew described this lack of acknowledgment:

It's almost if we request it [support], they'll give us some lip service or allow us to do whatever it is, but I don't think anyone has done any background research or any evaluations of even what it is that we're doing to determine whether they think that one program is the way to go or this is the way we want to try it. And, again, like I said, when we requested that feedback just recently, we really didn't get it back. We did not get the answers, nor did we get even a response that I thought we would get. (Interview 2)

Lew continued to explain in this same interview how he was used to the lack of support and why the teachers continued in spite of it:

I think years ago, Tanya and I realized that if we were going to do this, we had to do it the way we saw it because if we wait for their input, we would really be frustrated and kind of hanging out on the mountain because we've asked for that kind of input before. . . . We've never gotten the guidance from anyone with expertise to say, hey, if this is the program, this is the model of the program. We've never gotten anything specific, nor has anyone ever sat down with us and said, okay, exactly what is it that you are doing, and as a result, hey, we like this or this is what we see as being beneficial to our kids. There has never been any assessment. We feel very strongly about what we've done, and that is why we work so hard to try to keep developing it even with bringing the new guys into it, but at no point have they given us a forum to say exactly what it is that we are doing so that we let them know. We would like to know if what we are doing is right. (Interview 2)

Through the course of this same interview, Lew was able to articulate why the lack of guidance and support went beyond their own limitations and uncertainty to the bigger scheme of hurting education itself. He used the example of the way the other team was implementing interdisciplinary teaching, which he believed was slighting the students. Since the other team chose to use Drake's model of interdisciplinary curriculum, they emphasized student choice over content. Therefore, if a theme was labeled "moral responsibility," the students were allowed to choose what they wished to study. Thus, some students were researching the Vietnam War while others were looking at another historical event. Lew, who views history as a content driven by chronology, did not agree with this method of interdisciplinary teaming if it meant losing content, such as the Holocaust. Given the laissez-faire approach from the administration, Lew believed there was no forum to question these differences to arrive at the best model. He explained:

I really, really, really have a problem with the way that history is being taught over there because I was talking to one of their students, and they said that in this choices' theme, they are allowed to choose different eras of history, and so right now we have kids at this point in time in our curriculum doing Vietnam. So my question is, if at any time that they choose to be a history major or involved with a social studies era, they would have no chronological background. They may miss quite a bit of history because if they have a chance to choose, they are going to choose the ones that they either heard of or are familiar with or something that they have some attachment to, and then they are going to miss all the ones that the kids may consider boring, which is still just as important, and so those are the kinds of questions I want to propose to [central administrator] and the powers that be, and say, is this what you are asking us to do because then I do have some arguments to state that I don't believe that is the right way to go about it. So there is no way to combat it, there is no way to bring it to the forefront at this point in time without probably stepping on a lot of toes and causing a lot of problems.

I know I've talked to different people about it. Sometimes around here we step out of the area of professionalism because it becomes more personal when there actually is a question of, is it the educational thing to do, and people would take it as a personal swipe if you say that they aren't doing something that should be done in education, and again we never get any support otherwise. (Interview 2)

The teachers felt that it was the administrators' job to know what the teachers were doing. Corbett, Dawson, and Firestone (1984) report that building administrators can facilitate change by engaging in informal talks with the faculty, by discussing issues regarding the innovation at staff meetings, and by including staff progress toward the building or district goal on the formal evaluation. Both Tanya and Lew discussed their experience when the two of them teamed together as feeling unappreciated. They thought it was ironic that the administration discovered what they were doing through avenues other than directly observing or communicating with them:

It is kind of ironic because when Lew and I were doing all of this two years ago, we really started, and I think we did some things that were neat. It wasn't outstanding, we weren't the best teachers in the world, but it was making sense to us. The kids were getting things out of it and for ninth grade they were producing some really neat things—papers, projects, artifacts, plays—and our ninth graders were doing senior work. I am convinced. I have papers from my ninth graders that were better than any papers I got from seniors. We really didn't do anything with it. We showed it to parents when they came in. We didn't know we had to take it elsewhere. I didn't know I had to send copies of papers that kids had done to the principal. I thought that was his job to know what we were doing. I assumed he knew. He didn't know. I assumed our central office administrator knew. He didn't know. I think the team has to be aware of that, to broadcast. . . . For Parents' Day [the year before], I said, hey, Lew, nobody knows what we are doing, let's do a big display case. He let me go. We put this table out, we had a big glass display case, and we put out two of these tables. I covered them with construction paper, put a little border right around it and a little skirting and it looked like a little wedding party there ready for the cake, and we were doing World War II at that point. The kids had made tanks and these warfare trenches that they created. There were grenades, flags, sashes, medals. They had done all kinds of neat artifacts in addition to papers and a skit. So we put out a couple of the research papers, we put out the tanks, we put out some of the stuff the kids had done, and the whole school stopped by. [The central office administrator] came and said, this is a great job, this is what it is all about, this is the way to go. I thought, we have to do this every year. Really at that point we were in our own little world. (Interview 1)

Lew also talked about this need to display work to be appreciated and the resentment it caused inside him:

Years ago, they had given me a rating which was on an average level, and I had top ratings all other years, and I documented all the things I had done within a portion of the year, which ended up being four pages long, and I presented that to him [the principal], the central office people and everyone else who I thought should get one. All of a sudden everyone was amazed, "I had no idea what you are doing." Well, why don't you? This is why you have to sell yourself. No, I don't. All I have to do is teach. All I should have to do is teach, and you should be aware of what it is that I am doing, and as a result, I gained some respect, but I also probably gained some negatives because I was like forcing their hand to make a change that they never had to do before. (Interview 1)

Since the teachers did not receive any guidance or feedback from the administrators, they tended to look to others for support and to count on outside "scoops" to gauge their progress. One group they looked to for support was their fellow team members. Gary stated:

It was really nice having people there to support you and encourage you and give you ideas and feedback. So I think, I wasn't sure how well that was going to work with five people trying to work together, and again I was pleased with the way things worked out with our team. I guess I was a little surprised by the lack of support we actually got from the administration, and basically we were kind of out there on our own. (Interview 3)

Another source that gave them some acknowledgment was nonteam teachers who heard the administration was pleased with the work being done. Although they appreciated the comments, they resented hearing them secondhand. Lew said:

I guess I was talking to one of the teachers yesterday, and it came out that it seemed the administration was pretty well pleased with what the teams had shown them in the work we had done over the summer, and so they are not concerned about observing us and what we are doing because they feel that we are on track, so they are going to spend a lot of their time observing individual teachers. My first comment was that I don't appreciate that because if I put that time in, . . . I would like somebody to come along to see if that's what we are doing, if we are on the right track, and if that is the direction we are trying to go in. So, again, we are kind of left to ourselves. (Interview 1)

The policy that the administrators were following in not observing teachers who were on track made clear to the teachers that they were practicing a deficit model of teacher supervision and evaluation. The message was "no news is good news." Their final source of acknowledgment for the work they did came from their evaluation at the end of the year. Although they appreciated this praise, they felt it was too little, too late, and too ingenuine. Tanya shared her feelings:

> [Assistant principal] gave me this glowing report at the end of the year, and Lew got this wonderful report, and it just makes you feel like, well, I guess you are doing okay. All they had to do at the end of Jurassic Park was come up and say— it would've taken 15 minutes—tell me the best part about Jurassic Park and that's really neat, wow! I just think they don't realize the power of that . . . and they don't know what we're doing. Really they don't know. They've never asked to see a lesson plan. They've never asked to see any products of what kids did, and we're not the type of a team to go in and say, look, look, look. (Interview 3)

Conflict with Other Team

An issue that arose in the spring before implementing the restructuring mandate was a disagreement about classroom space with the teachers on the other team. The Apex teachers believed that the lack of administrative leadership to resolve this initial issue fueled the conflict between the two teams. This discord between the two teams sustained itself because of the lack of a common bond in the understanding and implementing of the innovations and the competition the restructuring project created.

The room disagreement began the spring prior to the implementation. Both ninth-grade teams decided that they wanted their five classrooms to be in proximity to each other for obvious reasons of facilitating group work and having easy access to each other. As team members negotiated classrooms near each other, one room appealed to both teams. This room sat in the middle of the hall that separated the two teams from each other, although it was closer to the other Apex rooms. It was a huge classroom with two big closets and a side hall that could be used for independent work. It also contained a water source. The math teacher who was originally a member of the Apex team had occupied that room for 15 years, which was the duration of his tenure at the high school. Thus, Apex assumed that it would remain with their team.

Unknown to them, the other team decided that they wanted the room and told the math teacher that they were claiming the room. This math teacher, near retirement, did not want to cause any arguments. However, when the other Apex teachers found out, they were furious. They had assumed from the beginning that it was their classroom, especially since it was already occupied by a team member.

Eventually, the two teams were unable to resolve the issue, and they approached the principal to decide whose room it would be. He refused to do so. He likened his involvement to feeling like Solomon and refused to participate in the conflict. Instead, he told the teams to go back and fight it out among themselves. Again, the teachers were unable to reach a compromise. After weeks of conflict and several fruitless meetings which sometimes ended in teachers being extremely angry with each other, the principal finally awarded the room to Apex and found a room with a water source for the other team. The other team saw this decision as a "win" for Apex, resulting in a competition throughout the remainder of the study. Both teams also left the situation with no improvement in their conflict resolution skills. As a result, they were in no better position to resolve conflicts which developed later. Had the principal helped the teams to develop a win-win approach to conflict resolution, each team could have gotten its wishes, and all the teachers would have learned some valuable conflict resolution skills. As a result of his refusal to become involved, the principal allowed a potential win-win situation to deteriorate into a win-lose situation, which caused lingering resentment and ill will.

Tanya captured the complexity of the room situation, explaining the beginning roots of the competition between the two teams and the negative feelings it created:

[Other team member] came to [math teacher who had been occupying the room] and said, we need this room, you are going to have to move, and to tell someone who had been in that room for 15 years. . . . This man has just been thrown on a team, doesn't really want to be on a team, the teaming bullshit is up to here with [the math teacher]. . . . I don't think it went over well. So [math teacher] brought this up to Lew. . . . We ended up writing a note to [the principal] that we need the room, you can't take the room. At that point, [the principal]—I think his intention was to let us hammer it out between the two teams, which when you have a situation with teaming there is a natural competition going on, you don't want to add any competition where you start to argue with each other to get the room. Their team was well versed. So they tried to get the room, and Lew and I have been passive at this point. Throughout the years any comparisons that were made between the two teams [English and social studies], we knew in our hearts we were doing what we were supposed to do. We weren't about broadcasting and advertising, get us in the fact sheet, get us in the [local newspaper]. We are not interested. We are doing what we are doing and don't have time for that stuff. We really didn't, but at this point they got us. No, no, you are not taking our room. We had planned activities. We needed the space to do some activities. When we get to the Wild West, you will observe how the floor is being used and how that big room will really facilitate. . . . Plus Lew and I saw that red brick area [between controversial room and Tanya's], and we thought we could use that. This will be our room. From your room to my room and everything in between is our room, and if people don't like it, they can take the other stairs. So, we wrote a letter to [the principal], explaining that we need the room for such and such reasons. He said to fight it out. That's when everything got nasty. That's when Gary [not yet a member of the team] was looking, saying, these two teams are at each other's throat already. I don't even want to be a part of teaming. The whole school kept saying, look what teaming is doing. Look, look, everybody is fighting with each other, and that's where the whole competition thing came from, I believe.

Two years previous to that, [the principal] was at a meeting and said a statement such as, I am paraphrasing now, that if it weren't for one team this teaming would never work anyway, and it was in reference to [other freshman English and social studies team], not Lew and I. At that point Lew and I had just finished all this work with the Wild West project. We had research papers of eighteen pages from ninth graders with internal citations and a bibliography page, and we had big performances in the auditorium where kids were cowboys and Indians and doing camp songs. All kinds of real learning activities. We thought, it's not working? At that point he [the principal] had never been in either of our rooms throughout the course of teaming. To make a statement like that really bothered us. So we called him on it right away, and that started a little bit of competition. The other team wasn't in the office saying, we do this and this, either. However, their team teaching, they both teach in the same classroom, so it appears—I am not even sure what goes on—it appears as though the two teachers have given up all boundaries and are just teaching. So it appears to be very interdisciplinary, so the principal assumed they were and we weren't.

So that started the competition. This room thing carried out the competition. The other team wanted a water source. It wasn't so much the room; it was the water source. They found another water source. We had these morning meetings where we sat around this big room, the conference room, and it ended up we were yelling, not yelling, discussing with one another a rationale for why we needed the room. Well, both teams thought their rationale was the right rationale, so we pounded heads back and forth. I'm not sure what the right rationale was, but we knew that they were trying to take a room that was on our team that we had a use for. If [original math teacher] was not a team teacher from the start, it wouldn't have bothered us. Take whatever rooms you want, and we won't argue about any of the other rooms. You just can't take a room from our team, and we wanted to stand our ground there so that if there ever was another situation, don't take our stuff. We are teaming, we work together, don't step on our toes and they really stepped on them there. So we stood our ground, we ended up with the room. [The principal] made the decision, found another water source, and I still think that bothers the other team, and I think it would have bothered us if we didn't get the room, and I think that is natural. (Interview 1)

Martha explained that the meeting that Tanya referred to as "yelling" and "discussing" had a feel of condescension, which made them feel guilty for asking for administrative assistance to resolve the issue, even though everyone knew a need for conflict resolution existed:

I don't appreciate [the principal] coming in that day—he was settling the room thing—and saying, . . . "I am sitting here with a room full of the most talented people I have ever met, and they can't work this out, and you, you"—it was all this "you, you" stuff—"you want me to back off always and let you have say, and here I am giving you say, and this is what you do with it," and we all sat there because we knew he was right. We couldn't work it out. Well, then, we said, we can't work this out. We asked him for help. If you ask someone for help, shouldn't you get it? (Interview 1)

Tanya believed that this room incident, which might have seemed trivial to everyone else, was really a part of a bigger issue, that of having no input into any aspect of the restructuring. Thus, when something came along where they had a voice and where they perceived a legitimate need to control the situation for the sake of their teaching, they had to fight for the room:

When we had the room battle at the beginning and ending of last school year. That really bothered a lot of people, rubbed the other faculty members the wrong way that we would even argue with the other team over a room, that this is trivial, we are fighting over a room. But what they didn't understand was the bigger picture that it wasn't just a room. It was the railroading of ideas, and we weren't getting any input, and no one was listening to our concern. It was all focused on the other team, so we kind of had to fight or get run over for the rest of the school year. (Interview 2)

Martha validated Tanya's assessment of the situation:

It became . . . for Lew it was survival of our team at stake. If you don't see in our favor because this was our room to start, then you don't want us to succeed. He said it in those words, and he was going to say that to [the principal]. If that happened . . . [the principal] let us have the room, thank God. He's fair. He's fair. I think it was the right way although [foreign language teacher from other team] does not to this day. To this day she calls it a victory for me. When I walked in that morning, she said, "Well, you won." I had never viewed it like that. To me there was no winning or losing. It was our room. It should never have left us. (Interview 1)

A second conflict that occurred in September, which seemed to cement the animosity between the two teams, dealt with using the computer room. When the administration was working on the logistics of teaming, they decided to create a computer lab, which would be shared by both teams, without a teacher or an aide to monitor the computer lab. The Apex teachers voiced that they preferred a few computers in each classroom so that students could be involved in simultaneous activities and the teachers could monitor everyone. The other team of teachers, however, liked the idea of a lab, and one of the teachers mocked Apex for being "behind the times," something that annoyed the veteran team of teachers. The administration decided to put all the computers in one lab. This decision may have been a not so hidden attempt at evening the score by providing a win for the other team at the expense of Apex.

The incident that sparked the argument occurred on a Friday. John sent some students to the lab, but he remained in his classroom. A teacher from the other team saw John's students unattended and became angry. Tanya realized this incident might cause another confrontation; therefore, she told the assistant principal about the incident Friday afternoon before she left school for the weekend. The following Monday, Tanya took her students to the computer room so they could write a midquarter progress report to send to their parents and houseparents. When she arrived with her students, a teacher from the other team yelled at Tanya, because she thought Tanya and Apex had run to the administration to "squeal" on Friday's incident. Tanya explained to her that she did not run to the assistant principal for his intervention, but to state her case. Although Tanya tried to keep her composure, the other teacher yelled at Tanya for making the computer lab a big issue and running to the administration.

Both teams then devised a sign-up plan for use of the computer lab. The teachers found, however, that they all seemed to want to use the lab at the same time on the same day. They even tried to divide a class period, allowing members from each team to use it for half a period. None of these efforts seemed to resolve anything, and it eventually came to a head between Tanya and a teacher on the other team. Martha explained the incidents leading to the argument:

> Tanya had sent a couple of students or somebody had, and they were there and it ended up the other team person yelled at our students and then it escalated into an all out fight about the other team signing up for more computer time way far in advance, and first off we never said we wanted the computer room. All of a sudden it comes together—it's the computer room being shared by two teams. We had never sat down with them to discuss rules or signing in or sharing and it became a big headache. (Interview 1)

This fight over the computer room seemed to end any possibility of a collaborative relationship developing between the two teams. Apex teachers felt that Tanya was unjustly treated by the other team member. Thus, even though both teams were in the middle of planning a ninth-grade pep rally and cheering together at a football game, neither activity occurred. All their plans to work together were abandoned.

As the teachers continued to refer to these two incidents throughout the course of the study, other issues surfaced, explaining some of the underlying hostility between the two teams. All these issues were exaggerated because of the lack of administrative leadership. Lew expounded:

> The administration sometimes seems to back off from directly approaching a problem because they don't want to hurt people's feelings, and I think a lot about that, but that's not the best way to deal with it. I mean if there's a problem in education, that means a problem with kids, and it should be dealt with directly, and many times that's not done because of personal restraints. (Interview 2)

Without a written curriculum or a model of interdisciplinary teaming to adopt as a school, the two teams went in different directions from the start. As stated in chapter 3, there was no written curriculum or articulated goals for the restructuring project. Also, there were no plans to evaluate the restructuring project. Therefore, the two teams did not have any common bond to keep them accountable to each other.

The teaming did make the five teachers become more accountable to each other and played an important factor in their commitment to the team (to be discussed in chapter 6). However, the lack of common goals for the entire restructuring eliminated a need for close linkage to the other team. Linkage refers to "the degree to which parts of a system can function independently of one another" (Corbett, Dawson, & Firestone, 1984, p. 90). These two factors created balkanization that was stronger than they had experienced as members of their subject-area departments. Hargreaves (1994) describes balkanization as follows:

> The balkanized form of teachers' cultures, like all other forms, is defined by particular patterns of interrelationships among teachers. In balkanized cultures, these patterns mainly consist of teachers working neither in isolation, nor with most of their colleagues as a whole school, but in smaller subgroups within the school community. (P. 213)

Hargreaves cites four qualities that generate and sustain balkanization, all four of which apply to Apex. The first is low permeability. The Apex teachers predominantly belonged to their team. Their rooms were in proximity, and their schedules incorporated a team planning period every other day. They tended to eat lunch together, at least on the days of team meetings (three days out of a six-day cycle). Since they were separated from other teachers by proximity and time, they spent their nonteaching time with each other. They all said that they never visited the faculty room any more and that they rarely attended department meetings. Thus, as Hargreaves maintains, their professional learning (what teachers come to know, think, and believe) occurred mainly within their own subgroup and varied considerably from that of the other freshman team teachers.

The second quality Hargreaves labels high permanence. Once established, groups tend to remain together throughout the years, thus cementing their beliefs and values. This bond was apparent between Lew and Tanya, who had teamed together for three years before the new restructuring project.

The third quality, personal identification, rides tandem with high permanence. Because these teachers formed a tight bond, they began to identify exclusively with their teammates. Because they inducted themselves into a subculture, they distanced themselves from their other colleagues. This singular identification undermined their capacity for empathy and collaboration with others.

Lew seemed to understand the way these qualities, coupled with a lack of administrative leadership, caused the balkanization. When asked to explain the friction that existed between the two teams, Lew explained:

> It goes back again to, I think, administrative guidance. They allowed us to get together and call ourselves a team, and we met, I guess in the very beginning the four of us, and it was almost like they [administrators] said, go to it, we are with you 100 percent of the way. Then, after we started to go, nothing materialized in guidelines because we were supposed to meet periodically and see how each team was doing, what and how we were working, and we never did that. Never. There was never a time when we sat down. The one time we sat down in an in-service time—we asked for some time—we discovered that their philosophy was totally different from ours. We said, how about the projects we were trying to create and the things we were trying to do. They were like no, no, we are not into projects. So, right away, we kind of put up a shield, hey, this is our baby, this is what we do, and they are saying, no, no, we don't buy that. So, I am sure they did the same thing. So, right away, there was distance put between us, and we didn't see any real need to come together and work together. But as a result of not having [administrator] or whoever it was supposed to be to pull us together and make us bring these things out, it just got us further and further apart. (Interview 1)

The final quality that Hargreaves attributes to balkanization is political complexity. Hargreaves explains this quality as follows:

> Teacher subcultures are not merely sources of identity and meaning. They are repositories of self-interest as well. Promotion, status, and resources are frequently distributed between

and realized through membership of teacher subcultures. These goods are not distributed evenly, nor are they contested by different subcultures on equal terms. . . . In balkanized cultures, there are winners and losers. There is grievance and there is greed. Whether they are manifest or muted, the dynamics of power and self-interest within such cultures are major determinants of how teachers behave as a community. (P. 214–215)

Because Tanya and Lew believed that they had been ignored in their dual teaming endeavors, they sensed the political issues early in the project. They felt that the other teaching dyad of English and social studies had received all the accolades for interdisciplinary teaming the previous years, yet no one knew what they were accomplishing in their classrooms because they did not have the time or inclination to publicize. The room conflict, especially when the other team reported the results as a win for Apex, set the political agenda for both the teams and the administration. Therefore, when the administration ruled that the computers would be housed in a lab as the other team requested, the score was tied, 1-1, and the politics stayed at the forefront.

Other issues that divided the teams might have appeared small on the surface but aggravated the situation between them. The Apex students told their teachers that the other team of teachers said they stole their incentive idea of giving tickets for good grades and citizenship. In addition, the Apex students told them that the other team of teachers did not think candy was an appropriate item to be purchased with the tickets. The students told their teachers that the other team of teachers said the competition between the teaching teams was good because it made them better teachers. The Apex teachers disagreed, stating that they were good teachers for their students' sake, not for competitive reasons.

These issues cropped up because of philosophical differences between the two teams. Tanya explained the differences that she perceived:

Well, it is a philosophical difference. I think we look at our kids more as kids, and they look at them more as students, which they can be both together. When I talk, I don't say *students,* I say *kids,* and even when I'm writing formal papers, I catch myself writing *kids* instead of *students* . . . To go to a different level with kids, you have to cross over that line that everybody's in a little row and all feet are on the floor and all pencils are out. Especially with our kids. I'm confident enough with what I'm doing and what I know that I don't need that. I still want classroom management, but I don't have to have the kids raise their hands when they say something anymore unless the activity really needs that in it. . . . I have different ways to do it, and they [other team teachers] are still in that disciplinarian structure boot camp mentality, and I think that's why we are not into the orientations in the beginning of the year, and it's ironic because we don't need to stay overnight with our kids. Here, let's be buddies. Let's sleep over and then [in class], don't talk, are your papers folded, detention, stand up, you forgot your pencil. You wouldn't do that to a friend, and that's what they want them to think of them, as their friends. So, yeah, there is a philosophical difference. And if we'd get together more, they would feed off maybe some of what we do. (Interview 3)

The teachers were also upset when they discovered that the other team was making presentations about interdisciplinary teaming at the Association for Supervision and Curriculum Development's annual conference. They were appalled that the other team had submitted a proposal three months prior to their actually implementing the restructuring project. Lew stated:

The fact that they are going out to present at the ASCD conference, and we are thinking, why? They don't even have the experience to present yet. They haven't assessed the program. I don't understand why that would be allowed to happen, that you are out there teaching somebody else about something you are trying to figure out yourself. (Interview 1)

The other team later went to Atlanta, Georgia, to assist a school that was embarking on a similar restructuring project. The Apex teachers were surprised and hurt. They felt the other team could have at least come to them for some suggestions.

All these qualities led to a lack of trust between the two teams. Murphy and Hallinger (1993) offer three reasons why trust is difficult to obtain, especially in school restructuring projects. First, in many schools trust is a structural phenomenon, spelled out in contracts, guidelines, and operating procedures and policies. In restructuring, however, trust must be less structured and more relational. In restructuring, "game rules" change, and people find themselves in different roles. Second, restructuring creates conflict, confusion, and ambiguity, conditions that are not amenable to trust. Third, restructuring entails risk, which entails possible failure. The right to fail, however, is not a part of the school culture in this country. Therefore, failure is more likely to be viewed from a finger-pointing blame than a supportive stance.

Lew summarized why the trust between the two teams was broken early in the restructuring project and how it impacted on everyone:

> We would bend over backwards sometimes to meet and try to bridge the gap, but it is just something that just doesn't seem to be there because I believe we have a lack of trust at this point. We see a lot of the underhanded things that have taken place, and they [the other team of teachers] do things for reward and they seem to get it. That is the sad part about it, and we do things for a different type of reward, the intrinsic reward, and that doesn't get the same kind of slap on the back as some of the other things. So, again, it is just kind of a feeling of disdain. It just won't go away. And it's sad because it is really a detriment in some way to the ninth graders as a whole. I really do feel bad about that part of it. Because even some of the comments that the kids make to each other, like they might say to our kids, all you guys do is fun and games, but they have no idea what we are really doing, and then we feel that in their area, all they are doing is memorizing material, and so you have two different philosophies, and the kids are kind of like against that and each other, and it is just not the best thing in the world, and again that's an administrative situation that they should definitely step in and take control, which we don't have. (Interview 1)

Hargreaves (1994) believes that a way to solve the issues of balkanization is to produce a mosaic culture in which teachers have membership on multiple working groups within the school such as interdisciplinary teams, subject area departments, and student assistance programs. Through the boundary crossing which occurs in these various working groups, faculty members have the opportunity to develop shared, whole-school commitments to missions and visions of educational purpose. Lew explained the lack of wholeness that began four years ago with the dyads of interdisciplinary teaming and continued into the new teaming formation:

> We were given no set curriculum to follow. We were given no set guidelines on what the team approach was all about. So they [the other team] automatically went in one direction, and we totally went in another. For example, they didn't see that the interdisciplinary approach was even important as far as projects and things of that nature, and we felt very highly that that was what it was all about, to bring it together and the kids could become creative in that range. So right away you have two different philosophies, and no one stepped in to say which one was the direction that the school wanted to go in. So even as of today with the two teams, their team is totally doing something different than what we are doing, and I don't think that is fair to the kids because, if we bring the kids together, we don't know which one is more effective, because no one has really tested that yet either. I wonder if they will. But it is not fair to have the same grouping of kids being taught two separate ways with totally two separate curriculums. You know, because I doubt that they are covering any of the materials from what I can tell that we are covering and vice versa. Which one is the way to go for the school? (Interview 1)

Gary expressed that he doubted the possibility of the two teams finding a common ground since they were so far removed from each other:

> Well, there doesn't seem much concern about getting the common ground together. I think we're just so far apart right now that it's going to take a lot to try to pull it back together again. Now one thing they [administrators] did mention was actually, if we ever get a curriculum together, where we both would be following kind of the same curriculum, it might help,

but, yeah, we kind of follow the thing with Lew and Tanya in what they had set up for theirs, and we tie our own work into that, whereas I don't even know what the other team really does. So I'm not sure what they do use as their foundation. (Interview 3)

Tanya seemed to validate Gary's fears, stating that the schedule for the following year already made it impossible for the teams to meet. Even though the administration had said the two teams would meet on a regular basis the following year, the new schedule showed no common planning time for both teams to meet.

Gray (1989) warns that conflict is common even in collaborative groups who have a shared vision. The conflict arises when people have different ways to implement the vision. It can, however, be productive as long as the participants understand that conflict often arises from individual assumptions.

Gray notes the following assumptions. The first is that people believe that their way of viewing a problem is the best, which may really mean the most rational, the fairest, the most intelligent or perhaps the only way. These people lose sight of the possibility of multiple approaches to a problem.

Tanya believed that Apex was correct in their implementation because of a comment written on her evaluation:

I feel confident sending the kids to the teachers [next year]. I just wish that they would do more as a team. If that's what the school wants you to do, that's your job, you do it. That's how I thought about it from the start. That's what they want me to do. Whether I agreed or not, this is the curriculum, do it. Which I'd still like to see. Use the map. Even [assistant principal] put in my evaluation something about the curriculum and about I was right using the maps. Well, if I'm right, then someone's wrong, and please tell them to use the same thing. (Interview 3)

The second assumption that Gray notes is that people believe that different interpretations are opposing interpretations. If people work through these interpretations, they often find that they are sharing the same concerns but have framed them differently or not listened to them carefully because of their own strong convictions.

The third assumption is that people stereotype others, thus discounting the legitimacy of another point of view or restricting the flow of information between the stakeholders.

Even when the principal tried to get the two teams together near the end of the year, the teachers felt the meeting was hopeless. Tanya explained the meeting:

> [Principal] said what a wonderful job we've done, but I don't really think he knows what we've done. He just blanketed all of us with what a wonderful job we've done, but we've gone our separate way as teams, and now we need to come back together and to maybe come up with common objectives, and Lew's question was, well how do you come up with objectives without a curriculum? Oh, we have a curriculum, he said, and [teacher from other team] said something about the thirteen desired results, yet there was no curriculum written from the thirteen results. So he [principal] wants us to do some objectives, and we still need that big curriculum. And although he says next year we're going to focus on writing curriculum, I think this [restructuring endeavor] could've waited until we had a curriculum. It would've been much more successful. (Interview 3)

The teachers realized as early as the spring prior to the implementation that they were not in agreement with the other team's philosophy. In the minutes of their March 14 team meeting, they recorded the follow: "We are in agreement that we are not in competition with [other team] but reserve the right to respectfully disagree and travel different paths to reach the same goals." However, since the teams had no forum to meet and discuss nor a written curriculum to follow, they were unable to agree to disagree. Therefore, all three of the previously discussed assumptions remained, and the teams had no chance to reconcile.

Conflict cannot be ignored or dismissed, although the most common and most mistaken response to conflict in a school is to avoid it (Glickman, 1993). This avoidance leads to fragmentation and division among faculty. Avoidance of conflict can undermine communication and prevent resolution because a norm tends to arise that coerces people into hiding their feelings and emphasizing the rational parts of their interaction (Maeroff, 1993).

Martha tried to be the peacemaker between the two teams, especially since the one teacher on the other team was a good friend of hers. Martha talked about how she felt at the height of her frustration over the room conflict:

I am evaluating relationships with people right now, deciding which of them to continue and which to stop. Because I can't take it. Every time I turn around, there is another little headache between the two teams. I spent two weeks with [a female member of other team] trying to get our teams together just for something as simple as a pep rally for the ninth graders. Through a communication difficulty, Lew was waiting for [a male member of other team] to come to him, and [a male member of other team] was waiting for Lew to come to him, and if [a female member of other team] and I hadn't talked, they would've both sat in their rooms waiting for the other one to come, and I went in to Lew and said, "Lew, [a male member of other team] is waiting for you," and then he e-mailed [male member] and we met. Something as simple as lack of communication, which we do a lot with this other team. (Interview 1)

The teachers resented that the conflict was being ignored and felt bad about the animosity between them even though they did not know how to resolve it themselves. Tanya explained:

One of the most disappointing aspects is still the relationship with the other team. I feel very disappointed in that I can feel it getting better, but I still feel that we get the cold shoulder, and I still think that we give the cold shoulder to an extent in our interpretation of what is going on, and I think that could be handled by giving us time together in a non-competitive atmosphere to talk about what we are doing by an outside facilitator maybe. That way we could vent our anger on them [the outside facilitator]. (Interview 2)

The teachers felt sure, however, that the administration would continue to ignore the conflict between the two teams and to remain uninvolved in the intricacies and details of implementing the restructuring initiative. The teachers felt, too, that the lack of administrative leadership was detrimental to them as individuals and as a team and helped lay the foundation for the tension created between their desire to remain loyal to both their subject area and the other team members.

6

Subject Loyalty versus
Team Allegiance

Problems are the route to deeper change and deeper satisfaction.

—Michael Fullan (1991)

Overview

A theme that became increasing prominent throughout the study was subject loyalty versus team allegiance. As the teachers struggled throughout the year to blend their curriculums, they became concerned with the loss of subject-area content. This struggle between fulfilling content requirements and remaining loyal to the team's goal of interdisciplinary work created individual and group tension. When one of the researchers accompanied the teachers on the site visit to another school that was described in the previous chapter, she was struck by their individuality and unfamiliarity with each other:

> This team doesn't really know each other. They are still be-coming acquainted with each other. Something I found inter-esting is that each one made some individual content area comment that showed their excitement about their subject. They still seem to be trying to figure out where they fit into the team picture. (Field Notes, April 5)

These early perceptions were correct, and the study showed how their differences would surface. The mandate for interdisciplinary teaming did indeed allow the teachers to risk and experiment. It also did help assure for the administration effective implementation of the imposed restructuring project. However, the nature of interdis-ciplinary teaching created issues that undermined the teachers' in-dividuality and caused them concern. Although it is a very common move in secondary restructuring efforts, attempting to move teach-ers into interdisciplinary teams and away from subject-centered departments typically creates conflict and threatens teacher identity to some degree (Siskin and Little, 1995).

Letting go of old beliefs, although critical in order to design interdisciplinary curriculum, can cause anxiety and fear. Drake (1993) writes that there are ten assumptions that hinder the imple-mentation of interdisciplinary designs:

1. Students will not learn basic skills.

2. Optimum learning moves from basics to more complex issues.

3. Content is most important.

4. Course content will not be covered.

5. Integrated curriculum is superficial.

6. Knowledge belongs in discrete categories.

7. A specific subject is a "force-fit."

8. Teachers do not know enough.

9. Integration is only for gifted students.

10. Students are passive learners. The way to overcome these false assumptions is to empower teachers to make decisions

about the connections so that they identify and plan how and when to make the connections. (Palmer, 1995)

Palmer (1995) warns, however, that empowering teachers to make decisions has its own set of problems. Because they must negotiate in order to make curricular connections, teachers must have the ability to work as a team, listen to another point of view, and change long-held practices or beliefs. Negotiating refers to the process of planning for interdisciplinary teaching and learning that requires give and take on all sides and is achieved over time within a trusting, collegial situation. Beane (1995b) concurs, noting that teachers' identities are tied to status associated with subject area.

As these interdisciplinary teaching assumptions and empowerment issues came to the forefront, the teachers continued to struggle with their own identity and competence. In addition, the lack of a shared understanding of the mandate and the lack of a written curriculum added to the tension, leaving the teachers to grapple with intrapersonal tension and interpersonal conflict, on the one hand, and their professional commitment, on the other.

Intrapersonal Tension

The teachers did not sense an attack on their individual subject content. Instead, they felt remiss for the loss of content that was specific to their subject area and part of the common knowledge that, they believed, is requisite to an educated person. John struggled with his frustration at having to eliminate content yet wanting to be a contributing team member. Asked to explain if he made any changes in how he teaches, John responded:

Actually, I've made a lot of changes in how I teach, but I think it's more in what I cover. I don't cover as much, and I have a problem with that, and I brought that up to the team because I believe we are trying too much to coordinate what we're doing with what's going on in the social studies area, and I can't always fit in, and I had a problem because we're trying to get the Science Department to come out with outcomes' standards, and then, once the kids reach those standards, have them move on, and then we're watering down with this teaming and with these themes, even though they are good, and you know, I have certain things that I'm supposed to cover in this course, and I'm not getting them covered, and if I stop what I'm doing to do some teaming things, then I lose a lot, and I've lost a lot this year, so I kind of told Lew and the team that, look, I have things to cover and I can't be part of—I think it was Immigration—and, you know, I didn't play a big role in the Wild West, although we did do a lot of things, I thought, in the Wild West. But I just had to cut back and really concentrate on the few areas I felt my students were weak in that we had to cover, and now with World War II, they are doing the Holocaust, but that doesn't gel with what we're doing in here. We're doing in here, more or less, with World War II, the advancements and science and technology. So, you know, we're not right in line with them, but at the same time, we will be able to contribute to what's going on. (Interview 2)

Gary added that the lack of a written curriculum not only aggravated the uncertainty, but also added to the intrapersonal tension:

We have to decide, are we going to follow a curriculum by departments, or are we going to be really creative and come up with a curriculum for ninth graders and then follow through with it for tenth grade, and maybe, I mean, we've been talking about setting benchmarks and doing those kinds of things. No one seems to have made those kinds of decisions, and that's why I feel we are floundering cause we have so many things in the air yet. I mean we started last year with benchmarks and then that kind of—I guess that's still around—and we're still working on it, but it seems to be a very slow process that they're going through, and I've kind of taken the attitude that I will make sure I cover certain things in Algebra I and geometry, but if I don't get as far as I hoped to get, well, then, I just can't do everything. So, I mean, I think, I know John wants to make sure he has everyone as well prepared as he can, and that's exactly what I want to do, too, but I think we have to look and say, which is more important? (Interview 2)

John became even more exasperated when he felt that the students might also be missing out on skills, as well as content.

Very frustrated by the poor test scores on the students' final exams, John reflected:

> The only thing that I can say about it is probably for them [students who flunked] going to summer school will be good and might implant in them the idea that, hey, finals are important. Maybe taking tests are important, and maybe I should sit down and do some good studying so that I don't have to go to summer school. I don't know. But I'm not happy about it. I don't like it. I was really surprised, to tell you the truth. And the whole thing was, my final was not that difficult. The other thing I have a problem with is with all this communication and all the stuff that I've heard about on the team. One of my questions on the final—there were three essay questions, and one of the essay questions . . . was like, if you took the earth and moved it between Mercury and Venus and then you took it and moved it between Jupiter and Saturn, what would happen to the oceans? Describe and compare what would happen to the oceans. I thought that was easy. I didn't think it was that hard. All I wanted was that if it is between Mercury and Venus, it would probably boil away and evaporate because of it being closer to the sun, and if it was between Jupiter and Saturn, it would probably freeze because of being further away from the sun. That's all I wanted. (Interview 3)

John's third issue with the interdisciplinary teaming revolved around his perceptions of a lack of academic rigor:

> When you get caught up in teaming and themeing and everything else, it is very easy to lose sight of what your goals are because you can do some cutesy little things that are fun to do and the kids really have fun at it, but it doesn't mean that the kids are learning. That's something that we're going to have to learn, too. Just because a kid's having fun does not mean the kid's getting everything out of what you are doing in class. (Interview 2)

Gary did not see the projects and activities as an academic problem, but he had a concern about their value if the students did not continue in this learning style:

There were times where I think kids were always doing projects and skits and activities and those kinds of things, and, yet, if they leave this team and don't do any of that stuff anymore, I don't know that we prepared them the right way. Because they are going to go into a situation where they are going to have to do more textbook work, and they are going to have to do more traditional learning, they may not be as ready for that. So, I think we need to kind of think about what types of things we have done, how good were they, and were they beneficial overall for the whole process, or do we need to kind of maybe back off a little bit on some things and emphasize others that are more important. (Interview 3)

John resolved his inner conflict by the end of the year by deciding that he needed to remain loyal to science even if it meant relinquishing his position on the team. Upset with the lack of time to have students involved in science activities, the loss of content and poor final exam test scores, John demonstrated how he reached his decision:

I'm not so sure about not covering as much content. I didn't get to a lot of things that I usually get to. I didn't get to meteorology, I didn't get to rocketry, and I'm not sure that's good. . . . It's the content that is important, and all that stuff that flows along with it. . . . At the end of the school year, I am not happy with some of my students. I'm not happy with their attitude toward the exam. I'm not happy with how they did on the exam. I failed more students this time than I have in a long time. I failed seven students. . . . I think I was stretched to the limit this year, and I'm not going to be stretched to the limit next year, and I'm going to be able to do activities, and I'm going to be able to do science in my room, or else I'm going to look for something else. I mean that's what I do and that's what I do well. . . . I don't know, maybe it's the end-of-the-year blues or something. . . . Maybe there has to be a better way to do this, mixing all these different groups and stuff. But I think if we have students who like science and want to do science, then damn it, we should offer courses that challenge those students and that really get those students involved and let them show their talents. . . . My loyalty is science. That is my area. That is what I'm good at, and that's what I'm going to stay good at, and I can't give that up for teaming. (Interview 3)

Although Gary never considered leaving the team, he acknowledged how drained he felt at the end of the year:

I think it really started to take its toll at the end of the year, especially in my position where I had to cover the math curriculum plus the other team things, and it really became difficult toward the end to make sure I was getting both things covered. . . .

I became kind of frustrated towards the end where I knew there were things I needed to cover yet, and I didn't get to them, and there were things that I wanted to do and I wasn't going to have time for them. I really felt drained by the end of the year. (Interview 3)

Martha felt that she, too, had to work through a lot of issues to decide if she wanted to continue teaming. She felt very pressured to cover a department-specified number of chapters so that the students would be ready for the next level of foreign language study. She had to deal with preparing the students for the Foreign Language National Exams in the spring while internally questioning whether those exams were still pertinent. Even though she saw the exam as a good test-taking experience, she was not convinced that they were a valid gauge of her students' achievement since the interdisciplinary teaming created different objectives that eliminated time to teach the content requisite for the exam. She also had to face the possibility of relinquishing all chances of teaching French III and IV the following year in order to commit to the team full time. Martha explained why she decided to continue to team in light of all this uncertainty and frustration:

I had to weigh last night—I bounced it off Jay [her husband]— am I going to stay on this team and give up that French III and IV that I would love to have, or am I going to get off the team and take those two classes? I said, you know what it boils down to, I'm enjoying this. I like doing the Holocaust. I like doing Jurassic Park, and I think that I'm getting more out of this new teaching than I'm not. So I think I'm willing to give up—

these are kids I've had for two years now in French and they are going to be French III—I think I'll give them up. If I can't do it, I can't do it. I feel myself being pulled in two directions, though. I wish they [team members] would just say to me, "Teach four classes. Don't join us for Special Projects [fourth-period class], and take French III and IV. We can see that's what you want, Martha." But nobody's saying that. (Interview 2)

By the end of the year, Martha realized that she would be able to teach upper-level French anyway. This opportunity occurred because the team decided to allow the German teacher to be a member of their team so that the students would be allowed to take German, as well as French and Spanish, an issue that was debated for months. When Martha found out that allowing German on the team gave her the opportunity to teach the upperclassmen, she expressed relief and joy:

I didn't realize my attachment to the Foreign Language Department and how I would not want to pull out, and that's why I'm secretly and now verbally happy about having French IV next year off the team, and I'm glad that my team let me do it. They gave me the flexibility to still have upperclassmen because you can see I love them and I want them. I want them— that's what it boils down to—and I cannot teach ninth graders all day every day for a year and stay sane. (Interview 3)

The other team members assumed that Lew and Tanya were satisfied with their content coverage since the team was using the curriculum that Lew and Tanya created. This belief, however, was not the case. Tanya explained why adding teachers to the team complicated her teaching:

I am happy to have more people aboard because we are doing a lot more. It is hard, though, because Lew and I understand what we can do and we have a system kind of in place. We want to do the Wild West unit and all these other units, yet getting everybody on aboard to those units might be a problem instead of creating new with everybody. We want to keep what we are doing the same. We know we can't do that. So we are going to have to change eventually. That has been difficult. (Interview 1)

Tanya seemed to understand the difficulty that everyone was having. She continued:

> You can't keep old curriculum and try this new. This is not a different theory. This is a whole new concept. It is not a theory. It is not a different way to do the same thing. It is something totally different. It is not me still teaching English. I have to give up some of those English skills, some of the English jargon that I like to teach, and teach more life instead where it fits which is really what I think English is all about. In fact, it's a whole new paradigm. It is hard for high school teachers to give up that "This is my curriculum," "I am an English teacher," "I am a math teacher." Well, you are, but you are also more than that which is why most teachers went into education. It is hard to give that up, but I think the longer you have been teaching, the harder it is. I am lucky I got into teaming my second year because it might have been more difficult. There are times that I wish I could just close my door, and I would have those twelfth graders back, and I could teach whatever I wanted out of whatever book whenever I wanted because it was easier. It was much easier. I had more of a life at home. I felt more like a college professor where you can have an in-depth conversation with some students. That is hard to do with ninth graders. (Interview 1)

Tanya voiced her belief that Lew would never give up his content because he had a strong belief that all curriculum should be driven by history in chronological order, a conviction that Lew himself articulated:

> I'm actually trying to drive the curriculum based on the social studies curriculum that I've kind of developed over the years that I've been teaching. It's based on what we said we were going to do from the very beginning of my teaching about nineteen years ago, which is based on a chronology of after the Civil War up until the present time. I developed curriculum throughout every era that I thought was important, and I'm trying to now make that the basis for what everyone else teaches in the team. It is something I guess I learned from Dr. Taylor from going to some of his conferences, and he always proposed that history drive the curriculum, and I can see why,

it makes so much sense. Even when he did it, I was thinking, yes, that makes sense because everything is tied to social studies in the long run. . . . I selected the textbook and everything. The textbook is one that I thought fit right in with what I was trying to get the team to base theirs on. Tanya is totally tied into it at this point in time, and now it's just a matter of getting the other people. . . . I guess it's not falling 100 percent in line because no one wants to lose what they consider their curriculum, but I think it could be all inclusive. I think it can all be tied together. (Interview 2)

A very clear example of Lew's loyalty to social studies surfaced when the team discussed participating in the orientation weekend for the incoming freshmen the following year. The orientation the previous year was run mostly by the teachers from the other team. This program involved an overnight stay at the high school during a weekend in the summer so that the students could become familiar with the high school, team build, and socialize with their teachers. Because of the room conflict with the other team (discussed in chapter 5), Martha was the only one who participated in the orientation program the previous year.

The orientation for the next year included giving the incoming ninth graders a team learning packet to complete over the summer months. Martha hoped that this class's orientation would include more Apex teachers and tried to actively recruit them, a difficult mission since the animosity between the two teams still existed. When Martha stated at a team meeting that she needed their assistance, Lew replied that he would come and assist in any aspect of social studies and nothing else.

Tanya voiced on several occasions, besides on the preceding interview transcript, that she would like to close her door sometimes and go back to teaching the content that she loved. Hargreaves (1994) writes that this desire for classroom isolation is a welcome measure of privacy for teachers because it protects them from outside interference from what they often value. However, he adds that this privacy also isolates teachers from getting adult feedback on their value, worth and competence.

Lew explained that Jurassic Park was difficult for him to incorporate into an American history curriculum that started from the 1860s until the 1950s. He explained why he agreed to include that unit into the curriculum since it did not follow the curriculum that the teachers previously agreed on:

> It was difficult. It was a challenge to me, too, and I took the challenge because I kept saying to myself, there has got to be a way that I can tie that in and still be within my area within the content area. And I think that is almost like my responsibility. I guess I have to do things like that to show everyone else that it would work and that's it. That is true. Tanya and I talk about it. You know, we feel that we have done some very strong and quality projects over the past couple years, and we hope that we can bring the same type of quality out of all five of us, which we think would be remarkable. . . . In our first year [of English and social studies teaming], it was just as difficult. Just understanding the concept of interdisciplinary was hard, and people seemed to think that they know, and we thought we knew, but we didn't. I mean that first year, I mean we look back to what we did that first year, what we did that third year, it was like worlds apart. . . . So if we stay together, we probably could do something good for education because if we can show it works, you know, we would be happy, we would be very happy. (Interview 1)

Interpersonal Tension

Two issues directly related to the restructuring project created interpersonal tension. The first issue dealt with trying to form an interdisciplinary curriculum without any written single-discipline curriculums. Without any schoolwide written curriculums in the individual subject areas to examine for possible integration, the teachers did not know how to deliberate across the five curriculums to formulate common themes. The other issue dealt with teaming or collaborating, which human nature demonstrates causes conflict. Although the teachers knew this interpersonal conflict existed, they seemed to have a difficult time resolving it.

All the teachers concurred that they chose the English/social studies' model because it already was in existence. They added that they included Jurassic Park in the beginning of the school year to give John the ownership that they felt he needed to become a "believer." Tanya and Lew knew all along that they wanted to keep their units as they were and hoped the other teachers would agree to it. The biggest obstacle was John, who did not see how his curriculum could fit into the historical units. In addition, Tanya and Lew wanted to digress from the historical perspective to begin the school year and include a unit that would contribute to team building. Tanya said they talked about trying to incorporate ideas under the theme of "community." She explained how the tension between the team members, especially Lew and John, started early in the teaming. Asked to describe how the team chose the opening unit, Tanya expounded:

> Lew and I were thinking about community for the first few weeks, and we were trying to come up with this idea to get everybody together. John kept saying about Jurassic Park, and John would go from Jurassic Park all excited to what we were talking about couldn't fit. So we thought the best way to get John into this was to do Jurassic Park. I liked that idea. The book sounded good to me. The kids would like it. It would get them on board right away to teaming. I could see a lot of activities I could do. The problem was I could see Lew frustrated because he really can't fit that well with Jurassic Park. If he would've given up history all together, he could've taught morals and values. I think of the history teacher, and it is something inbred in them. They always have to stay on a time line. They have to get the material covered. The book has to be covered. . . . So, we did it [Jurassic Park] because of John. (Interview 1)

John had been introduced to Jurassic Park as an interdisciplinary theme at a science conference over the summer. He stayed an extra day at the conference to attend the workshop, "Jurassic Park: A Walk in the Park." The workshop was crowded, and John returned to the team very excited about the possibilities that the unit had for them. The team, however, greeted him with nonchalance, the same way they reacted to Martha's excitement when she returned from the Association for Curriculum and Supervision Development's annual conference in the spring (discussed in chapter 5).

John understood that the team included Jurassic Park to appease him. He felt, however, that everyone saw its benefits and potential and hoped that experience would broaden possibilities for themes. He explained how he realized a unit can grow and the teachers only became believers as they implemented the unit:

> As far as teaming is concerned, I feel, that first of all, when I brought up the Jurassic Park thing, I was real enthused about that. It was not received well. As a matter of fact I have to say this, I feel that the other members of the team, more or less, said, well, okay, we'll do it for you because they already had their stuff together, and I was glad they accommodated me, and I've been trying through the year to accommodate them. But I think it was the way that after they saw it, saw the possibilities, it started to grow, and it was almost like a flower blossoming and it kind of, I'm not sure that it got out of control, but it kind of went into areas that I never thought it would go in, and it kind of became bigger than I ever thought it would become, and it kind of became something that was almost, could've taken over the whole year. I mean it was unbelievable. I was very enthused about it, and I just felt it was a good learning process for the kids and for the teachers. (Interview 3)

Jurassic Park, then, became the symbol for the struggle with ownership and control that the teachers had to face. Hargreaves (1994) writes that ownership suggests that teachers have prime and maybe even sole responsibility for their classes, that students somehow belong to their teachers, like possessions. This ownership can carry characteristics of possessiveness, which becomes an issue when teachers' ownership is threatened.

An example of this possessive ownership came to the forefront when Martha tried to help a student with a science concept. Martha felt she successfully assisted the boy and reported that fact to the team at a meeting. John would not acknowledge Martha's comments, and Martha eventually stopped talking about it. John told one of the researchers later that Martha should have referred the student to him when specific content was in question instead of trying to explain it herself. Lew felt this incident demonstrated that walls can be disassembled when teachers team if all the teachers are in agreement:

> There was an incident the other day that was kind of interesting. Martha, in our last meeting, had said to John, which I wasn't even aware of, she said, "Oh, how did you think I did

the other day?" and he [John] didn't make any comment. She said, "By the way, guys, I was teaching science to Awan yesterday," and, so, then, we said, "Oh, really?" She said, "Oh, yeah, I was teaching him various things. Well, how did I do, John?" No response. "Well, John, do you think I did a good job?" He kind of just shrugged his shoulders. So he had to leave. It was kind of interesting. . . . And so then she [Martha] said, out of nowhere, "Do you think I stepped on John's toes?" I said, "What do you mean?" [Martha said] "Because I got a cold feeling from him for the last couple of days since I tried to teach Awan science. Do you think I stepped on his toes?" And when she said it, immediately I said, "Yes, you did." Then she said, "Well, I didn't mean to." I said, "That's all right because it doesn't matter. You can do that. It shouldn't be on his toes. That is something he should accept and feel good about." I wouldn't care if someone started to try to talk about historical events because, more than likely, they are going to come back to me and ask me some information about what else can I do to share these ideas with them, and that's what I thought he should do. . . . I said, "Look, if we're a team, our job is not to give up on the kids, and if any of us can get to any kid in any way, that's all that counts. (Interview 2)

Hargreaves (1994) explains:

Control in social settings comprises the ability to regulate, determine and direct the course of one's life or other lives, and to avoid or resist intrusions and impositions by others which interfere with that ability. Control over one's destiny and over the destinies of others has both positive and negative implications. The bounded classroom where the teacher has almost exclusive contact with and responsibility for the development of impressionable young minds is rife with control implications. Indeed, there are elements of the control impulse that attract many teachers to that setting. (P. 175)

The teachers believed that covering their subject-area content was their moral and professional duty. Hargreaves (1994) found in his studies that any initial loyalty that teachers might have felt toward a group became subordinated to deeper department loyalties, especially when curriculum content came into conflict with the new initiative. Santee-Siskin and Little agree with this assertion based on their research on departmental structure within high schools: "Research has framed teaching's pedagogical practice and the school as the relevant organizational context, yet teachers framed their work in terms of the subject and their organizational environment in terms of the department" (Siskin & Little, 1995, p. 152).

The Apex teachers definitely felt responsible for their students' receiving the requisite content in their discipline. Since John, Martha, and Gary were additions to the team, their struggle was more difficult. They knew that the thematic approach was one way to integrate the disciplines, but they did not know how to develop a way to create themes. Lew realized this frustration but did not want to accept it:

> I really do think that we've come a long way. I think that we've started out as a splinter group with no real direction, not sure, very unsure as a matter of fact, probably protective, and I think we've broken down a lot of doors, and I think we've already become real close, and I think that's gonna get closer as time goes on if we stay together. And, as I said, I guess a little struggle from time to time to try to get everyone to understand that yes, you have a curriculum to teach, but you have to become creative on how you teach it based on what we're trying to do as a team. So, if we can keep the team concept in their minds and thinking about their curriculums, it can be done. I 100 percent believe that. So I think that is my hardest fight right now is trying to keep that going. (Interview 2)

All the teachers except Lew came to believe that the historical approach was not the best model for them. They sensed that they needed broader, more encompassing themes, but they did not have an alternative plan. In addition, the lack of time to change in the middle of the implementation process added to the frustration and created more tension.

Sometimes, in spite of their willingness to incorporate a unit, the lack of research materials or small glitches hindered them. For example, Gary decided that he would incorporate the Santa Fe Trail into a math project for the Wild West. He took a lot of time to find maps of the original Santa Fe Trail and to photocopy them and plan a lesson. He eventually ended up having to abandon the activity, however, because he realized that none of the maps included names of the cities, making it impossible for the students to follow the trail. Thus, he decided to try again the following year.

Another time Gary spent endless hours in the library and on the Internet to find raw data that depicted the number of immigrants by nationality who came to the United States during the start of legal immigration to the United States. For several weeks he searched for raw data in vein, finding instead all sorts of graphs and tables that contained pre-analyzed data. He finally dissected the treated data to obtain the raw numbers and planned a lesson in which the students analyzed and graphed the data for themselves. Serendipitously, as he was searching for the data on immigration, he came across a web site on Ellis Island which allowed students to vicariously experience the process of moving through the immigration experience at Ellis Island. He informed Tanya about the web site, and she eventually used it to have her students create immigration short stories from the first-person point of view. The time he spent simply looking for the information, however, made him realize that he could not continue losing math planning and teaching time to accommodate the themes.

Team members were frustrated, too, when they had ideas they wanted incorporated into a unit but were ignored, instead, by their colleagues. Almost all of the Apex teachers experienced the feeling of having their suggestions ignored at some point during the year. Lew was frustrated because he could not complete the Wild West living museum. He hoped other team members would volunteer to allow students to use some of their class time to complete the project, but no such offers of extra time were forthcoming. John wanted to hold a square dance for the team as a Wild West activity. He thought the students would enjoy it since country-western dancing and music is so popular. Everyone quickly nixed the idea. Gary wanted the teachers to read a novel that he had read by a minister who experienced Dachau. When everyone said they did not have time, Tanya said she would take the book if Gary did not need it back quickly. Martha could not get team members to assist in planning a pep rally or joining her in community service projects, such as helping at the local soup kitchen. However, she was able to have everyone agree to read Ruth Hartz's book, which she became familiar with at a foreign language conference.

John sensed this apathy toward each other's ideas. When asked to respond to how the team affected him, John expressed very positive attitudes with regard to working with the other Apex teachers. He added that, at the same time, he felt some ideas were railroaded and equally good ideas were ignored:

At the same time I feel that sometimes my idea about how something should be approached and other members of the team and their ideas are not similar at all, and I believe that you have to be giving and you have to at the same time iterate what it is that is important and work toward that goal. I believe that teaming enables you to do that, but I believe that we have a lot of areas that we need to really look at and we need to try to figure out how we're going to approach them in the future, and we have to approach them looking at all the standards that we have, and are we covering those standards, and are we hitting the ones that are important. (Interview 3)

When Martha, John, and Gary did find ways to incorporate a theme, it often meant they needed to work with just each other rather than the group of five. This small grouping became an issue in itself. Lew saw it as a division while the others saw it as a way to incorporate a theme. For example, Gary and John decided to pursue a scuba diving activity to relate to the World War I unit. They knew a staff member who had a scuba diving license, and they were able to secure time at the school's swimming pool. They hoped to use this experience to have students develop a deeper understanding of submarine warfare while at the same time developing an understanding of concepts such as pressure and its relation to depth. Coordinating this event became difficult because not all the teachers wanted to relinquish their classes to accommodate the dive. Therefore, Gary and John had to prolong the activity since they could only conduct the activity when the students were in their classes.

Although Gary and John were very happy with the results of the activity, they realized that the other teachers were not a part of the activity. They also realized that this kind of small group teaming might be the way to incorporate some of the historical themes. Martha seemed to understand the tension:

If Lew would just give them a block of five hours and let John and Gary go off by themselves, Gary may be able to affect a change in John that Lew can't because Gary got John to do the scuba diving. So, Lew has to back off the need for all five of us to always be on task at all times and let two of us do some things together. I could've done much with John, like when he did weather, I should've been doing the weather, but I didn't have time. We were so focused on team activities. I think I need to mention that to Lew to let me go off sometimes with just John and Gary. (Interview 3)

Tanya seemed to agree, too, that, if some members needed to separate to achieve a team goal, they should be encouraged to do so:

Gary is getting together with John on his own, which is a good sign. If those two want to get together, that's one way that we can get them in, I think, we should let them. But Lew doesn't see that as being good. He sees them as trying not to meet with us, as trying to do their own—which is fine as long as they—then they'll come on board. You just have to let that happen. (Interview 3)

The small group activities demonstrated that the teachers were willing and able to participate when they felt ownership in them. As much as Gary and John were frustrated by the other teachers' lack of interest in becoming part of the scuba diving activity, Lew felt the same way regarding the Wild West living museum he wanted to build and showcase. Lew described his disappointment attached to the incompletion of the museum:

There is something I feel bad about, and I guess you wonder why I kind of backed off a little bit from the museum. . . . it was hard to ask, and no one volunteered their kids, knowing what I was going through in the struggle to get this done. I didn't get the feedback from the group, and I wasn't going to step on anyone's toes at that point. I wasn't going to, you know, force my hand and say, "Guys, guess what? If I had these kids everyday"—which we could easily do, we could give up these kids everyday—"I could have that museum done before Thanksgiving," but I was saying to them every meeting, "You know, the museum is coming along. It's really a struggle. I don't have them all the time. I can only take so many at a time. I can only do this," and no one ever . . . Martha went down and saw it. I don't know if Gary ever went down. I don't know if John ever really went down to see exactly what it was and how monumental it was, and then I think that if they would've pulled together and . . . if I would do it again, I would definitely demand it almost, say, "Hey, if we're going to do a project of this nature, everybody, come on." That's the same thing that happened with this. When I was saying, "Hey, let's get involved with this Wild West project," it was, again, like, "Well, I've got to teach this," and "I have to teach this," "I don't see where I fit in." So, as a result, they didn't get on the ship as to what I was trying to do with the actual building of the museum, and I feel bad about that because that is a project . . . I don't like to have projects hanging the way this one is hanging, but I'm dead set on completing it. It is going to be completed one way or another, but they made me alter my plans in so many ways so many times because at the end of this every other day schedule, it really created a big crimp for me and then not having the kids for like a three hour block of time, I had them for one and a half hours. Then, all of them [the students] don't go to Tanya, because Tanya would let me have them, but then the other group [of students] wouldn't, and then a couple of times when I asked to take kids out, it was a big concern. . . . I'm saying if we're doing things together as a team, those are the variables that we have to overcome because then the kids can get some real understanding of the group because now look at that, we can actually leave all our classes all of the day to get this one project done. (Interview 2)

Another issue that clouded the teaming was the teachers' nonunderstanding of the content of the individual disciplines, as well as the inherent difficulty in matching the discipline to the historical themes. For example, when Lew wanted everyone to become involved in the Immigration unit, he could not understand John's unwillingness to participate. John told the team that the students needed time to understand atomic molecular theory. John believed it was imperative that the students understand this theory, a very difficult theory, because it is the basis of all scientific under-standing. Lew believed that John could incorporate atomic molecu-lar theory into the general idea of immigration if he talked about some of the German scientists involved in its existence. This situation was exacerbated because the teachers never discussed their individual content before designing their model of interdisciplinary teaming. Lew rationalized:

> I just want John to recognize that he could probably even tie atomic theory into immigration even if he did it in the more present sense, if he talked about atomic theory involving some of the German scientists and some of the other people that brought it in and then talked about different groups of people and immigration. There's a lot of ways it can be done, and that's why I think sometimes it doesn't come to light yet, that we haven't reached that level with the other three. With Tanya and I, it's automatic. You know, as soon as the topic comes up, she can think of literature, or she can think of different areas that she can bring in, and she started thinking about different authors, and all kinds of things come to her mind immedi-ately, but we aren't at that point, which is understandable being less than a year. (Interview 2)

As well as not understanding each other's content, they did not always share the same philosophy regarding teaching techniques and assessment. Whereas Lew and Tanya had become involved in authentic assessment over the years, Gary, John, and Martha re-lied on traditional methods of assessment. Traditional assessment was especially important to Gary, whose students had to pass com-petency tests, and Martha, whose students took the Foreign Lan-guage National Exam and had to be at a certain proficiency to continue to the next level of study. John, who had become very concerned with science standards, explained how he viewed the other disciplines vis-à-vis his:

> I think at the beginning of the school year, even though we did a lot of stuff on Jurassic Park, I did not put emphasis on tests and testing, and I intend to put more emphasis on tak-ing standardized tests because I found at the end of the year, students were like, "I didn't bother studying for that test.

Can't I do a book report? Can't I do a collage? Can't I do some art work?" I'm like, "No, you have to show me you know this material, and this material isn't just solar power, it's the whole sun, how does the sun work." And I said, "You have to show me that you know something about that whole concept," and I just feel that they were out of it. I feel that part of it is in other classes, I don't think they are held to know this much material, you know, from Civil War to the 1980s or whatever it is. I think they just do these little projects and they write these little poems, and I'm not sure if they get credit for that, and if they do flunk, then they can just do a little book report or something, and that suffices, and I don't think that's giving them the message that they have to learn to sit down—I'm talking about 18 vocabulary words in a chapter—and they can't sit down and learn 18 vocabulary words so they can do well on a test. I have a real problem with that, and I never felt that way before. Some students wouldn't study for tests, don't get me wrong, but not like this year. I had students come in who slept during the final, and that is just really bugging me, as you can tell. (Interview 3)

Tanya seemed to understand best why the interdisciplinary issue was so difficult. She was able to understand everyone's frustration. One reason for her understanding was the reading and researching that she did prior to and during the implementation for her master's degree program. She realized already in September that the themes that they chose were impeding successful implementation. She vacillated from using broad themes, such as "leadership" or "individuality" to believing all subject-area content must be assimilated into an interdisciplinary curriculum. As the year progressed, she really began to question the themes they chose in light of the five-member team:

I would say that history chronological order at this point is driving the curriculum, and I think that is becoming somewhat . . . I think we have to pick up a strategy, stick with it and move the rest of the curriculum to fit. Right now, John can't fit because of the timing. Gary is having a tough time. We need to take a look at the chronological order of history and decide if we want to keep that as our [curriculum] map, so to speak ... I can match wherever. I really don't have a problem with American literature. Martha has a problem, depending on when she can match. (Interview 2)

By the end of the school year, Tanya was convinced that the model they chose could not accommodate a five-member team even though they all tried to the best of their ability. Asked to comment to what extent the year met her expectations, Tanya replied:

I think I expected less than what we did, which is funny because I know Lew expected more than what we did, but with Gary and Martha and John, I think they did as much as they could feel comfortable with and still tie themselves to their curriculum. They didn't want to give up things, and to be successful, you have to give up things. But it was easier for me to do that, much easier than it is for Martha because she has things that need to be taught for next year, and Gary has a competency test at the end of the school year, and John is just so tied to the curriculum—he's been teaching it for years—he is not going to give it up. (Interview 3)

Tanya also seemed to realize at the end of the school year that, in order to move away from their present model of interdisciplinary teaming, they would need to examine all the curriculums:

I would like to consider changing the whole organization of what we do from post Civil War to current. We might still be teaching the curriculum that way, but we might be able to pick up different themes out of those eras to teach that maybe John will feel more comfortable fitting in and Gary could feel more comfortable. Instead of having to do the Roaring Twenties or the Wild West, maybe there is a concept that we could talk about more. I'd like to see—do we have to do chronological? Maybe we don't have to. Maybe we could take ... I'd like to look more at what their curriculums actually are, because I don't know them and I just assume they could fit and maybe they can't, and maybe it would be better if Gary and John did more things together and Lew and I and Martha fit with whatever—almost like two teams within a team—and then have a major like the Holocaust. (Interview 3)

While they all struggled with their own content issues, John seemed to become the most disillusioned and separated from the group. Although all the teachers actively participated in the field trip to the museum at the natural history museum to culminate the study of Jurassic Park, John did not reciprocate on the other two field trips. When the team went to see the play *The Immigrant* in a neighboring city, John was in the midst of studying for a midterm exam. Although he considered missing the field trip, he did attend. On the way to the play, he asked one of the researchers if anyone would be upset if he studied in a side room instead of watching the play. The researcher did not offer any opinion, believing that others would be upset but also believing that it was inappropriate to say so. John did choose to study rather than attend the play, and Lew was upset.

Lew eventually confronted John about the lack of participation at the play, as well as some other incidents that Lew did not appreciate. He and John talked about the issues, and John thanked Lew for bringing them to his attention. Lew felt, however, that things remained unresolved and John became more reserved. Lew felt sorry about that. He explained:

> He backed off. I didn't want that either. I was just saying, "Let's work with the issues at hand. Let's try to make the best we can out of what we're doing," but it wasn't long after that day he got silent. (Interview 3)

By the end of the school year, John realized that he was not fully contributing to the team. He also felt guilty because he felt misunderstood and not attached to the other team members. When asked to talk about his low point of the year, John reflected on the complicated feelings that he experienced:

> I think my low point is the fact that I get the impression . . . I don't feel that I fit into all these themes that they do. My low point is the fact that if you are on a team, I think you have to work together, and I want to work together. I like the people on the team, and I want to do things with them, but I kind of felt like when we went to the Holocaust Museum in Washington, I kind of felt like a third-wheel type of person because I really was not involved with that very much. I kind of felt

that when the person came here, the lady [Ruth Hartz, the Holocaust survivor who spoke at their school], I wasn't involved that much, and I felt kind of funny almost, getting any recognition for that. I really didn't want recognition for anything. I just felt like a third wheel because I really hadn't been that involved with that aspect of that, and I kind of feel like I wish I could've been involved somehow, but I don't know how. I know people have given me stuff about genetics. I don't do genetics in earth-space science. People have given me stuff about medical experiments and stuff. I don't want to get involved with that type of thing. That's not the way I approach science, and it wouldn't be in earth-space science anyway. So I think that—I kind of have the impression that Lew doesn't understand what I do here, and Tanya. Gary understands more, I think because we worked together on some things, and Martha is just Martha. But I kind of feel it would be good if—Lew doesn't come down here very often—I kind of think it would be good if he came down here and saw what we do down here. (Interview 3)

Gary, too, felt disappointed by the end of the school year and realized the team had separated:

Generally, it [school year] was really good as far as the support we gave each other, I felt. I was a little disappointed towards the end of the year. I think the past couple months, we kind of separated somewhat. I don't know if it was because of being together all year long, or if there were simply other aspects distracting us, but we didn't seem to have the continuity here the last few weeks that we had all year, and I know other teachers are involved with different things, and I know I was trying to get other things done, too, and there were some problems that arose in the end, I think, that caused a little bit of conflict. (Interview 3)

As Gary said, the team did separate at the end of the year. Lew stopped calling team meetings, and no one went to him to ask why, even though they expressed concern among themselves. Lew did continue to communicate with everyone through e-mail, but the team became distant without meetings. Everyone speculated why the meetings were canceled. Some said that the Holocaust unit ended their teaming, so they did not need to meet anymore. Others said that Lew was frustrated because he felt that the Holocaust unit became a showcase for one or two subject areas rather than the whole team, plus he was unhappy with some of the team members' lack of involvement in the unit. Another said they probably just all needed a break from each other.

All these speculations probably did have an element of truth. Martha received schoolwide attention by booking Ruth Hartz, the Holocaust survivor, to speak to all the juniors and seniors and foreign language students about her childhood experience. The most active participants in the assembly were the nonteam upperclassmen, who obviously had a deeper understanding of Ms. Hartz's plight because of their maturity.

Gary and Tanya received a lot of media attention for the projects that they incorporated into the unit. Gary had 1,000,000 sunflower seeds in a coffin displayed to represent the one million children who died in the Holocaust. He then had all the students on the team participate in planting 250,000 seeds in memory of those children. Gary and the agriculture science teacher planned a fast and efficient way for each student to participate in the planting, which received both newspaper and television coverage. Tanya's students wrote moving poems about the Holocaust, which were published in the local town newspaper.

All this attention intensified John's guilt for not participating in the unit. Lew felt that the individual subject attention took away from the interdisciplinary teaming, which was the purpose of the unit. Lew explained why he stopped the meetings:

> The enthusiasm that was there for Jurassic Park just wasn't there for the Holocaust, and I kept talking about that throughout the year, "Guys, okay, you guys are hitting and missing and not jumping on with the Wild West. You didn't really do a lot with Immigration. There were a lot of other areas that we could've done great things with, so let's at least make the Holocaust our second greatest project . . . ," and I felt that when we got to the Holocaust, it was a great unit only because of Tanya and I. Again it goes back to that, and I feel bad about that because we knew what we wanted and what it would take, but I felt there was a lot of drop off from the other three

members about that point. I know they think I'm like a work dog, they don't know where I get it from. . . . You know, I have to always remember that I can't take it personally. I really can't, but at the end of the year, I really got frustrated, and I just shut down the meetings, and then everyone was wondering what was wrong. I'm glad I got the response I got. They could've just walked away, and that would've been a totally different story, too. We need to get together, but I just got a little break from them. (Interview 3)

Tanya realized that stopping the meetings was one way of dealing with the conflict that the team was encountering. She predicted that this conflict might arise. In her first interview, Tanya stated that one of her fears was that they would all get sick of each other and not want to team anymore. She said that she and Lew had gotten to the point in their teaming when they would separate from each other for three or four days after a major project was completed.

She articulated in the second interview that she did feel all of them becoming frustrated with different issues, but she felt they could work them out because they were all intelligent enough to know that people are different. By the third interview, she realized that she did not like the tension and hoped that at some point in their teaming that they would be able to face the conflict rather than avoid it. Tanya explained, too, that she did not feel comfortable as the middle person between Lew and the other team members:

Lew has stopped the meetings, and everybody came to me, why is he stopping the meetings? They think that I'm the closest one to him. I probably am on a hall of five. . . . I think we were more close this year than we ever were. This year I think pushed us even closer. But they wanted to know why, and I feel as though John comes to me when he is upset about some things, yet I'm hearing John's side and Lew's side, and I don't feel comfortable saying, "Okay, guys, let's get into a room and duke this out." I like to see everybody happy, and it bothers me when people are mad at each other, and I saw times this year when John was mad, Lew was mad, Gary was mad. I don't like it when people don't get along. (Interview 3)

This loss of contact at the end of the year seemed to confirm that the collaboration in which the teachers were engaged was contrived in spite of their willingness to work together. Hargreaves (1994) notes that collaborative cultures are working relationships that are spontaneous, voluntary, development-oriented, fixed in time and space, and predictable. If these conditions are not present, *contrived collegiality* is present.

He submits that the following criteria can create contrived collegiality. First, teachers are required to meet and work together, which makes the collaboration administratively regulated and compulsory. Second, teachers are required to implement the mandates of others rather than programs decided on through discussion. Third, teachers only meet at the particular time and place that has been mandated by the administration. Fourth, the collegiality is designed to have a high predictability of outcomes since the administration has control over its purposes and regulates its time and place.

All four of these criteria were present when the teachers entered into their teaming initiative. They tried from the beginning to work through their different values, beliefs, and curriculums to form a coalition. Unfortunately, because of the lack of professional development to assist them in their effort, they were forced to remain at the level of contrived collegiality. Thus, when Lew stopped calling meetings, the other teachers wondered why, but no one tried to reinstate them.

Fullan (1991) warns that the more an advocate is committed to a particular innovation, the less likely he or she can be effective in getting it implemented. The reverse, however, is not true. Commitment is essential, but it must be balanced with the knowledge that people may be at different starting points with different legitimate priorities. Also, the change process may result in transformations or variations in the change. These different starting points and different priorities did affect the teachers' original agreement to follow the English/social studies' interdisciplinary model, no matter how committed Lew and Tanya were to keep it intact.

Tanya realized that the team did start out strong because of Lew's leadership and initial prodding that they all work together. She reflected:

Lew, no doubt, carried the team this year, no doubt, and if he wouldn't have demanded meetings, we wouldn't have had meetings, I don't think. But once we started having them, people just got used to that's the way it was and came to a meeting and that's what was expected. He put the status quo up front at the beginning of the year, and I am happy with the work and the willingness to try. (Interview 3)

Instead of true collaboration, the teachers engaged in "interactive professionalism," which Fullan (1991) describes as teachers and others working in small groups, interacting frequently in the course of planning and testing new ideas, attempting to solve different problems and assessing effectiveness. Although the teachers did not try to meet when the meetings were stopped, they were not happy. They knew that they still wanted to be part of a collaborative group even though their curriculum issues appeared unresolvable. Plus, there was not any sense of immediacy to stay together since they could function in their teaching duties alone.

Lew, as team leader, often felt responsible for the team's effort. He appreciated that the teachers chose him to be the leader, but he saw it as a challenge because he always felt that the team's actions reflected on him. Early in the teaming, he talked about the responsibility he shouldered as leader:

I appreciate the fact that they respect me enough to put me in that position [team leader], so, you know, there is admiration there. It is a major challenge because I always feel like whatever we do weighs on my decisions, to think that I pushed them to do something, so it keeps me on edge all the time. . . . It makes me constantly stay on check with myself, what I'm doing because I want to make sure that I believe in what I am saying and believe in what I am doing, and if I am modeling it in anyway, then I am doing the right thing. (Interview 1)

At the end of the year, Lew reflected on his effectiveness as leader. Asked to describe the year in terms of a metaphor, Lew compared his duty as team leader to that of his role as head basketball coach:

I would definitely put it on the line of a basketball game, and a kind of basketball game where you start off blowing a team out in the beginning, and you're up twenty points in the first half. Then, around the middle of the game, you start to make turnovers, and suddenly the team is creeping back in, and then the panic sets in, and then some people on the team get a little bit depressed and don't know how to regain the energy and strength, and the coach calls time out and tries to rally them through with words of encouragement and a sense of mission, saying we were winning, so we know we can win, but it's a question of whether the desire is there to win or how much effort are we willing to put out to win, but definitely the abilities are there, and so you go back out on the court, and now you pull yourself together and again you get the game back under control, but as always, in most games, you get to fourth quarter and you get a little tired because it's not over until it's over. And then again, with more guidance and with more, even sometimes hollering and irate messages sent out to the players on the court, through the grace of God or however it works, you do win, but you only win by a few points. So you're satisfied that you won, but in your heart you know that your team didn't play well, not as well as they could, so you are happy and satisfied with the win because you know that's what you came here to do, but you also know that before the next game you'd like to improve those errors and those miscues in the things that were done because you know you have a great team and they can win on a higher note with a lot more satisfaction. (Interview 3)

Another possible negative outcome to collegiality is *group think.* Fullan (1993a) defines group think as "the uncritical acceptance and/or suppression of dissent in going along with the group decisions" (p. 82). Therefore, it is important for the stakeholders to realize that collaboration does not require consensus. In addition, Fullan (1993a) warns that a majority decision does not necessarily mean sound judgment. Thus, questioning an innovation, especially at the early stages, should be welcomed. Festinger (1957, as cited in Nias, 1987) explains that people are psychologically uncomfortable holding views that are mutually incompatible or acting in ways that are inconsistent with others. This discomfort creates "cognitive dissonance," which people resolve by modifying their views to align them with their colleagues.

John became concerned that some members were becoming a part of *group think*. The team presented their interdisciplinary unit of Jurassic Park at the regional Council of Teachers of Mathematics' annual conference in March. All of the Apex teachers took turns talking about teaming and then presented their contribution to the unit. John told me he was surprised when Martha stood up and talked about the benefits of teaming, which she said so outweighed content that she was going to stop her students from participating in the National Exam. She continued to say that teaming was easy and that she could incorporate her discipline into any theme. John could not understand why Martha changed her mind, especially since, he said, national exams are important.

Martha's comments were surprising. She had always said at team meetings that she was frustrated because she could not cover her objectives. When she voiced concerns about not being able to cover the content, Tanya would remind her that interdisciplinary work meant doing less and she should tell her department she no longer could cover twelve chapters. When the students wrote reflections on Jurassic Park, two of them wrote that foreign language was not incorporated into the unit. Martha protested that was not true. Tanya then read the two students' statements. Martha was hurt and she again denied the charge.

Professional Commitment

In spite of all the tension, the teachers had a professional commitment to each other. They were as committed to the team's mission as to their subject-area content. Thus, the teachers were able to retain a team spirit that transcended their conflict.

A large part of the commitment to the team mission was probably because of the team building that occurred in the beginning of their formation. The teachers knew they needed to understand teaming; therefore, they all attended a team-building conference together the spring before the implementation. Maeroff (1993) writes that part of what is important to team building is the attempt to alter the culture of the school; the ways that teachers do their work; and the content, manner, and quality of their interactions with each other. Since only Tanya and Lew knew each other, all the teachers realized that they needed the time to understand who they were and what their mission would be. Therefore, their immediate chore was to examine the beliefs and values that already existed in each one of them.

Lew explained how the team slowly became familiar with each other by trying to understand who they were and how they could interact together:

> I guess in the beginning it really was a feeling-out process, and again this is where we differ from the other team. The other team felt they knew everybody, they knew each other, so they could just jump on the ground and start running, whereas we definitely had a different feeling about it because we had never worked together as a group. So, it was a feeling out process where we sometimes just talked about backgrounds and things of that nature to get a feel for each other and where our frame of reference was and things of that nature. Then as we got to know each other, we started to try to come to some decisions on what we were even doing together. Trying to decide ourselves—nobody is telling us what to do—so we just tried to develop a framework for where we wanted to go and the things that we wanted to do, and each of those days that we had it seemed like you could feel that there was a closer bond than in the beginning, and it was beginning to connect. . . . after we got past some issues [room conflict with other team and original math teacher who did not want to be on the team], we really tried to lay our groundwork for our philosophy, who we were and what we wanted to try to promote this year coming into it. . . . We were trying to put some connection to it. . . . So, for the most part, that was what we did. It was really just a building process of finding out who we were, what our mission really is, and then how we would go about putting that together. . . . So, it was kind of like a hodge-podge come together, which means that we did take a little more time to get to know one another, which I think is a lot more healthy, to tell you the truth. (Interview 1)

Another important element of their team building was to find a team identity both outwardly and inwardly. They spent time discussing names for their team, finally agreeing on Apex, whose acronym represented "accountability, pride, exploration, and excellence." They used a mountain as their symbol and incorporated the motto, The view at the top is worth the climb. They spent numerous hours working on every detail of their roles as teachers and team members. They devised an incentive program for students who demonstrated good academic work and citizenship. They devised these five goals for the team: community building, study skills, higher-level thinking skills, accountability, and growth in moral and ethical behavior. They devised their own achievement scale as follows: 92–100 = A; 84–91 = B; 74–83 = C; 65–73 = D; and 0–64 = F. They included a list of general guidelines that addressed academic and classroom expectations, as well as effort and conduct. They created a timeline that showed their interdisciplinary endeavors on a monthly basis.

All these meaning-making endeavors gave them a sense of team spirit in spite of their concerns regarding specific subject-area content. Their commitment to who they had become was cemented when the principal, unsuccessfully, asked them to give up the team name in hopes of eliminating the competition between the two teams, which was already apparent. They started the year strong, and this strength was apparent to the students on the first day of school. Whatever curricular issues remained unresolved, the students saw only a group of dedicated teachers starting the year as a team and inviting them to be a part of it.

All the teachers explained that the outside obstacles that they faced in the beginning of the teaming also brought them closer. Tanya remembered that their first two days of team meetings dealt with negative comments from some members who kept complaining how all five subjects could not fit together. Worse, though, she felt was dealing with the original math teacher on the team who did not want to be there. She said that they gauged a successful meeting by their ability to talk him into putting down the *USA Today* newspaper and joining in their conversation. The room conflict with the other team also made them band together at a critical time. Although they were having problems connecting the curriculums, they did not want to be attacked by an outside team. Therefore, even though the curriculum issues remained, their allegiance to each other grew.

Martha explained the outside obstacle that moved her to full team status. The teachers' second pull-out day to discuss teaming, the spring of the year before implementation, they decided to meet at Tanya's house instead of in the conference room at school. As discussed in chapter 1, the teachers also planned to meet us there so that we could discuss the purpose of the study. The teachers had cleared the decision with the administrator who was in charge of the restructuring project. Two hours into their meeting, Tanya received a telephone call from the principal who was irate that they had left the school, especially without his permission. They were ordered to return to school immediately. Tanya was in tears. She felt responsible for asking everyone to meet at her house and hurt for being treated so nastily over the telephone. The other teachers were angry that the principal had upset Tanya and that he treated all of them like children. The teachers lost the team workday because they had to return to the school and confront the principal about the way he treated them.

Martha felt it was her turn to speak up against the injustices done to the team because others had dealt with the other issues. She believed that her role as spokesperson that day led to a strain in the relationship with the principal that finally resolved itself by the end of the year. Martha explained the circumstances leading up to the confrontation and why she believed her support that day gave her team identity:

> We got nothing done that day except that whole uproar. ... Tanya cleaned, got food, and we were on a roll, we were actually getting something done. It was embarrassing to have you [the researchers] there and for us to be treated like children. ... I was really upset to have to do that [tell the principal he was unfair to them], but Lew was watching me. He wanted me to become a team person, and I just felt the time was right, and Tanya was worth defending. You shouldn't just make somebody cry like that. The mother in me came out. (Interview 2)

Wideen (1992) writes that people learn, become inspired and find their identity within the group; therefore, the group setting is a powerful vehicle for bringing about change. He adds, though, that certain norms, beliefs, expectations, and support—such as ethos that allow for risk-taking and for slower-paced implementation—

are needed within the group setting for any change to occur. Lew explained why teaming is difficult, describing his initial teaming endeavor with Tanya:

> At first I probably would not have been coming into it [teaming] because I had my own values and beliefs and my own way of teaching. Then we were forced to go into this process [English/social studies teaming], and it just so happened that I was fortunate to latch up with Tanya, who also really worked with me personality-wise and things of that nature, so things got off to a good start as opposed to getting off to a bad start, and then we kind of developed it along the way after hitting bumps and bruises, and as a result, I can see where it works. (Interview 2)

Schools that are characterized by norms of collegiality and experimentation are much more likely to implement innovation successfully (Fullan 1990). Successful school improvement can only result if the environment supports collaboration and risk-taking in an atmosphere of trust and support (Goodlad, 1984, as cited in Stoll, 1992). Because of his previous teaming with Tanya, Lew understood why successful collaboration is a long process:

> [Collaborating] really opens the doors to other people observing your teaching. I guess that's what it amounts to, so there is almost no place to hide, and you can't be in your own little secluded world anymore, and so I think some of the teachers who are just coming on [the team], that is kind of a hard mix right now, and they are not always in favor of that, of somebody stepping into their territory. I think as time goes on and if we stay together, we will learn to trust each other more. Like Tanya and I, we have no barriers at all in what we have done because we've been together so long. But in the meantime these people are still new to the whole concept and the idea. So, it's like . . . sometimes I see it as a slight annoyance as well as sometimes a real plus. . . . it has its pluses and minuses, but I think in the end, it's an overall plus, because in the end, we will start to reach a higher standard as we start to understand what it is that we are trying to do. (Interview 2)

Lew continued to explain that his previous teaming experience made him feel responsible for leading the team. Lew explained why it was incumbent on Tanya and him to guide the team:

> I think what happened was the experience that Tanya and I gained from those three years and how we struggled and how we pulled ourselves together and then we started to feel good about what we were doing was like a guiding force because right away when all this started to come together, she and I were in constant contact and conference, kind of saying that if we do this, we have to do it right. We got to get it going in the right direction. We know better and we know more about it. So, if we let it flop, then we are going to be right back where we started from. So it became one of those things, and it was like she was pushing me because she felt that I could take the lead. It was almost like I couldn't be involved with anything that was not right, not quality, that's not really trying to accomplish something. Whether we accomplish it is another story. But at least I know that we are putting out the best effort, and I'm not the type of person that would step out in general and take the lead. I like to stay in the background and still get the job done and just kind of enjoy life in that kind of certain mode. But I also knew that if I did that or chose to do that and someone else became the head and they didn't really take it in the right direction, I would be hurting in the whole process. So, it almost became a baby of mine, something that I had to take charge of based on what happened and then try to encourage everybody that if we are going to do this, we have to do it properly. So I am taking credit, but not really. I am saying it is something that evolved over a period of time based on what we went through for the three years and how we saw it, and that's why Tanya and I are always still in close contact and making sure what is happening now, is everyone on board. Right now with the Wild West project, we are looking at it and we are not happy because it is our project [Tanya and Lew's], but we don't want it to be our project. We want to see how we can bring everybody in. So I think the people involved, they picked up on that, and as a result, they are good people, too, and they

decided that okay, let's go for it, let's go at it in spite of the administration or lack of their involvement, in spite of all the other things you can think that are being done unfairly and under the table that we just don't think is right involving both teams, leaving it open like that to create conflict and nobody stepping in to really try to solve it and make sure that things are working smoothly. In spite of all that, we have a job to do and we still make the kids our number one priority. They still have to be the ones that come out of this with something good. (Interview 1)

Little (1981, as cited in Grimmett & Creehan, 1992) reports that group work allows teachers to attempt curricular-instructional innovations that they probably would not have attempted on their own. Grimmett and Creehan (1992) found that it is not just the teamwork that creates the willingness to attempt new endeavors, but the joint action that emanates from the group's purposes and obligations as they shape the shared tasks and outcomes. Finally, Barth (1990) concludes that teachers working in a group are provided with a built-in support system, having someone to talk to about their teaching and learning.

All the teachers reflected that teaming gave them the opportunity to interact with adults. They liked the support and encouragement that working together offered. Gary expressed his feelings this way:

One of the true benefits about this whole thing has been I've really gotten to know the other members of the team, and I kind of see what they do and get different views from them as far as what we are trying to accomplish, and fortunately, I think we all seem to get along very well and try to complement each other. . . . Just getting some reinforcement from other people, getting ideas, being able to share ideas with them has really made a difference, I think. (Interview 2)

The teachers felt that their teammates also supported them in the individual decisions they made. Martha explained how depressed she was at the end of the year when she decided to teach French off the team the following year. As much as she was happy with the decision, she could not feel relieved until her colleagues assured her that they supported her decision. As Martha recounted the difficulties that were related to her decision, she described how the team supported her:

I'll stick to it. I told you I was thinking of getting out [of team completely]. I was in the pit, but it worked out. My team backed off and let me make this decision for myself. I don't know what guided them to do that, but they did, and one day they all, except for Lew, gravitated into my room when I was . . . in the pit . . . and I didn't even know they knew I was in the pit. It was Tanya, Gary, and John. They just sat in my room, and we all talked. It was good. We decided that we had done a lot of good this year. We should try it again. You know, Tanya is so cut and dry when I was asking about turmoil in the English department. She said, "Martha, I don't get involved in that. I have ninth graders to teach and that's what I do." She is so focused on the ninth grade. So I need to focus on the ninth grade, and whatever I can accomplish with French IV will be icing on the cake. (Interview 3)

Besides support and encouragement, the teachers also felt that teaming gave them more energy, which was transferred to the students. When asked about the positive effects of teaming, Lew commented:

I would seriously have to say it still is the energy that we can generate as an adult team first. . . . when we do go after things on a creative and professional manner, it's really pleasing to see five people working together, and then, on the other hand, when we culminate that and bring it together with the students and they're all bubbly and we really see them involved, that makes me happy. That makes me very happy to see that we can pull together our project. (Interview 2)

Maeroff (1993) warns that teams often become overly enthusiastic and take on too much responsibility, trying to perform as superheroes. This ardor makes them more vulnerable to disappointment when things do not go well. Therefore, team members must continue to monitor, counsel, and console each other. The teachers as individuals believed that they were trying to do too much, but felt so accountable to the team that they did not try to slow things down. Adding to this fast pace was the fact that a few team members were perfectionists. Three of the five teachers referred to perfectionists in the group, and John described that quality as follows:

> We've done some great things. We have done some great things, and at the same time, you want to do more great things. I think that's another thing that's wrong with us. I think we have too many perfectionists—people who really want to do good and really want to do everything well and really want to get across to the kids. It's really frustrating when you find out that we didn't get across to these kids. (Interview 3)

Tanya seemed to have the most realistic expectation of the teaming and reflected on the year:

> I think for the first year we are doing well. I think looking back on the only experience I ever had was teaming with Lew, and it was rough the first year. I think all of the people on our team have been very willing to try anything within the extent of their comfort level. Some are willing to try more new things than others. I think that is just human nature. I think we are doing the best we can under the given situation, and everybody does want to meet this summer for another one hundred hours. So, I think that is very positive, that we are interested in refining. (Interview 2)

The team spirit of caring for their students overpowered any struggle that they encountered. This team spirit was fostered by several factors, perhaps the strongest being a sense of who they were as individuals. All the teachers brought their individual styles of caring to the team setting and blended them, creating a wealth of strategies and techniques to take care of the students. With five teachers to care about them, the students always had someone to turn to in time of need. The teachers, too, had the advantage of working together to deal with student behavior. Thus, the students could not "fall through the cracks" and were held accountable for their actions and work.

Many incidents happened over the course of the year to demonstrate the individual caring of the teachers. We saw each one of the teachers make some profound gesture to assist a student in learning or coping with an outside issue. The most moving story that we saw unfold, however, involved all the teachers and displayed their team spirit.

Awan and Terrell were two boys on the team who tended to get into minor trouble. The teachers felt that Terrell was probably the ring leader and Awan, the follower. This particular incident began in Martha's Spanish class. She passed around photographs of the scuba diving activity for the students to see. When the class period was over, a picture of Awan and Terrell in their diving attire was missing, and Martha asked for it back. Awan and Terrell said they did not have it. Tanya tried to get the photograph back the next period, but they still would not admit they had it. The teachers knew that the two were lying, but they were not sure which of the two took the picture. They decided to confront the two of them during their pull-out day for curriculum work.

The two boys came into the conference room. Awan did most of the talking and tried to divert the attention away from the picture-stealing incident. He said that they liked Martha because she had a good rapport with them, but they did not like Tanya because they did not trust her; therefore, they could not tell her they had the picture. Tanya looked hurt and Martha seemed embarrassed by the comment. John gazed straight ahead. Gary, who was usually the most reticent member of the team, became red faced and started reprimanding the boys. He told them they had no right to attack Tanya and demanded they apologize to her. Lew then brought the issue back to their stealing and lying. Awan finally apologized, and Terrell did, sort of. Martha thanked the boys for telling the truth and reminded them that all their teachers cared about them and would not allow them to lie or steal. After the students left, the teachers decided they would separate the two boys so that they would no longer have classes together. Martha said she was afraid they would see that as punishment since she had promised them they would not be punished if they told the truth. Everyone else said that it was not a punishment, but a new beginning.

We found this incident very powerful. We watched Awan try to pit Martha and Tanya against each other. It reminded us of the classic way that students try to "work" teachers, to divide and conquer. But their strategy failed. We felt a synergy in the conference room that is difficult to convey in words. The teachers mixed their individual styles of dealing with students and became a potent force in showing the boys that they would not be duped. The balance of anger and care was delicately weighed, and the teachers felt a sense of accomplishment in dealing with the situation.

This ability to work together for the good of their students was one of the strongest qualities that the team possessed. Because of this skill, the teachers experienced feelings of accomplishment and rewards, feelings that overpowered the difficulties they encountered trying to blend their curriculums.

7

Craft Pride, Caring,
and Moral Purpose

We do not remember days. We remember moments.

—Cesare Pavese (1961)

Overview

In spite of all the obstacles that the teachers encountered, they continued to persevere with the restructuring endeavor. Their heroic efforts at implementing the restructuring initiative defied the generalized notion that imposed change inevitably leads to low morale, dissatisfaction, and reduced commitment, as well as resistance and sabotage (Sikes, 1992). Rather, this team of teachers became a modern-day Sisyphus, the figure in Greek mythology whose daily task was to push a boulder up a mountain only to have it roll down the moment he reached the top. Louis and King (1993) explain:

Sisyphus is a symbol and touchstone for all committed professionals who believe that we labor long and hard at tasks that,
at best, we can only partially or temporarily accomplish. We
admire Sisyphus. He perseveres, his will undaunted by impossible circumstance. . . . At the same time, though, we mar-
vel that he keeps struggling up that mountain without
analyzing why he cannot accomplish his task. If evidence
repeatedly suggests that a job can't be done, isn't it better to
reorganize the activity so that you can at least accomplish
something of worth? This essential dilemma—between com-
mitment-perseverance, on the one hand, and practicality-com-
promise, on the other—is played out repeatedly in the life of
educational reformers who work in schools. (P. 217)

Lortie (1975) writes that teachers experience craft pride when
they succeed in reaching work goals that are important to them.
He reflects on the findings from his research study:

The activities which generate pride among respondents are
teaching duties; as with hoped-for outcomes and the effects
of outstanding colleagues, craft pride is centered on instructional outcomes and relationships with students. Scant attention is paid to other aspects of the teachers' role; pride is
not evoked by participation in schoolwide affairs. The classroom is the cathected forum—not the principal's office or the
professional association. . . . psychic rewards associated with
achievement center on the instructional tasks of the classroom teacher. (P. 131)

The Apex teachers' work was deeply connected to craft pride,
and they measured their accomplishments by their success in developing two well-integrated curriculum units, by their ethic of
responsibility and caring, and by their sense of professional growth
and renewal.

Well-Integrated Units

The Apex teachers were extremely proud of two particular interdisciplinary units which they were able to develop over the course of

the year. The first unit, Jurassic Park, was designed during the 100 hours of paid summer curriculum work while the second, The Holocaust, was designed during the course of the regular school year. All of the members of the team saw both units as being very well integrated across content areas although in each case one team member felt that his subject had played a relatively minor role. In the case of Jurassic Park, Lew felt that he had not contributed as much to the unit as the other teachers did, and John had similar feelings about his contribution to the Holocaust unit. Even though there were differences in the depth of individual pride concerning the two units, all of the teachers pointed to them as the team's shining moments. Though the other units on Immigration, The Wild West, and World War I were gratifying for individual teachers, none of these units was considered to be a real team success.

Jurassic Park

Science. Jurassic Park, as noted in previous chapters, was John's brainchild. He had encountered the idea at a National Science Teachers Association Conference and came back to school intent on having the other teachers adopt this theme for one of the units. Though none of the other teachers was particularly enamored of the idea initially, they all eventually agreed to give it a try. Their agreement was based on the fact that John was displaying genuine enthusiasm about the teaming prospects for the first time, and no one wanted to discourage him. Once they agreed on Jurassic Park as an opening unit, the team members spent the bulk of the 100 summer hours of paid curriculum work planning activities for this unit. The goals of the unit were:

(1) to establish a link between all team disciplines using the Jurassic Park theme; and (2) to demonstrate growth and understanding in the following areas: research, analysis, reflection, technology, the writing process, communication and presentations, use of time lines and graphs, use of learning logs, and critical thinking. (Team Curriculum Meetings, Summer)

In his science classes, John used Jurassic Park as an opportunity to focus on the scientific method, paleontology, evolution, fossils, plant and animal classification, and critical thinking. Three activities that John planned proved to be extremely exciting for students. The first activity was a simulated dinosaur dig. After watching a "Nova" video on paleontology and discussing the painstaking work of finding and preserving fossils, each pair of students went to work as paleontologists. John had obtained multiple balsa wood dinosaur kits from a science materials distributors. Each kit contains replicas of the bones of one type of dinosaur that students typically assemble in order to learn about the structure of dinosaurs. John, however, wanted his students to understand the work of paleontologists; therefore, he prepared an activity to have them "find" the dinosaur bones first. He did this by burying all of the pieces from each kit in an individual shoe box filled with sand. He gave students small wooden digging utensils and told them to dig carefully through the sand to remove the dinosaur fossils. He then asked them to construct the model of the dinosaur from the "bones" and conduct research in the library or on the Internet to find out what type of dinosaur they had constructed. The field notes from one of the researchers described the scene in the classroom that day:

> John passed out the "dinosaur kits" and told the students that they were paleontologists on a dinosaur dig. They were instructed to carefully remove the bones from the sand without destroying them. John noted that the digging tools would be very important in avoiding damage to the fossils. He told students that they could spread out around the room or even go out into the hall to complete the dig. (I expected students to just dump the boxes over and pick out the bones. To my amazement, they actually used the digging tools and sifted through the sand boxes very carefully as if they were really going to damage precious fossils. I would never have expected this from ninth graders.) (Field Notes, September 18)

A second activity that proved particularly interesting was the fossil preservation activity. One of the major premises of the book, *Jurassic Park,* was the preservation of insects who had bitten the dinosaurs in amber or hardened tree sap. The fossilized insects could then be used to produce dinosaur DNA. After the students read this section in the book, John explained the basic notions about DNA and the preservation process. He then conducted an activity in which students preserved their own insects in "amber." John sent the students on a mission, both inside and outside the school, to collect as many bugs as possible. The students returned with an abundant supply. Using ice cube trays and casting resin, the students then preserved these already dead insects in cubes of amber.

A final activity, which would be a precursor to some of John's later work with the students on topology was the task of mapping Isla Nublar where the novel is set. The students mapped the island by establishing compass directions in relation to other land and water masses mentioned in the book. As they were reading the novel, John directed the students to take notes concerning the relative location of buildings, dinosaur paddocks, and other landmarks. Using these pieces of information and some lessons on latitude and longitude, students produced detailed maps of the island.

The student maps, amber cubes, and assembled dinosaur kits were proudly displayed in the display cases outside John's room. These displays attracted the attention of many other teachers in the school who began sending articles, web site addresses, and notices about TV shows concerning dinosaurs to John and the other Apex teachers.

Spanish. Martha, who is always enthusiastic and supportive of both students and her colleagues, wanted to endorse John's ideas, but she was baffled at first as to how she could integrate Jurassic Park into her first- and second-year Spanish curriculum. She reflected: "I spent a lot of time trying to figure out what the heck I was going to do. These students just can't handle heavy reading yet" (Field Notes, September 26). She eventually settled on several different strategies. She decided to begin the year studying the geography of several Spanish-speaking countries in Latin America. Naturally, she began with Costa Rica, the setting of Jurassic Park. After studying the geography, climate, and ecology of Costa Rica as well as the Spanish influence in that country, she turned her students' attention to other Latin American countries. Pairs of students studied individual countries, focusing on two major questions: Why did Crichton choose Costa Rica as the setting? Would there be a Latin American country that would have been a better choice, in your opinion? Martha felt that this activity really enhanced her students' research skills as well as their knowledge of Latin America.

Martha also found that she could use the novel to sharpen students' pronunciation. She found a Spanish translation of the novel and used the Spanish cognates for many of the dinosaurs to help her students understand the differences in pronunciation between Spanish and English. She believed that by starting with the cognates her students would see the task as achievable since the words looked like English. It also provided a nice opportunity to compare and contrast various vowel sounds within the two languages.

Martha's final use of the novel was in teaching some grammatical concepts. Students were introduced to interrogative forms in Spanish using questions about the novel. They were also taught gender and number rules using examples drawn directly from the novel. As she proceeded through the unit, Martha discovered a number of other possibilities for integration that she would use in following years, including writing paragraphs describing the characters or the plot in the novel and making a Spanish video to act out one of the scenes from the book.

English.   The major activity in English was the reading of the novel. Through the reading and analysis of the novel, Tanya was able to illustrate a variety of concepts, including characterization, plot, point of view, and literary devices, such as personification and foreshadowing. Tanya also attempted to develop a better sense of media literacy on the part of her students through an analysis of the film version of the novel. The students viewed the film as the final event in the unit. After viewing the film, Tanya asked her students to complete an analysis of the movie focusing on two specific areas: 1. the differences between the novel and the film, including both plot and character; and 2. the film techniques used to produce suspense and to entice the audience to identify with the dinosaurs as well as the people.

To synthesize their learning about the novel and movie, Tanya required her students to complete a learner/response log on a daily basis and a reflective analysis paper that pointed out the integration of the novel into all of the other subject areas. She also gave her students a variety of other possible activities to pursue. She assigned each activity a certain number of points, and required students to choose activities whose point value added up to a specific point total. These optional activities included character sketches, role playing, creating commercials for the novel, creating music about the novel, writing a eulogy for one of the characters, writing a children's book about Jurassic Park and reading it to a group of elementary children, writing poetry about the novel, writing an editorial about the establishment of a Jurassic Park in the United States, and drawing cartoons or caricatures depicting scenes and characters in the novel. As a result of these optional activities, several children's books were written and read in elementary classrooms; and a variety of posters, eulogies, short stories, and cartoons were displayed in the hallway showcases between Tanya's and Lew's rooms. These activities and hallway displays brought a great deal of notoriety to the Apex teachers throughout the entire school. Teachers, administrators, visitors, and we, the researchers, were impressed by the quality of student work.

Social Studies. At first Lew was the most reluctant participant in the Jurassic Park unit. He had envisioned the entire curriculum as being driven by historical themes in chronological order, beginning with the United States Civil War and moving to present times. He did not see how Jurassic Park could possibly fit into his curriculum and did not see the need to deviate from what he and Tanya had been able to do successfully over the previous three years. However, given John's enthusiasm, Lew felt that it was best for the team's unity that he go along. He also did it as a form of modeling for the other teachers. He foresaw even during the previous summer that integrating their content areas with historical themes from U.S. history might be very challenging for some of the other Apex teachers. Lew explained, "I went along with Jurassic Park because I wanted to show them that if you worked hard enough at it, integration could be accomplished no matter how far-fetched it seemed at first" (Interview 1).

Lew was able to accommodate this theme by focusing on learning and thinking skills that he knew would be important to succeed in his classes in U.S. history. He emphasized the following skills in his unit: creating timelines, summary writing and note taking, comparing and contrasting, cause-and-effect relationships, outlining, research skills, and political cartooning. He used the novel to have students develop timelines of the key events in each section of the text, to have students write short summaries of various sections of the text, to have students practice outlining sections of the text and taking notes on other sections, to have students compare and contrast the viewpoints of various characters in the text, to have students identify a variety of cause-and-effect relationships within the text, to have students research a particular topic introduced in the novel, and to have students draw cartoons that depicted various characters or events in the novel. Lew felt that he was very successful in teaching students important skills and in modeling how integration is possible across disciplines for his Apex colleagues.

> I feel that the study of American history should offer more than just names, dates, and events. It should go beyond the facts and provide a challenge, and an opportunity for our students to think, analyze, explore, understand, and create. Keeping this in mind, I was able to incorporate my original curriculum and our Jurassic Park theme to create an exciting series of lessons which are crucial to the study and understanding of my content as well as the content of my teammate's individual disciplines. (Apex Conference Presentation, March 19)

Math. Although Gary actually spent far less class time in math on topics directly related to Jurassic Park, his projects brought a great deal of publicity to the team and its Jurassic Park efforts. Gary actually incorporated Jurassic Park into his algebra and prealgebra curriculum in the following four ways: 1. through a brief discussion of fractals and chaos theory, 2. through the use of some data drawn from the novel for graphing activities, 3. through the creation of a 40-foot timeline of history, and 4. through the creation of a life- size Tyrannosaurus Rex on the school parking lot.

The timeline was an activity designed to sharpen students' understanding of graphing and proportion. Students were required to work together to produce a timeline of history, which would represent 570 million years of actual time. Working from a scale in which 1 inch represented 57 million years, students worked in groups to create a 40-foot timeline that depicted the Paleozoic, Mesozoic, and Cenozoic periods. The timelines were then hung in the school hallway outside Gary's room.

It was the life-size T-Rex activity, however, which really put Team Apex on the local map. The project began with an 8-by-10-inch drawing of a T-Rex. Gary decided that he could use this activity to help his students better understand scale, ratios, and proportions, as well as give them a much better understanding of the size of real dinosaurs. The first step was for students to conduct research to identify the actual size of a T-Rex. Using the research that had been completed on the assembled dinosaurs in John's class, students decided that a T-Rex would be about 24 feet high, a measurement that is difficult to fathom. Gary decided that the only way to impress the students with the massive size of a T-Rex was to actually re-create a 24-foot dinosaur somewhere on the school property. His first inclination was to paint the life-size dinosaur on one of the outside walls of the school. When the principal nixed that idea, Gary turned to the parking lot. Students worked together to create a scale for the dinosaur on the pavement, divided the scale into rectangles that corresponded to rectangles on an enlarged poster version of the 8-by-10 drawing, and then took responsibility in pairs for painting several rectangles on the parking lot.

The school's public relations office heard of this parking lot activity and sent a notice to local newspapers, radio stations, and TV networks. On the day that Gary's students were applying the finishing touches to their life-size T-Rex, three film crews appeared from three different local TV stations. They filmed students as they painted, interviewed students about the project, and also interviewed Gary. All three stations aired two- or three-minute segments about the project on their local news shows that night. The teachers and students in Team Apex became local celebrities overnight.

The culminating activity for the teachers and students was a field trip to a museum of natural history. One of the researchers accompanied the students and teachers on the field trip. When the students were brought into the large lecture room of the museum, one of the tour guides greeted them and spoke with the students about dinosaurs. He was holding pieces of the dinosaur models that are typically used to introduce guests at the museum to the study of fossils and dinosaurs. The guide began the lecture assuming a very low level of understanding on the part of the students. As he began to ask questions and students responded accurately and confidently, the level of complexity in his description grew by the minute. Midway through the talk he was so impressed with the students' understanding that he went out and brought out a real dinosaur fossil instead of the plastic replica that was normally used for such talks. He informed the group that their clear understanding of what paleontologists do and of how important fossil preservation is had convinced him that he could risk bringing out a real fossil. He confessed that this was usually not done with groups of school students. Students were allowed to touch and hold the real fossil and asked a host of intelligent questions of the guide. As the talk ended, he reiterated how deeply impressed he was with the students' understanding and behavior. On the way back to the school, John remarked, "Wow. What a change. Tour guides usually say, 'Get your kids out of here. We never want to see them again.' Today they were encouraging us to bring them back again" (Field Notes, September 27).

The combination of the students' behavior at the museum, the notoriety gained by the hallway displays, the local TV coverage, and the fact that all of the teachers were able to incorporate some Jurassic Park content into their respective disciplines convinced the teachers that the unit was a resounding success. Perhaps John said it best:

> I feel that first of all when I brought up the Jurassic Park thing I was real enthused about it. It was not well received. As a matter of fact I have to say this, I felt that the other team members, more or less, said, Well okay, we'll do it for you because they already had their stuff together. But I think it was the way that after they saw it, saw the possibilities, it started to grow and it was almost like a flower blossoming, and it kind of—I'm not sure that it got out of control— but it kind of went into areas that I never thought it would go into, and it kind of became bigger than I ever thought it would become. It kind of became something that almost could've taken the whole year.

I mean it was unbelievable. I was very enthused about it as we went through it. I was really enthused with what the kids did within, and I just felt it was a good learning process for the kids and the teachers. (Interview 3)

Although the Jurassic Park unit would fall short of true curriculum integration as some theorists see it (e.g., Drake & Beane), for Gary, Martha, and John it did represent a first attempt at crossing subject boundaries. They ventured into this territory cautiously and planned for it diligently during the summer. Their efforts were rewarded and they were convinced by their own reactions, by their students' reactions, and by accolades received from others that the venture had been a great success. This initial success represents what Kouzes and Posner (1988) call planning small wins. As a result, the team members left the first month of school on a real high. They were a team, a successful, winning team. This perception is critical to understanding the Sisyphus-like behavior we documented during the remainder of this initial year, a year that turned out to be much bumpier and lonelier than its start.

The Holocaust

The Holocaust unit represented a second high point for the team in terms of curriculum integration. Though John opted not to participate in this unit as noted in the previous chapter, the other four members of the team viewed it as a great success. The unit focused around the theme of the children of the Holocaust and was developed jointly by Lew, Tanya, Martha, and Gary. In contrast to all the other units that were taught during the year, these four team members all felt a great deal of individual ownership for this particular unit. John was the primary owner of Jurassic Park, and Lew owned the others.

The central integration structure consisted of students and teachers reading the novel, *My Name Is Renee*. This novel depicts the plight of a young Jewish girl who flees with her family into France during the Nazi persecution and is eventually hidden away by her mother in a Catholic convent. The child protagonist, Ruth Hartz who is now a mature educator living within 100 miles of the school, came and spoke with the students after they had read the novel. Apex students in foreign language studied the impact of World War II on France and Spain. The French students learned how the Holocaust played itself out in France, and the Spanish students compared the Holocaust to the Spanish Inquisition. In addition, upper-level French and German students who were not a part of Team Apex also read the novel and heard the author's speech. In social studies, Lew, who until that point had not been a heavy Internet user, found a web site that contained a significant amount of information about the impact of the Holocaust on children. Students researched the lives of particular children who died during the Holocaust, wrote papers about their lives, and then wrote and acted out skits that depicted historical events in the lives of these children. In English class, students read the novel and wrote short stories and poems depicting the events of the Holocaust for children.

As was the case with Jurassic Park, Gary probably devoted less actual class time to the Holocaust than the other teachers, but he developed a project that brought much attention to the team. He found a coffinlike box with a clear plastic lid on the top. He challenged his students to find a way to figure out the volume of this irregular structure and then to estimate how many sunflower seeds would be required to fill it. After working on the problem for several days, Gary and the students actually filled the "coffin" with sunflower seeds and placed it in the hallway between Lew's and Tanya's rooms with a sign informing all who passed by that each of the sunflower seeds represented a certain number of the more than one million children who had died in the Holocaust. One of the agricultural education teachers saw the display and asked Gary if he was interested in actually planting the sunflower seeds in one of the fields owned by the school. He and Gary worked out a plan to plant a million sunflower seeds. Each sunflower would represent one child and the seeds that would be harvested after the sunflower seeds had grown would represent a lost generation of children. When the project was actually carried out, it was possible to only plant approximately 250,000 seeds.

The Apex teachers arranged a ceremony to honor the children of the Holocaust. This ceremony consisted of Apex students planting several thousand seeds by hand (the rest were planted by machine) and reading poems that they had written about the

Holocaust. Again, news of this event was communicated to the local media by the school's public relations office, and Team Apex students and teachers appeared on the local news shows again. Several of the student poems were reprinted in the major newspaper that serves the surrounding metropolitan region.

The culminating event for this unit was a field trip to the Holocaust Museum in Washington, D.C. One of the researchers who accompanied the students and teachers on the trip recorded the following observations in the field notes:

> I have never been so deeply impressed by the behavior of ninth-grade students as I was today. Nor have I ever been as proud to be associated with a group of students. I had hoped that the students would be respectful and well behaved given the power of the museum. Their behavior went beyond respect. They were empathic, morally outraged, and moved emotionally. Many cried, the girls openly, the boys secretively. They clearly knew what this was all about. (Field Notes, March 26)

Though the unit was not perfect by any means and despite John's inability to participate in it, the other Apex teachers saw this unit as a resounding success. It boosted their morale and reinforced their purpose—especially through the course of a year that had been filled with disappointments, conflicts, and tensions. It allowed the teachers to move toward the end of the year again feeling that they had been able to accomplish some important goals for their students.

Ethic of Responsibility

Ethics of responsibility and caring are the requisite components for teachers to attain psychic rewards (Hargreaves, 1994). In an ethic of responsibility, professional obligations are emphasized and improvements to planning and instruction are stressed, while, in an ethic of caring, actions are motivated by concerns for care and nurturance of others (Hargreaves, 1994). These psychic rewards, the joy and satisfaction of caring for and working with young people, revolve around classroom achievement (Lortie, 1975).

All the Apex teachers cited examples of student learning as a source of pride and sense of accomplishment for their efforts. Tanya best demonstrated the balance between care and expectations:

> When we look at our honor roll statistics, I would love to take the time to look at last year's makeup and how many kids are on honor roll now compared to how many we had on honor roll last year because I know we haven't lowered the standards. . . . My one class, I about died, this hasn't happened since my first year—and my first year I didn't know any better. The one class has one C, two B's, and all the rest A's, and I just can't believe that those are the grades. When I look back through, that is what those kids deserve and that doesn't go with the curve. . . . Yet for failures for the year, I have six, and last year I only had three. So I think our standards are higher. I think when we talk about kids at meetings, it helps, whereas before I might have thought they [the failures] were my problem, that maybe I am judging too harshly. But when I hear the names brought up [of those who are failing], it's better then that the students have to stay and make up the course work if they're not ready to go on. I feel bad about failing six kids, but it's going to help them if they take advantage of it. . . . Some kids we could have helped more, yet to balance how much emphasis you put on the kids who really need help with those on the top who need help, too. You need to put time into the TIC-it program and incentives and so you have to balance, and I think we've reached a lot more kids this year than we ever did. I'm closer to more kids than I ever was. I would keep these kids next year. (Interview 3)

John explained why he was unable to balance the components of care and expectations that are requisite to attaining psychic rewards. Reflecting on the poor test results on his final exam and the knowledge that students had cheated on the test, John explained his dissatisfaction and unhappiness with the restructuring endeavor:

> I think the beginning of the year for me, I was really on a high and felt that things were working out really well. Toward the end of the year, after seeing the exams, after listening to

people saying that they didn't cover their content, knowing that I didn't cover my content, I'm not quite sure if we are moving in the direction that we should be moving. We did a lot of things that were neat, a lot of things that were fun, but I'm not sure that when I see my exams and I see how the kids did in the exams—and some kids did well and others didn't— and I see that we didn't cover as much content as what I think we should've, as I go over these [science] standards, I have some real questions about teaming or at least the way that we're doing the teaming. When I look back at the Jurassic Park theme and then I look back at the work that the kids did then and some of the things that were accomplished then, I'm very happy about that, but when I look at the Holocaust, I really have some questions about the Holocaust theme because we have an element in our team of students who I don't think learned a thing from the Holocaust as far as a moral responsibility is concerned. We have some students who I feel have "borrowed" answers and handed in work that wasn't theirs as you would with any class at any time. But we spent a lot of time on the Holocaust and a lot of time going over that, and we have students who stand by and let these students get away with it, and that was the whole crux of the whole Holocaust and my thing is, hey, I'm kind of a little bit frustrated because I know and have heard what's going on as far as that's concerned, and I'm not happy with the students' response and the way they handled that. I think that after the unit the kids should've handled it much better just being aware of the Holocaust. (Interview 3)

Gary expressed how his concerns at the beginning of the school year dissipated when he saw the student results:

Going into the year not knowing really well some of the people and the willingness to work together sometimes, I was a little reluctant probably at the beginning as far as what was going to get accomplished, but I really feel when I look back at some of the things the kids did, it was a success because some of the ideas that I saw presented by the kids and some of the materials they created definitely shows that there was some learning that took place, and I think what really drove that home was the thing with the Holocaust poems that Tanya had them write. Some of the depth that the kids put into those was amazing, and I look back at myself in ninth grade and I don't think I could've done anything that deep at that point in time. I certainly think there is still room for improvement. I think there are a number of things we can still work on to make it better, but I would say that overall it was a very beneficial experience. (Interview 3)

The student writing that Gary referred to was poems that the students wrote after studying the Holocaust unit as described in the previous section. As noted, some of the poems were printed in the local newspaper, and Tanya said that her husband, too, was moved by the student writing. Tanya explained how seeing the poems in print affected her:

[The staff from the local newspaper] picked out parts of the kids' poems, Heather's poem, Jessica's. Jessica was a C student for me, and then she wrote this poem, and I thought, wow, I did something with Jessica this year. She is a good kid and she is a neat writer, and I think she really likes English now, and that's all I really wanted to do in ninth grade was make them like it and feel they are good at it even if they totally stink. . . . They put parts of their poems [in the newspaper], and my husband read the article and he said, "Those poems are wonderful," and he is not a poetry person at all. Someone wrote into the editor saying that they were just so moved by parts, and these were just snippets of the poems, and I thought, those poems are really good. My kids did that. And then to see them in print in the paper, I thought, wow! (Interview 3)

This kind of successful display is very rewarding for teachers. Lortie (1975) explains why:

Displays dramatize the teacher's achievements, giving high visibility to efforts which generally take place in private. . . . Success which is witnessed, applauded, and remembered by others (including adults) has greater psychological substance than the evanescent flow of everyday teaching. People can recall the event and refer back to it. Learning and involvement are demonstrated; and since rapport is often high on such occasions, the visibly loyal conduct of the students testifies to the teacher's relational skills. (Pp. 126–127)

The Apex team experienced many public displays of their work as described in the previous section. The students were very pleased and proud to see themselves highlighted, especially since the teachers emphasized the coverage as the results of the team's effort, not an individual's.

The teachers also mentioned other ways they measured student achievement. For example, Martha noted better class participation, especially obvious to her in a mixed class of foreign language experience. Martha explained that students with no foreign language experience were mixed with those who already had a year of the language. Normally, the students with no experience were too intimidated to participate, but she found the reverse this year. She also noted better behavior in her classes. She rationalized the better behavior as a direct result of teaming:

I usually have a lot of talking in my class, like chit chat on the side and stuff, and possibly because of the other teachers on the team, I'm having less of that this year because they come from one focused, really focused teacher, and then they come to me where I have a more open classroom, and they still are carrying the same thing from John or Lew or Tanya into my room, and I can count on my hands the number of detentions I had to give this year for kids off task or where it has annoyed me while I'm teaching. (Interview 2)

Martha, Lew, and Tanya all commented on the students' ability to see connections in their learning, being more interested in the content because of these connections, and retaining more information than before. Lew added that he felt that teaming transformed students from "very slow or very lethargic—not wanting to be involved—to by the end of the year or by the middle of the year, to be totally go-getters and to be totally aggressive and to be totally committed learners" (Interview 2).

Lortie (1975) found that teachers place value on the grateful comments of former students because they see the students' testimony as trustworthy rather than "calculated flattery." Both Lew and Tanya used examples of former students who were part of their teaming dyad as a measure of student achievement. Tanya commented on the sophomore teachers who have complimented her for the writing and creative ability of her former students. Lew explained why he feels the students have achieved:

> I've said to [principal] and some of the other people at times—and I think they think I'm giving them lip service—but we've actually been able to sit back and say, remember when this kid was doing this and look at what he or she is doing now. Even right now some of the kids that are in tenth grade, some of the kids that started off as some of our worst kids in the beginning with attitude problems are some of the same kids that come back and talk to us now. They kind of want to hang around our room. They want to be part of what we're doing. They come to check back, "Well, how are you all doing this year? How are these guys doing for you?" You know, they know what they came through and they remember the experience, and they seem to have enjoyed or at least gotten something out of it. So that's what I look at, absolute results. (Interview 2)

Gary conducted a student survey at the end of the year in order to obtain feedback from the students, especially since there was no evaluation planned by the administration. The teachers realized that the student surveys only gave them limited information. Nevertheless, they valued the students' comments and found the surveys helpful in planning for the following school year. In tandem with the surveys is the evidence of student interest that the teachers acknowledged as a measure of successful implementation. Lortie (1975) explains this concept as follows:

> When students exert more than usual effort or show special enthusiasm, some teachers feel self-approval and pride in their craft capacities. One can conceptualize such student behavior—as perceived by the teachers—as "voluntary contributions" to their joint enterprise. To have meaning to the teacher, such contributions should constitute a surplus beyond what he normally expects of students. (P. 129)

Lew gave a clear example of this student interest when he explained the card he received from Jenny, one of his students who, unbeknown to him, had a crush on him and often vied for his attention. Her silly ways of getting his attention often annoyed Lew, who would admonish her to be more serious. Lew explained how she touched him when asked to talk about the high point of the year for him:

My highest point always comes from the kids and their reactions to what we've done, and I guess Jenny gave me a card the other day—I'll show it to you—and I didn't even know she gave it to me. We [team of teachers] were sitting in a meeting, and I opened my grade book and it popped out. I said, "Who's this from?" When I saw the handwriting, I said, "Oh, it's from Jenny." Knowing Jenny—I know how she can be—I'm thinking, what nonsense is she leaving me with? I opened the card later on and I read it, and there are a couple of things in it that always makes me feel like I'm doing my job and it comes from them [students]. Basically, in it, she was saying that she appreciates all that I've done in trying to help her and that I don't have to worry about her because next year she is going to really turn up her grade point average because she wants to go to college and she does want to make a change in her life. She is going to really work, and she talks about the grade point average she is going to have, and she said she knows sometimes she got mad or upset with me, but she always got over it, but the reason she got mad was because she knew I was right. . . . And she mentioned that I've been a father or a friend that she really needs. She appreciates all that I've done, and at the very end she said I shouldn't worry because she's not as wild as she sometimes seems or something along that line. That kind of thing—incidents like that where kids, I can tell that I've gotten a kid from point A all the way to now, and I see a maturity and a difference and in the end if they can say that in some small way that I had something to do with it, then I really feel good about everything. That is a high point for me when kids come back in some way and say thank you, a small thing, a little thing. (Interview 3)

The teachers also expressed a change in their teaching because of the positive results in student achievement. Martha explained how everything she learned in life made her the teacher she is today; therefore, she wanted to help the students see how learning takes place in wholes rather than in pieces. Gary explained how and why he changed his teaching style:

> I think I am more aware of trying to incorporate real world experiences or outside experiences into the classroom. I have seen how using the theme in certain areas really helps deliver the point and make it more meaningful to the kids, and that has made a big difference, I think, in my outlook as far as what I want to try to do. (Interview 3)

Ethic of Caring

In tandem with an ethic of responsibility was an ethic of caring that was equal to and perhaps greater than any other characteristic the teachers shared. In other words, even though they might have differed in beliefs about teaching and learning, teaching techniques and content issues, they shared a genuine care for the welfare of their students. This sense of caring kept the teachers connected to each other and sustained their team purpose even under the most trying circumstances. Martha, when asked to explain why the teachers were working so hard to implement an initiative that they did not have any input into, responded by expressing her feelings about students.

> There is something about these kids in this school. I always taught the same way, but I am more attached to these kids than I have ever been and the same at the school for the blind where I taught. It appeals to some instinct in me that wants to protect these kids because they have been through enough. I would go to bat for any of these kids. So maybe it is something inside each of us that's making us do it for the kids. I've seen Lew do it for the kids; I've seen Tanya do it for the kids, . . . They are different from the kids I had in public schools. Those kids had their moms and dads. It's nice to build relationships with them, but I want to take these kids to Europe. I want to see the looks on their faces when they see the Eiffel Tower for the first time and climb it. So there is something in

this school that breeds a sense of family, but they have tried to kill it over the years with paperwork. All the demands. Throwing too much at us. In the past if a kid was crying, I took him home for the weekend. Let him live with a family, eat a family meal. Lots of teachers used to do that. If you get too busy, if you spend the whole weekend doing paperwork, then you just can't do that. That is one of my goals again this year, to take needy kids home again. (Interview 1)

Hargreaves (1994) explains the importance that teachers attach to care: "In the main, existing evidence suggests that for teachers as for many members of other 'caring professions,' care appears to be interpreted as the interpersonal experience of human nurturance, connectedness, warmth and love" (p. 145). When asked to reflect on her low point of the year, Martha referred to the picture-taking incident with Awan and Terrell (previously discussed in chapter 6) and Awan's and others' cheating. She explained why she was disappointed and hurt, feeling as if perhaps they, the teachers, had failed their mission:

A team low point would be the Terrell-Awan incident. When they treated Tanya with disrespect, that really bothered me. I thought, here's your chance, boys, to just apologize and mean it, give the pictures back, and say, "When Mrs. L asked for the pictures back from us, we should've given them to her." They made a mistake and they didn't admit it. And, I had to acknowledge, John said they were worthless—and I can never write a kid off as worthless—and then that's what went through my mind when I caught Awan one more time cheating. . . . I thought, yeah, we gave Awan ample opportunity to get help and try to improve, and he just never changed his color, and John always said that, and I had to like say, well, you told me so. (Interview 3)

Tanya, too, talked about Awan and Terrell when discussing events that transpired during the school year. She reflected:

I think if I would've had Awan and Terrell together last year, I really wouldn't like them at the end of this year or at the end of last year, whereas this year I do. And Awan, his biggest thing—and if I would've realized this back in September—all he wanted was someone to care about him. He came and made up a story about three weeks ago that he was getting kicked out of school, he was being suspended all the next week, and my reaction was, what happened to Awan, tell me, and I ran and told Lew, and we got him together and asked, "Well, what can we do to help you? How can we . . . " and he said, "See you all do care about me." See, he made it up just to see our reaction. Now he'll come in and touch me on my back and stand at my desk and get closer to me. He actually sat—he pulled a desk back and sat by me the other day. All he wanted to know was that we cared about him, and I think that whole picture thing [picture-taking incident with Awan and Terrell] turned that around. Just because I didn't let him get away with it, he realized, well, maybe she really does care about me. (Interview 3)

The "little" extras that go without recognition or acknowledgment surfaced so many times to demonstrate that the teachers' caring was genuine, that it went beyond mere mimicking of words. The TIC-it (Ticket Incentive Center) program that the teachers devised encompassed stocking their "center" with items for the students to buy with the tickets they amassed. Tickets were given to students for a variety of reasons such as outstanding work, great effort, good citizenship, being helpful to teachers or students, and so on. The inventory went beyond the obvious school supplies of paper and pencils to objects young people would want to possess. Things such as earrings and candy were popular purchases. If a specific item did not sell, the teachers slashed the ticket price to sell the product so that they could replace it with something more appealing. A fun, relaxing activity was to help bag candy for the "center." We found this activity to be a time for the teachers to engage in small talk and bantering, a time to symbolically renew their commitment to their students and each other.

The teachers went to great length at the end of each quarter to conduct a team assembly to commend students for their work during the previous quarter. Besides recognizing those students who achieved Distinguished Honors and Honors, they acknowledged, by certificate, effort, conduct, most improved, most congenial and those who completed an extracurricular activity. The teachers deliberated very long and hard in naming the recipients of the certificates, and the students, especially those singled out for effort, conduct, most improved, and most congenial, were always very surprised, grateful, and proud.

The teachers also held a pizza party at the end of each quarter for students who received Distinguished Honors and Honors. The original plan was to take the students to Pizza Hut one evening after their awards assembly, but the teachers decided, instead, to hold the party in Lew's classroom. Besides pizza and soda, the students danced, played board games, put together puzzles, and shopped at the "center." The students enjoyed the evening with their teachers, and receiving an invitation to the party took on a symbol of status and accomplishment.

The party was important to the teachers, too. For example, the third-quarter party was difficult to schedule to accommodate all the teachers' commitments and school activities. The date they finally agreed on conflicted with a faculty outing that Tanya had initiated and planned. When everyone else said they were available that evening, Tanya said she would skip the faculty get-together, knowing full well that the faculty would be unhappy with her decision especially since she organized the gathering.

The teachers' sense of caring and unity was so outwardly demonstrated that many students began to model the same behavior toward each other. The best example of this modeling took place on the morning the students were going to watch the movie *Jurassic Park* on the big screen in another building on campus. All the students had received team T-shirts the first week of school and were told that they had to wear the shirt on any field trip they took as a team. All the students complied with the rule when they went to the museum of natural history. However, when the students were told they had to wear their shirts to view the movie the following week, one girl said she had lost her shirt. The teachers felt bad because the girl was a good student. Martha offered to wear her other team shirt and let the girl wear hers. Lew, however, stated that it was the girl's responsibility to take care of the shirt and that she would have to sit with him outside the auditorium if she did not find it by the day of the movie. The Apex teachers told Lew that perhaps they should just give her another shirt, that they did not want Lew to miss the movie. Lew remained firm that they had to stay committed to their rules. The students themselves resolved the problem. They collected TIC-its from each other and purchased a new shirt at the "center" for the girl. The students felt proud of their team effort to obtain a shirt for their peer, and the teachers were proud of their students' problem-solving skills and concern for each other.

This overall atmosphere of caring became the touchstone for Apex's success. Asked to talk about the effects that teaming had on the students, Martha explained:

> They [the students] had no sense of identity. Apex gave them identity. It gave them five of us to talk to if they needed to. They could vent on anyone of us knowing that we knew the other teachers in our group and we would listen. (Interview 3)

The students did seem to understand the teachers' dedication to them and to Team Apex. Student reflections included comments that acknowledged the importance of working together and striving for excellence. Even students who, at first, did not believe in the teaming, calling it too babyish since they had teamed in the middle school, sensed success and unity in the teaming.

Gary seemed to reiterate Martha's feelings and tempered his happiness with the realization that they might not have reached all the students:

> I think they've [students] realized that we as a team of teachers, we were not going to let them kind of slide too much. We tried to keep on top of students that were having trouble. We tried to reward those who were doing well, and I think they saw the results of that. I really, truly believe the majority of them enjoyed some of the activities they did. I think they found out it could be fun plus serious about getting their work done, so, overall, I think it was a good experience from a lot of the feedback I saw, but obviously there is still that group that we probably didn't reach. (Interview 3)

Lew, too, gauged the year's success by the students' response to it:

As far as the kids' production, I actually feel it is probably one of my most productive years for what I've gotten from the kids and their response to us. It is very kind of eerie right now because the kids have realized that we are coming to an end, and some of them have actually said verbally that they are dreading that or missing that, and they wonder what things are going to be like, so I know that we really made some contact with them based on things that we try to do. I really feel very good about what we've done as a unit, you know, with the kids overall. (Interview 3)

Lew also explained how he wanted to expand the activities period that was held every other day into a more productive time for the students. Although he decided to give up his Law and Youth class to devote more time to the team, he already knew where his extra energy was heading:

What I really enjoy is that even though I'm giving up my Law and Youth class, the fact that I'll be involved in team projects and I'm going to feel again what I was really trying to say before. There is a lot we can do with this that I don't want to make it [activities period] a study hall. I really don't. That's why Tanya and I have been coming up with all kinds of crazy games like I have a history Trivial Pursuit game—I want to turn it into club-type fun where they can get tickets and stuff to win. They can enjoy this and learn something along the way. Tanya has all kinds of word games that she ordered, too, and I want to give them a choice: "Hey, you don't have to be here doing this. If this isn't your bag, go over there and have fun doing something with that." So, I want to turn it into a real revolving learning. I look forward to that. (Interview 3)

Their deep caring for their students gave the teachers a strong sense of moral purpose about their work. They saw themselves not as restructuring, not as implementing someone else's ideas but rather as trying to do what was best for kids. There were many examples throughout the year of teacher's sacrificing for the good of students including giving up favorite classes (Law and Youth, French III) so that the teachers could devote more time to the team. One particularly pertinent example of self-sacrifice for the good of students concerned the issues of teaming and foreign languages. As we noted earlier, foreign language teachers were not intended to be a part of the original teaming design. Once they were added to the team, deciding which students would be assigned to which team became problematic since there were three foreign language options but only two ninth grade teams. In March of the first year of implementation a building level administrator came to talk with the Apex teachers during a team planning meeting. He wanted to discuss the assignment of students to the ninth-grade teams for the following year.

He began the conversation by informing the teachers that he and the other administrators had been discussing the foreign language issue and had pretty much decided to only allow ninth-grade students to take either French or Spanish. This policy would go into effect for the coming school year. Using this strategy, students who elected Spanish would be assigned to one of the ninth-grade teams and those who took French to the other. The teachers at first seemed receptive to the idea since this would make scheduling much easier for them. However, after a minute or two of thinking about it, John spoke out against the idea. He suggested that ninth graders should be having their horizons broadened, not closed. He posited that restricting students' choices for the sake of administrative convenience was not the right thing to do. The other Apex teachers agreed with him and finally convinced the administration to retain the three foreign language choices that would make their own scheduling more difficult. This is just one example of the multiple instances in which the Apex teachers chose what they believed to be right for students as opposed to what was more convenient for them.

This intense devotion to doing what was best for kids was both a liability and an asset in terms of its emotional impact on the teachers. On the one hand, they derived great satisfaction from successful experiences such as the well-integrated units, the parties, the certificates, and the "great shirt bail out" by the Apex students. When they were drowning in inner tensions and conflicts, this satisfaction from doing the right thing buoyed them up like a life preserver. On the other hand, their sense of uncertainty about the restructuring effort and the continuing tension between subject-area curriculum and subject integration had a much greater negative impact on the emotional lives of the teachers simply because they cared so much about doing the right things for students. If they had not cared so much, uncertainty would not have been so emotionally draining. If they had not cared so much, the more likely it would have been that any small effort they made was good enough, especially since they saw so many flaws in the change process. In Sergiovanni's (1997) terms, "satisficing" would have been enough. But they did care, and as a result they agonized about whether they were really preparing students well for the future. They worried constantly about any potentially negative impact of their curriculum on students. This worry carried over even into their successes. Tanya wondered out loud during an interview if all the extras that they had done would turn out to be a source of frustration for students in the future.

> I feel like we might have set these kids up in a way because they think next year is going to be like this too and it's not. It's not going to be like this, and I worry if they'll mind. I think they'll mind. They're going to wonder where their TIC-it program is and want to know where their pizza parties are, and I don't think they are going to be there. (Interview 3)

Professional Growth

By being connected morally and professionally through the ethics of responsibility and caring, the teachers felt both a personal and interpersonal sense of achievement. Espousing the team concept of working together, the teachers became products of their own design. They became more intensely committed to their mission and felt professional growth with each reward they experienced.

Personal satisfaction ranged from becoming more proficient in a skill to feeling individual success in the classroom or with a student. Lew felt personal satisfaction in his work with the Holocaust unit. He was very anxious to show the videotape of the students' skits about the Holocaust to demonstrate what students can do if they worked together. He acknowledged that he had become very fond of the Internet and intended to use it even more the following year. Lew tempered this satisfaction with a need to take time over the summer to examine the year to see if his feelings of success were accurate:

It seems like every year I have a different challenge, and this one was probably one of the most dramatic of all of them to try to pull five people together and keep us on the right track. As I said, class-wise, . . . it opened my eyes, it brightened my horizons, it gave me more energy, and as a result, I kind of turned that over into what I was doing with the kids. Now, I'm sure I'm going to look back and think about how much substance was within my curriculum as well. I feel it was very strong looking at it from the overview, but I'd like to look at it a little bit deeper because I did things again much differently than I would've normally done based on getting caught up in this frenzy of enjoying education again, not being concerned about written tests. I looked back at my grade book the other day, and I hadn't given a written test in about two marking periods. And I want to make sure that that's good, and in the end when I was giving my final, I said to the kids—you know, they were worried about what final I was going to give. I said, well, it wouldn't be fair that I would now come back and put everything on paper and say, "You now need to memorize and remember all these things." I said that wouldn't be fair because that's not the way we've been learning all year. So, as a result I created a final that was creative in nature that they had to do presentations that a lot of them really enjoyed doing. And so my grades were high. My grades were high overall, and I gave more A's than I've given, a lot more B's. The grades seemed to change, and I hope that's for the best. So they changed in the classroom, and I hope that's a positive. (Interview 3)

John explained the personal satisfaction he experienced when he and Gary walked through the Natural History Museum in Washington, D.C., during the field trip to the Holocaust Museum:

When we went down to Washington, we went to the Holocaust Museum, but we went—my kids and I—to the Air and Space Museum, and then we, Gary and his group and my group—

we were cutting through the Natural History Museum, and we said, hey we have time, let's look through here, it's pretty neat. As we went through that museum, there was a special exhibit on oceanography, and Gary and I are saying, hey, look at this. It was a lot of the things that we touched on in class this year. A lot of things we did when we did the water pressure and stuff and almost everything that we did this year was in that museum. Whether it was minerals, whether it was gems, whether it was—they had dinosaurs! There were a few things that we had not touched upon. But the kids who were in there could relate to all that stuff. So Gary and I were just walking around on air because we really felt good about the situation. (Interview 3)

The interpersonal satisfaction went beyond reaching the goals they set to the relationships that emerged from working together. The teachers cited satisfaction in terms of gaining respect from fellow team members, as well as simply feeling a sense of belonging to a group. Tanya expressed the value of teaming this way:

The value of teaming is that the teachers meet regularly, they can discuss problems with students, they can discuss curriculum, what the kids need to know. If one teacher is having a particular problem with one student, another teacher can try to get through to that student. You can pick out big problems that might be a problem in your room, but when you talk about it, it is a problem in everybody's room, and then you can plan together a strategy to deal with even the good kids, negative kids. You can deal with all kids.

I think one of the positives, I've had a lot of success with kids. By this time past years, I had certain kids that were starting to work on my nerves. But it seems as though we can talk through a problem with four other adults. I start to see ways to correct problems so I am not getting frustrated dealing with a kid, getting negative with a student. I have found ways to get through, pick up other ideas. (Interview 2)

By the third interview, Tanya still reflected these same feelings and perhaps believed in them even more strongly:

I changed as a teacher from meaner to a kinder sort of person because I think I was dealing with adults more, and I didn't get as uptight with the kids as I did last year and the year before because I didn't see adults other than Lew. This year Martha is always coming in, John's always stopping up, Lew's always over, Gary comes in. You have more contact with adults, so you kind of—working with ninth grade, you come to be a ninth grader by the end of the year with temperament, and with the adults I eased up on the kids but they're not worse than they ever were. They're actually better, and I'm going to miss more kids this year than I ever would've, and I put in more work with doing things because everybody is seeing what you're doing so you do have to instead of, okay, I'll just pull a lesson plan from—now you have to put more work into that. (Interview 3)

Martha expressed her acceptance into the group as very rewarding. Since foreign language was not originally slated to team, Martha felt especially sensitive about her importance and contribution to the team. When asked to comment on the most positive aspect of the school year to date, Martha responded:

Just the niceness at Christmas time, the team, we like each other. And what we've built in one year from not knowing each other and squabbles in the beginning, and also when I presented to them that foreign language teachers may be dropped from the team, Gary jumped in and said, "We'll fight for you, Martha." Even though he's the only who said it, I felt that Tanya appreciates it. I was never sure of Lew, but I do think he likes it. And John above all of them has voiced his favor of foreign languages. He thinks the kids should have more. So, the acceptance is nice. (Interview 2)

Nias (1987) found in her research studies that job satisfaction is highly related to the presence of a reference group within a school, particularly when the members are friends as well as colleagues. She explains that teachers speak enthusiastically about their working lives when they share basic assumptions and values with their coworkers. She adds that the situation becomes one of "absolute commitment" and "total fulfillment" when common perceptions are strengthened by affection. Thus, she concludes, "To believe and work and love together appears to be, for those teachers fortunate enough to find it, a potent and heady mix, rendering its members almost impervious to pressures from superiors and peers" (p. 10).

Gary captured the essence of working with a closely knit group as follows:

> They [administrators] said, "Don't expect to do too much the first year. If you pull one thing together, that's great." I think we certainly did that with Jurassic Park, and maybe we did set our goals a little too high, but I think that was one of the things . . . I mean we had certain ideas that we wanted to put together and a lot of them have come together, but there is still some work to be done. (Interview 2)

Gary still felt at the end of the school year that the team's cohesiveness led to their sense of accomplishment:

> I think teamwise we accomplished more than what I expected to do. Going into this, people were saying that it would be lucky if we could do one or two things together, and we managed to do quite a few things together. So some of the goals we had for the team and what we wanted to accomplish, I certainly think we went above and beyond. (Interview 3)

Besides the cohesion that sustained the team, the teachers portrayed a sense of commitment as a profession. Nias (1986) explains this type of commitment as "a dedication to one's skill as a teacher, involving a continuous search to improve one's knowledge and abilities, and to do the job really well" (p. 133).

Lew explained how they could and would go beyond other people's expectations to meet the goals they set for themselves:

> I think it is noticeable that we've done something different. Something unique to what has been going on around here, so I feel good about that. I guess just me being something of a perfectionist, I just know there are so many things we didn't do and if we just put a little more into it, it would be even more special than what it is at this point. So I definitely feel

success. I really do, but I'm looking forward and hoping that we can make even larger strides in the near future. That is the question they keep asking me, [principal and assistant principal], "How can you add to what you've done?" They have no idea. I have hundreds of ways that I know we can make it better because I'm never satisfied with just looking good. I know we have so much more to make it good. (Interview 3)

Finally, in succinct, clear, and deservedly proud words, Lew compared Apex in relationship to the entire school community:

Looking at the entire school family, I would probably say that we functioned best out of all that I'm aware of. I think we tried harder, pulled together more, had less back fighting or infighting. We actually did try to make the program work to the best of our ability. (Interview 3)

Part III

Conclusion

8

Deepening Our Understanding of Educational Change

If the artist does not perfect a new vision in his process of doing, he acts mechanically and repeats some old model fixed like a blue print in his mind.

—John Dewey (1943)

Overview

F ramed by phenomenological inquiry and symbolic interactionism, this case study examined the meaning a team of high school teachers made from a restructuring initiative that incorporated teaming, interdisciplinary teaching, and block scheduling. The following questions guided the study: What did these teachers experience? How did the teachers understand these experiences? How did their interaction with each other as a team contribute to their understanding of these experiences?

Summary of Findings

All five teachers held mutual perceptions regarding the implementation of the restructuring initiative. These perceptions formed the basis for the five themes that emerged: uncertainty; intensification and limited time; lack of administrative leadership; content loyalty versus team allegiance; and craft pride, caring, and moral purpose. Throughout the course of the one-year implementation, other issues and concerns came into play from time to time; however, these five themes dominated the teachers' perceptions and remained at the forefront from the inception of the study until the end. Thus far the themes have been discussed as separate entities; now their interrelationship becomes an element to be examined.

Teacher uncertainty, which has been documented as a major issue in restructuring projects (Fullan, 1991; Hargreaves, 1994; Sikes, 1992), was magnified because of the lack of administrative leadership, and its negative emotional impact was intensified by the teachers' commitment to doing what was best for students. Although any new initiative creates doubt and ambiguity, the lack of guidance and feedback from the administration left the teachers feeling alone and insecure. When they realized that they were unlikely to receive the administrative assistance they sought, the teachers became more cohesive as a group and struggled with issues without the expertise to deal with them effectively or expediently. Thus, they often floundered throughout the implementation, always questioning and wondering if their method of implementing the initiative was effective, or as they often pondered aloud, "Are we doing it right?"

Without any written curriculum in either the individual disciplines or across disciplines, the teachers felt abandoned and helpless, unprepared to create an interdisciplinary curriculum that would naturally fit all five subject areas. After attempts to engage the administration in assisting them failed, they realized that they were not going to receive the leadership they wanted. This realization, in turn, exacerbated their doubt because they came to believe that the administration itself did not understand the restructuring initiative and/or did not care if it succeeded or failed. Their belief that the administration did not care about them or the initiative was especially difficult to accept since the teachers themselves were so committed to the implementation and the impact it would have on student learning. Their confusion and sense of uncertainty were further compounded by recognizing that there were no national models of interdisciplinary curriculum that could serve as a guide for them. They also came to realize that experts in the field of interdisciplinary curriculum often used the same terms with completely different meanings.

The uncertainty, already magnified by the lack of administrative leadership, also intensified the teachers' work. Since they did not have outside assistance in creating an interdisciplinary curriculum or any training in interdisciplinary teaming, the teachers spent large blocks of time finding materials for their units and trying to "plug in" interdisciplinary themes in areas of study where they did not naturally fit. This attempt to make curriculum fit caused frustration and uncertainty on the part of the teachers whose subject areas did not lend themselves to the particular unit being studied. At some point during the implementation, every teacher on the team felt this anxiety except perhaps Tanya, the English teacher, who knew that her discipline and personality allowed the most flexibility in terms of presenting content to develop skills and concepts germane to her subject area.

As the teachers tried to make their interdisciplinary themes apply to all five disciplines, they became cognizant of their inability to remain loyal to both their subject content and team. This dilemma, more than any other, divided the teachers. The inner struggle that emerged not only magnified the uncertainty, but also caused stress and guilt, which had already surfaced from the intensified workload and limited time to do all aspects of their job well.

The teachers internalized this predicament. Although the concern for content loyalty often arose at team meetings, the teachers rarely let the issue blossom into a full discussion. If any talk of content seemed to become intense, the other teachers either dismissed it as the questioning teacher's being negative or uncooperative or as an issue for the administration to resolve. At the end of the school year, when the teachers were feeling most uncertain about the loss of subject content to fit the interdisciplinary units they had agreed on, the team leader canceled all meetings, and little interaction took place among the teachers together as a team during the final month of the school year.

The reasons for squelching full discussion could be many. First, the teachers did not have a solution to their problem. Six months prior to the implementation, the teachers agreed to enter into the interdisciplinary teaming that the English and social studies teachers had already created. However, the teachers were making a commitment at that point in time to a process whose personal implications were not at all clear. As Fullan (1991) suggests, this is the major problem in crystallizing a shared vision prematurely. Eventually the teachers came to realize that without administrative leadership to guide them through curriculum deliberation and goal setting, they were ill equipped to cope with the complexity of trying to integrate five subject areas using historical themes in chronological order. Also, without administrative leadership to facilitate the implementation as it progressed, the teachers did not know how to challenge each other about the best way to implement interdisciplinary teaming or to deal with the issues that arose.

What the teachers did recognize and want to preserve, however, was the spirit that existed among them as a team of people who cared about the learning, self-esteem, and character development of their shared freshmen. Therefore, they did not deal with their individual conflict as a team. Instead, when they became most uncertain about the effect they, as subject-area teachers, were having on student learning, they became silent and distanced themselves from each other. Although they felt uncomfortable with this result, they had all come to their own conclusions about how much content they could "compromise" for the restructuring initiative and so they continued to team within the parameters they set for themselves individually. They could not risk losing each other as friends or colleagues in spite of their individual dilemmas and curriculum differences.

The four themes of uncertainty, intensification and limited time, lack of administrative leadership, and content loyalty versus team allegiance would appear to prohibit any feelings of success in implementing the initiative. Craft pride, caring, and moral purpose, however, a powerful theme that dominated the study, gave the teachers the emotional fortitude necessary to persevere in spite of the obstacles they faced.

The teachers' sense of caring for their students transcended all aspects of their work. In the end it was their students who held them together. They saw themselves as more than teachers. They referred to themselves as mothers and fathers and brothers and friends to the students. They felt a moral purpose to equip their students with book knowledge and emotional support, as well as good character and citizenship. This craft pride in their work emerged through the intrinsic rewards that they enumerated throughout the course of the study. Every time students made interconnections in their studies or performed a task well or showed a trait of good character, the teachers felt renewed in their mission. Their students' successes were their successes, and those successes elevated their spirits and energized them.

In addition, the teaming created a bond among the five teachers. They sensed their differences in philosophies regarding teaching styles and techniques, but they knew they all wanted the best for their students. They also knew that they were alone without any other assistance in their efforts. Finally, if they were unable to agree on the terms of interdisciplinary teaming, they never faltered on the team goals they created: community building, acquiring study skills and higher-level thinking skills, accountability, and growth in moral and ethical behavior.

Conclusions from This Case Study

From the five themes of uncertainty, intensification and limited time, lack of administrative leadership, subject loyalty versus team allegiance, and craft pride, we have drawn the following eight conclusions.

First, the teachers wanted to implement the initiative because of their commitment to their students rather than to the initiative itself. The teachers were emotionally interconnected by their ethic of responsibility and caring for their students, but logically fragmented by their inability to implement an undefined initiative. Although they tried to impose both an individual and a team reality on the initiative, they had no common realm of understanding, which thwarted their efforts. This desire to improve student learning increasingly frustrated them and zapped their energy and enthusiasm as they continued to implement an initiative that they did not fully understand. They persevered primarily because of their commitment to their students and secondly because of their growing commitment to each other. Commitment to school restructuring and its concomitant pedagogical practices per se played no role in motivating these teachers to carry on.

Second, because they were emotionally interconnected by their commitment to their students, the teachers were able to collaborate effectively on those issues that they understood and valued. They realized throughout the course of the year that some issues were noncollaborative, nonnegotiable because their subject content and teaching techniques were fundamentally different and more aligned to their individual disciplines than to the team itself. Therefore, the teachers collaborated on those issues that were student-related but engaged in contrived collegiality in issues directly related to interdisciplinary teaming. Team planning meetings were used for curriculum talk during the Jurassic Park and holocaust units because the teachers felt that these units allowed them to integrate while remaining true to their content. During the implementation of the other units, team meetings were dominated by talk of students. Who was doing well and who was in trouble became the questions around which these teachers teamed.

Though they did not understand each other's content areas and did not place particularly high value on each other's content expertise, they did value and admire each other as teachers who could make a difference with students. The researchers sat in on approximately 60 team-planning meetings over the course of the year. We heard the names of countless students being mentioned as those who were having trouble. Every time a student's name was mentioned, there was at least one teacher on the team who reported working well with that student and volunteered to try to help. Never did a student's problems fail to solicit a teacher on the team who worked well with that adolescent. As a result, teachers came to depend on each other to reach their students. This is the essence of true collaboration.

Third, the top-down mandate did not allow teacher ownership in the restructuring initiative or understanding of how to implement it. Without input, the teachers did not know the mission, purpose, or goals of the project and felt that their concerns and expertise were insignificant. The lack of a written curriculum added to the uncertainty and left the teachers unable to develop the understanding necessary to feel competent and comfortable in implementing the initiative. With the school's past history of adopting change, the teachers struggled between the difficulty of implementing an unclear initiative and the feelings of potential sudden abandonment of the initiative in the near future.

Although lack of ownership is often cited as a major cause of resistance to implementation of change initiatives by teachers, that was not the case here. The teachers wanted to implement the project well for the sake of their students, but the failure to allow the teachers to engage in prior discussions concerning the rationale for the restructuring and the goals that were to be achieved resulted in a lack of understanding that inhibited implementation. Thus, it was lack of understanding, not lack of ownership, which was the debilitating result of the top-down decision.

Fourth, their uncertainty was exacerbated by the lack of administrative leadership. The administration was not visible and supportive from the planning stages of the restructuring through the implementation and assessment of it. Without this support, the teachers remained unsure of their technical skills and effectiveness. The lack of schoolwide dialogue and deliberation concerning any area of the restructuring endeavor left the team of teachers isolated from their other colleagues during their implementation efforts. Also, because of the lack of support, the teachers felt emotionally "shunned," which deepened their frustration when they felt unable to implement the undefined initiative.

The administrators tried to be supportive by providing for material needs such as release time and money. They then decided to leave the teachers alone so that the teachers would not feel pressured by constant administrative surveillance. The teachers who needed and wanted emotional and technical support felt abandoned, not empowered, by being left alone. It was impossible for us, the researchers, to dismiss the parallel to parents who provide for the material and physical needs of their children but do not give of their time and attention.

Fifth, creating teams of people to implement a restructuring initiative caused conflict between groups and alienated teachers from their nonteam colleagues. Although the administrators did intervene when the teams were unable to resolve issues, they did not use these interventions as opportunities to resolve the underlying issues that caused the conflict. Nor did they take any measures to equip the teachers with the win-win type of conflict resolution skills that would have served them well in the future. In terms of both technical expertise and problem solving skills, the administrative team acted as if they believed that it was really all a matter of will and that technical knowledge had nothing to do with it. Also, conflict and alienation were increased by a lack of administrative structures to facilitate the implementation by bringing individual groups together for goal setting and assessment of the initiative.

Sixth, this restructuring initiative intensified the teachers' work. Besides trying to implement the initiative, teachers felt overwhelmed with the aspects of their work that they could not control. The teachers forfeited an individual planning period (three times out of every six-day cycle) in order to meet with team members to work on team issues. In addition, the teachers added to the intensification by incorporating field trips, honor assemblies, and reward parties and incentives. The teachers realized that this intensified workload was separating them from their other colleagues. As they performed under this intensification, they often felt guilt and stress that they were not implementing the initiative effectively or expediently. Their workload and intensive team meeting time made them an island unto themselves that gave them nowhere to turn when interpersonal conflicts erupted among team members.

Seventh, although the teachers were willing to work collaboratively with their peers, they felt individually responsible for their subject-area content and gauged their collaborative efforts on the outcomes of student learning in their specific subject area. Because of this individual responsibility to their subject areas, the teachers struggled with both intrapersonal and interpersonal conflict. They struggled inwardly to provide their students with a solid knowledge base in their subject area. They struggled interpersonally trying to accommodate the previously agreed-on themes in light of their inability to incorporate them effectively or expediently. Their professional commitment to the team mission and to their students became the glue that kept the team together when the tensions became overwhelming.

Eighth, the teachers measured their success on the intrinsic rewards of student achievement and appreciation. These psychic rewards overshadowed the difficulties and uncertainties of the restructuring endeavor and allowed the teachers to persevere. In spite of their differences in pedagogical beliefs, they all genuinely cared for their students and were able to pool their individual expertise to assist their students and to stay focused on their mission.

Assertions: Refining Existing Ideas about Change

Commitment to Students and Colleagues Counts Most!

Fullan (1991) asserts that real change represents a "serious personal and collective experience characterized by ambivalence and uncertainty; and if the change works out it can result in a sense of mastery, accomplishment, and professional growth" (p. 32). He adds that the more familiar people become at dealing with the unknown, the more they can understand how creative breakthroughs are preceded by confusion, exploration, and stress, followed by periods of excitement and increasing confidence as they implement meaningful change or cope with unwanted change (1993a). It is imperative, then, that the following realities be recognized:

1. Teachers have different understandings of change.

2. Teachers have personal and professional needs.

3. Teachers need appropriate and adequate resources.

4. Teachers need professional development and continuous support.

5. Teachers want to be trusted and seen as capable professionals. (Sikes, 1992)

Lortie (1975) concurs and expounds:

Change is impeded by mutual isolation, vague yet demanding goals, dilemmas of outcome assessment, restricted in-service training, rigidities in assignment, and working conditions that produce a "more-of-the-same" syndrome among classroom teachers. (P. 232)

Change, therefore, must be a "negotiated process" (Fullan, 1991). It must be viewed as a journey by individuals who have highly idiosyncratic views and varying levels of understanding that are evident in the different ways that they develop through a change endeavor (Hord et al., 1987).

Much of the literature on change explains top-down mandates as most difficult to implement because the teachers do not feel ownership in the initiative and therefore do not exert a great deal of effort in implementing it (Fullan, 1991; Hargreaves, 1994; Sikes, 1992). Vague but demanding school goals create difficulties for teachers and contribute to a sense of nonaccomplishment (Lortie, 1975). Moreover, adults are more likely to realize the full value of and necessity for change when they feel they are in control of the process (Clark, 1992). Fullan (1991) adds that vision building "permeates the organization with values, purpose, and integrity for both the what and how of improvement" (p. 81). Hargreaves (1994) explains the importance of vision as follows:

Through building common goals along with a shared expectation that they can be met, missions also strengthen teachers' sense of efficacy, their beliefs that they can improve the achievement of all their students, irrespective of background. Missions build motivation and missions bestow meaning.... Developing a sense of mission builds loyalty, commitment and confidence in a school community. (P. 163)

In spite of all the difficulties the teachers faced implementing this initiative, they remained committed to their vision they, as a team, had created. Their initial attempts at implementing the initiative were based solely on their belief that perhaps implementing this initiative would have a positive effect on student learning. It was the only, and probably most compelling, reason they had to implement the initiative. They attempted to piece together what they did not understand and had only their trial-and-error efforts to gauge their practice. When they were unable to elicit feedback from the administration, they turned to student evaluations of the program and "rumors" of the administration's satisfaction with their work. The key to their perseverance was their commitment to their students and their craft.

In addition to their commitment to students that existed from the very first day of the year, the Apex teachers also developed a commitment to each other that grew as the year progressed. They found themselves going the extra mile and making compromises in their own beliefs and values (that were difficult to make) out of loyalty and commitment to the team. This commitment to the team coupled with their commitment to students can be used to explain their heroic perseverance through the difficult year.

Therefore, this study leads us to believe that teachers may not need to be committed to an innovation for them to work hard at implementing it. Commitment to students and colleagues, not a sense of ownership or commitment to the innovation, may be a more critical factor in teacher willingness to implement an initiative. When viewed from this perspective, a vision that focuses primarily on teacher commitment to student learning becomes the foundation for discussing reform. It may be more important for change agents to provide time and leadership for teachers to articulate and examine their commitment to student learning and use this commitment as a springboard for discussing, understanding, and making decisions about proposed initiatives. Administrators may find teachers more willing to implement change by honing their natural commitment to students rather than by developing strategies for building allegiance to the initiative itself.

Lack of Input Results in a Debilitating Lack of Understanding

A commitment to students, however, cannot transcend the frustration and eventual surrender of the implementation if teachers do not understand the initiative as it has been mandated. Developing a deep understanding of the initiative in terms of its meaning, purpose, and technical requirements remains critical. The teachers in this study tried diligently and persistently to implement the initiative in spite of having no input in the planning stages. Their lack of representation in the planning stages, however, created a void in their understanding of the initiative in terms of purpose, goals, and technical skills. This lack of understanding heightened their uncertainty about their ability and effectiveness and impeded their progress in spite of their strong desire to "do it right." In this case, then, this absence of understanding the initiative was a bigger factor in the impediment of the implementation than the fact that the initiative was not a grass-roots movement. The need for a deep understanding of an initiative is even more central to the successful implementation of a restructuring endeavor, especially if it is administratively imposed. Useful advice for initiators of reform efforts are as follows:

1. to emphasize teacher commitment to student learning as the basis for any restructuring initiative; and

2. to ensure that change implementers have time and opportunities to develop a deep understanding of any initiative. The need for time to develop deep understanding should be emphasized to an even greater extent when the implementers are not the initiators of the proposed change.

Collaboration Is a Complex, Multi-Faceted Phenomenon

Collaboration proved to be a very complex issue that unfolded over the course of the year and remains a difficult phenomenon to explain. On the one hand, Huberman and Miles (as cited in Fullan, 1991) write that collaboration and collegiality move teacher development beyond a personal, idiosyncratic reflection and dependence on outside experts to the ethos of learning from each other by sharing and developing expertise together. Hargreaves (1994) adds that collaboration gives teachers the confidence to experiment and take risks, which result in a committed professional obligation to continuous improvement. In addition, collaboration and collegiality are widely seen as ways of securing effective implementation of externally introduced change (Huberman & Miles, 1984, as cited in Fullan, 1991).

On the other hand, individuality, according to Schon (1983, as cited in Hargreaves, 1994) is important to teachers because it gives them the power to exercise personal discretion, initiative, and creativity through their work. Therefore, trying to eliminate individualism through collaboration and collegiality may undermine this individuality, which leads to a teacher sense of incompetence. Hargreaves (1994) reports from his research that threats to individuality—mandated requirements to carry out the less than fully understood judgments of others—are closely linked to senses of incompetence. Therefore, he warns that efforts to eliminate individualism should proceed cautiously so that they do not undermine individuality and the teacher's sense of efficacy that goes with it.

Hargreaves (1994) notes that collaborative cultures are working relationships that are spontaneous, voluntary, development-oriented, fixed in time and space, and predictable. If these conditions are not present, *contrived collegiality* is present. He submits that the following criteria can create contrived collegiality. First, teachers are required to meet and work together, which makes the collaboration administratively regulated and compulsory. Second, teachers are required to implement the mandates of others rather than programs decided on through discussion. Third, teachers only meet at the particular time and place that has been mandated by the administration. Fourth, the collegiality is designed to have a high predictability of outcomes since the administration has control over its purposes and regulates its time and place.

The Apex teachers engaged in contrived collegiality in terms of their interdisciplinary teaching but in true collaboration in terms of their focus on students. By the middle of the school year, the teachers seemed to have decided individually how they could and would fit into the interdisciplinary scheme. By the end of the year, they were no longer meeting about curriculum on a routine basis, and no one tried to reinstate the meetings although all expressed a concern to us about the stoppage.

The unique slant, however, is that the teachers continued to collaborate on student issues that affected them as a team irrespective of the interdisciplinary work. They wanted to work with each other in spite of the obstacles of the initiative. Therefore, they chose to collaborate on the common issues of teaching and learning that, collectively, would make them more effective. In other words, the teachers guarded their individuality in order to retain the integrity of their subject area. Yet they formed a powerful, effective union to collaborate on those issues where they found common ground. Little (1981 as cited in Barth, 1990) defines collaboration as the presence of four specific behaviors in adults:

1. They talk about practice.

2. They observe each other engaged in the practice of teaching and administration.

3. They work together planning, designing, researching, and evaluating curriculum.

4. They share craft knowledge.

Collaboration makes sense when stakeholders realize the potential advantages of working together, the interdependence to execute a vision they all share, and the interdependence to advance their own individual goals (Watson & Fullan, 1992). The stakeholders must see a compelling reason to collaborate; that is, they must believe that their interests will be protected and advanced throughout the process (Gray, 1989).

The teachers remained intact as a core who shared concerns about their mutual team of students. This phenomenon suggests that true collaboration does not have to encompass every aspect of teachers' work. Collaboration here appeared to be nonlinear and uneven across tasks. The teachers engaged in a true collaborative community around student issues, but engaged in contrived collegiality around forced curriculum integration. Teachers may feel comfortable collaborating on those aspects in which they share common goals and philosophies. They do not have to collaborate on all issues to work together, and administrators should look for the ties that can bind groups of teachers and nurture those relationships. This understanding of collaboration would allow teachers to maintain their individuality yet pool their expertise to affect a wider range of students. Collaboration framed in this way would place emphasis on the emotional commitment to students, the critical component when teachers implement an initiative.

Lack of Systematic Evaluation Exacerbates Teacher Uncertainty

Although teacher uncertainty is a core element of teaching as a profession (Lortie, 1975), it is heightened when change is first being implemented (Fullan, 1991; Hargreaves, 1994). Bolman and Deal

(1991) write that change creates feelings of incompetence and insecurity because it undercuts people's ability to perform their work with confidence and success. They use the example of surgeons who have adeptly performed a surgical procedure over a long period of time. When the use of the laser replaces the scalpel for the same procedure, the doctors' self-actualization may regress, leaving feelings of insecurity and incompetence until they receive training and support. Fullan (1991) adds that the difficulty of learning new skills and behavior and unlearning old ones is underestimated and that changes in beliefs, practice, and methods represent profound changes that affect teachers' professional self-esteem.

This study demonstrated that teachers do not necessarily become more certain through implementation. In other words, practice does not make perfect. Instead, without leaders to assist teachers in understanding an initiative and to guide them throughout the implementation, teachers may become more uncertain as time passes. This greater uncertainty may occur from not seeing desired results, not feeling more comfortable as they progress in the implementation or both. It is in the critical stage of implementation, then, that teachers will decide individually if they will continue their efforts in the restructuring endeavor. If the uncertainty is exacerbated, their frustration may cause them to abandon the initiative. In addition, the teachers may resent their struggle and the feelings of inadequacy that the struggle creates.

Compounding the effects of uncertainty was the failure of the administration to initiate any activities to evaluate the success of the initiative. Teachers reported that lack of evaluation was a hallmark of "how things are done around here." It is likely that the administrators were following an old bromide that suggests that teachers should be given time to learn new skills before any evaluation takes place. If this was true, unfortunately the administrators confused evaluation of a change effort with evaluation of the competence of the teachers. Clearly it is unreasonable to evaluate teachers' competence on the basis of knowledge and skills that they are just beginning to learn. To do so in a case such as this where little technical support is provided would be immoral. However, the same is not true for the innovation per se.

The Apex teachers perceived the lack of evaluation of the restructuring as an indication that the administrators were more interested in the appearance of change than in the quality of change. The message they received was, we just want to be able to say we are doing it; we are not concerned with how well it is done. Thus, building in an evaluation component from the very beginning of implementation would have served a twofold purpose. First, it would have communicated the message that administrators, too, cared about doing the right thing for students. Second, it would have provided some yardstick against which teachers could have judged their efforts at implementation and would have reduced both the degree of uncertainty and the emotional turmoil that those feelings of uncertainty caused.

Strong Team Identity Must Be Coupled with a Coherent Whole-School Vision to Avoid Isolation and Alienation

The literature addresses teaming as an effective way to implement change because it allows teachers to take risks and share information (Fullan, 1991; Maeroff, 1993). This study found the same results. However, the strong bond that the teaming created in this study alienated the teachers from their other colleagues. As the teachers became closer and their workload intensified, they became more isolated from the other faculty. They sensed a feeling of being perceived as a "club" and were unable to reconcile the issue. This isolation was compounded by the teachers' belief that the administrators purposely created competition between teams and did nothing to alleviate the conflict between them.

In this case the administrators simply sent the two ninth-grade teams on their own individual paths toward reform. There were no meetings to discuss common school goals, no sense among the teachers that there were common school goals or even common ninth-grade goals, and no written curriculum for the ninth grade. Each of the ninth-grade teachers on both teams lacked a sense of common mission or vision, which would have given the two teams a common underlying purpose. Because there was no shared vision, the two teams were unable to define themselves as simply two work groups traveling different paths to reach the same general destination. Instead they saw themselves as heading toward completely different end results. Teachers were haunted by the question of which end result or destination was better for students. As a result, each team defined itself in opposition to the other. We are not them, and they are not us. One critical piece missing from the entire scenario was this sense: "Each team is part of something larger that gives us both definition, and therefore, we do not need to define ourselves in opposition to the other." If the restructuring process had begun with both ninth-grade teams creating a vision by mutually agreeing on a set of common goals, then the paths the teams chose to meet their goals would not have been an issue. The sense of competition, fragmentation, and hostility would not have existed. Both teams would have been headed toward the same destination. The different routes to get there would have been natural and expected as they are in any other teaching context.

The sense of isolation from other faculty members may be especially harmful in a high school setting because of the strong ties that exist among department members. As is so often the case, this restructuring project disbanded traditional organizational groups that tend to rely on each other professionally and emotionally (Siskin & Little, 1995). High school teachers usually align themselves with other members of their departments for various reasons. First, they have similar teaching concerns and curriculum issues to discuss. Second, they are often in proximity in the school. Third, because of proximity and similar concerns and interests, they usually form friendships with each other that transcend their professional duties. By rearranging groups to interdisciplinary teams as in this study, the nonteam members of the department felt a sense of abandonment. At the same time, the team members felt close to each other but mourned the loss of contact with their other colleagues. The loosely coupled structure of the organization was perpetuated and perhaps magnified.

Curriculum Integration Is an Exhausting Balancing Act

The teachers' desire to maintain the integrity and rigor of their subject content was a struggle that was aggravated by the separation from their department members. Martin-Kniep, Feige, and Soodak (1995) claim that educators must realize that the design and the implementation of curriculums may unintentionally cause sacrifices in the name of integration, whether it be of content and skills or school and self. For example, in the implementation of a unit integrating social studies and English, perhaps writing skills will not be honed, yet the students have demonstrated their ability to incorporate different cultural perspectives and combine literary study with their personal needs. Teachers, therefore, must recognize these imbalances and find ways to avoid them by staying focused on the need to balance and by remaining loyal to prioritized objectives. By sharing philosophies and focusing on objectives or desired learning outcomes, the subject area teachers identify a theme that can be integrated yet still can remain loyal to the skills and knowledge assigned to an individual course of study (Drake, 1993).

On the one hand, the teachers did not have the understanding or skills requisite to deliberate and formulate an interdisciplinary curriculum; nor did they have curriculum models, interdisciplinary textbooks, or national standards about interdisciplinary curriculum content. The teachers really felt that they were out on a limb on their own. They had to rely completely on their own professional judgment about the right thing to do. This was a daunting responsibility for the teachers who received literally no guidance or technical support. As subject-area individuals on the team, they felt responsible to advocate for the importance of their content in relationship to the interdisciplinary themes. On the other hand, they validated interdisciplinary curriculum to their colleagues by their public displays of student work, activities, and commitment to the team. The teachers felt trapped in a catch-22, trying to balance their two loyalties while remaining unsure as to which allegiance could better meet the needs of their students.

The literature shows that implementing a restructuring initiative intensifies teachers' work (Fullan, 1991; Hargreaves, 1994). Directly related to this intensification are the time limitations that are germane to teachers' work. Hargreaves (1994) explains:

> Time is a fundamental dimension through which teachers' work is constructed and interpreted by themselves, their colleagues and those who administer and supervise them. Time for the teacher is not just an objective, oppressive constraint but also a subjectively defined horizon of possibility and limitation. . . . Time is therefore more than a minor organiza-

tional contingency, inhibiting or facilitating management's attempts to bring about change. Its definition and imposition form part of the very core of teachers' work and of the policies and perceptions of those who administer it. (P. 95)

Hargreaves (1994) posits a phenomenological dimension of time, which refers to the subjective dimension of time that perhaps clashes with the time senses of administrators and innovators on the one hand and the teachers on the other. Werner (as cited in Hargreaves, 1994) explains that these differences in time perspective come to the forefront during curriculum implementation. He presents data that show that, in the context of an innovation, teachers feel pressure and anxiety because of excessive time demands, along with guilt and frustration because they do not feel they are implementing the innovation as quickly as the administration wants or as they themselves believe they can. From the teachers' perspective, the requirements of the new program are imposed with little regard for their existing pressures and demands, as well as little or no guidance as to how the innovation can be integrated with existing practices and routines. It is at this point that the teachers usually request more time for planning.

This study, however, demonstrated that the intensification goes beyond the physical components of more paperwork and planning and beyond the emotional aspects of guilt and stress. The teachers in this study felt a mental strain in terms of always thinking about ways to implement. They described themselves as suffering a mental fatigue that resulted from their desire to do well. This fatigue was worsened by the uncertainty that pervaded every aspect of their work. Thus, even when they could enjoy a weekend free of stress and guilt because their paperwork and lesson plans were completed, they still felt the mental burden of questioning their methods and effectiveness.

Caring for Students Creates a Double-Edged Sword

Teachers are motivated by intrinsic rewards (Lortie, 1975). Hargreaves (1994) writes that the psychic rewards of teaching are central to sustaining teachers' senses of self, their senses of value and worth in their work. He explains the way teachers attain psychic rewards:

> When the purposes of care are balanced with those of group management and instructional effectiveness, and when care is construed in social and moral terms as well as interpersonal ones, its contribution to quality in education can be exceptionally valuable. Indeed, a strong care orientation, balanced with other goals such as ones directed to providing focused and intellectually challenging work, has been found to be strongly associated with positive school climates that in turn foster student achievement. (P. 147)

This study demonstrated, however, that these intrinsic rewards can heighten the uncertainty and compound the intensification. Since the teachers had a compelling desire to improve student learning, they worked more intensely and felt more guilt as they tried to deal with complexities they were unequipped to handle. Therefore, administrators must understand that the ethics of responsibility and caring are part of a teacher's make-up and must be respected throughout the entire implementation. No matter how "thing" driven the administration may be, the teachers will remain "people" driven. Therefore, impact on learners and learner reaction will be the deciding factor that teachers use to gauge the failure or success of school restructuring. There is the danger, as Hargreaves (1994) points out, that teachers will feel as if they can never do enough. Such feelings are likely to result in cynicism and burnout. Collegiality can be a key force in reducing uncertainty and helping teachers to recognize their limitations and come to grips with the acceptance of what they can and cannot do. Thus, providing time for teams to assess their progress by collecting data on the consequences of change initiatives for their students would appear to be a powerful mechanism for maintaining the positive aspects of caring while minimizing its potential down side.

Conclusion

As we noted in the preface, we do not see this effort as a failed change process though it was fraught with problems, issues, tensions, and shortcomings. As you have read, the Apex teachers were able to create some excellent curriculum units, to impact their students very positively, and to build a sense of colleagueship with each other. They did so, however, at the price of constant mental fatigue, continuing self-doubt, inner turmoil over loyalties and obligations, and an overriding sense of guilt at not being able to do more. We believe that much of this turmoil and mental fatigue could have been reduced and possibly eliminated if the change initiators had only understood what the phenomenon of change was like for these teachers.

One particular incident strengthened that belief and motivated us to attempt to write a text that contributes to the change literature by deepening our understanding of the impact of reform on teachers' lives. We met in May to interview a central office administrator about the project so that we could obtain a broader understanding of the entire school context. During the course of the interview, we asked him if he could imagine what the Apex teachers were experiencing. To our utter amazement he was able to articulate many of the same concepts that you have encountered in this book—uncertainty, lack of understanding, alienation, lack of day-to-day support, worries that the project would end abruptly as had happened so often in the past, divided subject-team loyalties, some sense of pride, and general feelings of being overwhelmed. As he talked, we both realized that he understood these concepts in a very rational, logical way. He had indeed encountered some of them in his readings about educational reform. His understanding, however, was inert and sterile. He had no conception of the depth of emotional turmoil and mental stress that these same concepts had caused in the lives of his teachers. As far as understanding what actually living these concepts was like, he was clueless. It is our hope that our contribution is to enable readers to gain a more powerful, more empathic understanding of what living through change efforts means for some teachers and to use that understanding to develop change strategies that are more sensitive to the daily lives of teachers and their commitments, understandings, hopes, and fears. For as Saranson (1971) suggests, it is very unlikely that schools will ever be better places for children than they are for teachers.

References

Ackerman, D. B. (1989). Intellectual and practical criteria for successful curriculum integration. In H.H. Jacobs (Ed.), *Interdisciplinary Curriculum: Design and Implementation*. Alexandria, VA: Association for Supervision and Curriculum Development, (pp. 25–38).

Apple, M. W., & Jungck, S. (1992). You don't have to be a teacher to teach this unit: Teaching, technology and control in the classroom. In Hargreaves, A. & M. G. Fullan (Eds.), *Understanding Teacher Development* (pp. 20–42). New York, NY: Teachers College Press.

Bacharach, S., & Conley, S. (1989). Uncertainty and decisionmaking in teaching: Implications for managing line professionals. In T. J. Sergiovanni & J. H. Moore (Eds.), *Schooling for Tomorrow: Directing Reforms to Issues That Count* (pp. 311–328). Boston, MA: Allyn and Bacon.

Barth, R. S. (1990). *Improving schools from within: Teachers, parents, and principals can make a difference*. San Francisco, CA: Jossey-Bass Publishers.

Beane, J. A. (1995a). Introduction: What is a coherent curriculum? In J.A. Beane (Ed.), *Toward a Coherent Curriculum: 1995 Yearbook of the Association for Supervision and Curriculum Development*. Alexandria, VA: Association for Supervision and Curriculum Development, (pp. 1–14).

———. (1995b, April). Curriculum integration and the disciplines of knowledge. *Phi Delta Kappan, 76*, (pp. 616–628).

———. (1997). *Curriculum integration: Designing the core of democratic education*. New York, NY: Teachers College Press.

Blumer, H. (1969). *Symbolic interactionism*. Englewood Cliffs, NJ: Prentice-Hall.

Bogdan, R. C., & Biklen, S. K. (1992). *Qualitative research for education: An introduction to theory and methods*. Boston, MA: Allyn and Bacon.

Bolman, L. G., & Deal, T. E. (1991). *Reframing organizations: Artistry, choice, and leadership*. San Francisco, CA: Jossey-Bass Publishers.

Burnaford, G., Beane, J., & Brodhagen, B. (1994, November). Teacher action research: Inside an integrative curriculum. *Middle School Journal*, 5–13.

Carnegie Forum on Education and the Economy. (1986, May). *A nation prepared: Teachers for the twenty-first century*. Washington, DC: Carnegie Forum on Education and the Economy.

Clark, C. M. (1992). Teachers as designers in self-directed professional development. In Hargreaves, A. & M. G. Fullan (Eds.), *Understanding Teacher Development* (pp. 75–84). New York, NY: Teachers College Press.

Corbett, H. D., Dawson, J. A., & Firestone, W. A. (1984). *School context and school change: Implications for effective planning*. New York, NY: Teachers College Press.

Darling-Hammer, L., & Wise, A. (1985). Beyond standardization: State standards and school improvement. *Elementary School Journal, 85*, 3. (35–37).

Dewey, J. (1943). *The school and society (Rev. Ed.)*. Chicago, IL: Chicago Press.

Drake, S. M. (1993). *Planning integrated curriculum: The call to adventure*. Alexandria, VA: Association for Supervision and Curriculum Development.

Erickson, F. (1986). Qualitative methods in research on teaching. In M. C. Wittrock (Ed.), *Handbook on Research of Teaching*, 3rd ed. (pp. 119–161). New York, NY: Macmillan.

Erlander, D. A., Harris, E. L., Skipper, B. L., & Allen, S. D. (1993). *Doing naturalistic inquiry: A guide to methods*. Newbury Park, CA: Sage Publications.

Evans, R. (1996). *The human side of educational change*. New York, NY: Teacher College Press.

Fogarty, R. (1991). *How to integrate the curricula*. Palantine, IL: IRI/Skylight Publishing.

Fullan, M. (1990). Staff development, innovation, and institutional development. In Joyce, B. (Ed.), *Changing school culture through staff development* (pp. 3–25). Alexandria, VA: Association of Curriculum and Supervision Development.

————. (1993a). *Change forces: Probing the depths of educational reform.* New York, NY: Falmer Press.

————. (1993b). Coordinating school and district development in restructuring. In J. Murphy & P. Hallinger (Eds.), *Restructuring Schools: Learning From Ongoing Efforts* (pp. 143–164). Thousand Oaks, CA: Corwin Press.

Fullan, M. G. (with Stiegelbauer, S.). (1991). *The new meaning of educational change.* New York, NY: Teachers College Press.

Fullan, M., & Hargreaves, A. (1992). Teacher development and educational change. In M. Fullan & A. Hargreaves (Eds.), *Teacher Development and Educational Change* (pp. 1–9). New York, NY: Falmer Press.

Fullan, M., & Ponfret, A. (1977). Research on curriculum and instruction implementation. *Review of Educational Research, 47* (1): 335–397.

Gide, A. (1927). *The counterfeiters.* (Dorothy Bussy, trans.) New York, NY: A. A. Knopf.

Gitlin, A., Bringhurst, K., Burns, M., Cooley, V., Myers, B., Price, K., Russell, R. & P. Tiess (1992). *Teachers' voices for school change: An introduction to educative research.* New York, NY: Teachers College Press.

Glaser, B. G., & Strauss, A. L. (1967). *The discovery of grounded theory: Strategies for qualitative research.* Chicago, IL: Aldine Publishing Company.

Glesne, C., & Peshkin, A. (1992). *Becoming qualitative researchers: An introduction.* New York, NY: Longman Publishing Group.

Glickman, C. D. (1993). *Renewing America's schools: A guide for school-based action.* San Francisco, CA: Jossey-Bass Publishers.

Goffman, E. (1959). The presentation of self in everyday life. New York, NY: Anchor Books, Doubleday.

Gray, B. (1989). *Collaborating: Finding common ground for multiparty problems.* San Francisco, CA: Jossey-Bass Publishers.

Grimmett, P. P., & Crehan, E. P. (1992). The nature of collegiality in teacher development: The case of clinical supervision. In M. Fullan & A. Hargreaves (Eds.), *Teacher Development and Educational Change* (pp. 56–85). New York, NY: Falmer Press.

Hargreaves, A. (1994). *Changing teachers, changing times: Teachers' work and culture in the postmodern age.* New York, NY: Teachers College Press.

————. (1996). Revisiting voice. *Educational Researcher,* 25 (1), 12–19.

————. (1997). *Rethinking educational change with heart and mind.* Alexandria, VA: Association for Supervision and Curriculum Development.

Hargreaves, A., & Fullan, M. (1992). Introduction. In Hargreaves, A. & M. G. Fullan (Eds.), *Understanding Teacher Development* (pp. 1–19). New York, NY: Teachers College Press.

Havelock, R.G. (with Zlotolow, S.). (1995). *The change agent's guide.* 2nd ed. Englewood Cliffs, NJ: Educational Technology Publications.

Herbert, G. (1651). *Jacula Prudentury.* London, England: T. Maxey.

Hopkins, D. (1990). Integrating staff development and school improvement: A study of teacher personality and school climate. In Joyce, B (Ed.), *Changing School Culture Through Staff Development* (pp. 41–67). Alexandria, VA: Association for Supervision and Curriculum Development.

Hord, S. M., Rutherford, W. L., Huling-Austin, L., & Hall, G. E. (1987). *Taking charge of change.* Alexandria, VA: Association of Supervision and Curriculum Development.

Huberman A. M., & Miles, M. B. (1984). *Innovation up close: How school improvement works.* New York, NY: Plenum Press.

Jacobs, H. H. (1989a). Descriptions of two existing interdisciplinary programs. In H. H. Jacobs (Ed.), *Interdisciplinary Curriculum: Design and Implementation.* Alexandria, VA: Association for Supervision and Curriculum Development, (pp. 53–66).

———. (1989b). Design options for an integrated curriculum. In H. H. Jacobs (Ed.), *Interdisciplinary Curriculum: Design and Implementation.* Alexandria, VA: Association for Supervision and Curriculum Development, (pp. 13–24).

———. (1989c). The growing need for interdisciplinary curriculum content. In H. H. Jacobs (Ed.), *Interdisciplinary Curriculum: Design and Implementation.* Alexandria, VA: Association for Supervision and Curriculum Development, (pp. 1–11).

———. (1989d). The interdisciplinary concept model: A step-by-step approach for developing integrated units of study. In H. H. Jacobs (Ed.), *Interdisciplinary Curriculum: Design and Implementation.* VA: Association for Supervision and Curriculum Development, (pp. 53–65).

———. (1995, October). School structures: Systematic design and redesign. *Restructuring Your School: Integrated / Thematic Curriculum and Assessment.* Conference conducted by the National School Conference Institute, New York, NY.

Joyce, B., & Showers, B. (1995). *Student achievement through staff development: Fundamentals of school renewal,* 2nd ed. New York, NY: Longman Publishers.

Kouzes, J. M., & Posner, B. Z. (1995). *The leadership challenge.* San Francisco, CA: Jossey-Bass Publishers.

Lieberman, A., & Miller, L. (1984). *Teachers, their world, and their work.* Alexandria, VA: Association for Supervision and Curriculum Development.

Lincoln, Y. S., & Guba, E. G. (1985). *Naturalistic inquiry.* Newbury Park, CA: Sage Publications.

Lortie, D. C. (1975). *Schoolteacher: A sociological study*. Chicago, IL: University of Chicago Press.

Louis, K. S., & King, J. A. (1993). Professional cultures and reforming schools: Does the myth of Sisyphus apply? In J. Murphy & P. Hallinger (Eds.), *Restructuring Schools: Learning From Ongoing Efforts* (pp. 216–250). Thousand Oaks, CA: Corwin Press.

Maeroff, G. I. (1993). *Team building for school change: Equipping teachers for new roles*. New York, NY: Teachers College Press.

Marshall, C., & Rossman, G. B. (1995). *Designing qualitative research*. 2nd ed. Newbury Park, CA: Sage Publications.

Martin-Kniep, G. O., Feige, D. M., & Soodak, L. C. (1995, Spring). Curriculum integration: An expanded view of an abused idea. *Journal of Curriculum & Supervision, 10*, 227–249.

Merriam, S. B. (1988). *Case study research in education: A qualitative approach*. San Francisco, CA: Jossey-Bass Publishers.

Moustakas, C. (1994). *Phenomenological research methods*. Newbury Park, CA: Sage Publications.

Murphy, J. (1990). The educational reform movement of the 1980s: A comprehensive analysis. In J. Murphy (Ed.), *The Educational Reform Movement of the 1980s: Perspectives and Cases*. Berkeley, CA: McCutchan.

———. (1991). *Restructuring schools: Capturing and assessing the phenomena*. New York, NY: Teachers College Press.

Murphy J., & Hallinger, P. (1993). Restructuring schools: Learning from ongoing efforts. In J. Murphy & P. Hallinger (Eds.), *Restructuring Schools: Learning From Ongoing Efforts* (pp. 251–272). Thousand Oaks, CA: Corwin Press.

Nias, J. (1986). Teacher socialization: The individual in the system. Victoria, Australia: Deaken University Press.

———. (1987). Seeing anew: Teachers' theories of action. Victoria, Australia: Deaken University Press.

Palmer, J. M. (1995). Interdisciplinary curriculum—again. In J. A. Beane (Ed.), *Toward a Coherent Curriculum: 1995 Yearbook of the Association for Supervision and Curriculum Development*. Alexandria, VA: Association for Supervision and Curriculum Development, (pp. 55–61).

Panaritis, P. (1995, April). Beyond brainstorming to planning a successful interdisciplinary program. *Phi Delta Kappan, 76*, 623–628.

Pate, P. E., McGinnis, K., & Homestead, E. (1995). Creating coherence through curriculum integration. In J. A. Beane (Ed.), *Toward a Coherent Curriculum: 1995 Yearbook of the Association for Supervision and Curriculum Development*. Alexandria, VA: Association for Supervision and Curriculum Development, (pp. 62–70).

Patton, M. Q. (1990). *Qualitative evaluation and research methods*, 2nd. ed. Newbury Park, CA: Sage Publications.

Pavese, C. (1961). *The burning brand—diaries 1935–1950* (R. E. Murch with Jeanne Moui Trans.) New York, NY: Walker.

Perkins, D. N. (1989). Selecting fertile themes for integrated learning. In H. H. Jacobs (Ed.), *Interdisciplinary Curriculum: Design and Implementation.* Alexandria, VA: Association for Supervision and Curriculum Development, (pp. 67–76).

Peters, T., Schubeck, K., & Hopkins, K. (1995, April). A thematic approach: Theory and practice at the Aleknagik School. *Phi Delta Kappan, 76,* 633–636.

Proust, M. (1981). *Remembrance of Things Past* (C. K. Scott Moncrieff and Terrence Kilmartin, trans.) New York, NY: Random House.

Robertson, H. (1992). Teacher development and gender equity. In Hargreaves, A. & M. G. Fullan (Eds.), *Understanding Teacher Development* (pp. 43–61). New York, NY: Teachers College Press.

Rosenholtz, S. J. (1991). Teachers' workplace: The social organization of schools. New York, NY: Teachers College Press.

Rossman, G. B., Corbett, H. D., & Firestone, W. A. (1988). *Change and effectiveness in schools: A cultural perspective.* Albany, NY: State University of New York Press.

Saranson, S. (1971). *The culture of the school and the problem of change.* Boston, MA: Allyn and Bacon.

Seidman, I. E. (1991). *Interviewing as qualitative research: A guide for researchers in education and the social sciences.* New York, NY: Teachers College Press.

Sergiovanni, T. J., & Starrat, R. J. (1998). *Supervision: A redefinition, 6th Ed.* New York, NY: McGraw Hill.

Sikes, P. J. (1992). Imposed change and the experienced teacher. In M. Fullan & A. Hargreaves (Eds.), *Teacher Development and Educational Change* (pp. 36–55). Washington, DC: Falmer Press.

Siskin, L. S. & Little, J. W. (1995). *The subjects in question: Departmental organization and the high school.* New York, NY: Teachers College Press.

Snyder, J., Bolin, F., & Zumwalt, K. (1992). Curriculum implementation. In P. W. Jackson (Ed.), *Handbook of Research on Curriculum: A Project of the American Educational Research Association* (pp. 402–435). New York, NY: Macmillan Publishing Company.

Stoll, L. (1992). Teacher growth in the effective school. In M. Fullan & A. Hargreaves (Eds.), *Teacher Development and Educational Change* (pp. 104–122). New York, NY: Falmer Press.

Strauss, A., & Corbin, J. (1990). *Basics of qualitative research: Grounded theory and procedures and techniques.* Newbury Park, CA: Sage Publications.

Waller, W. (1965). *The sociology of teaching,* New York, NY: John Wiley and Sons.

Watson, N., & Fullan, M. G. (1992). Beyond school district-university partnerships. In M. Fullan & A. Hargreaves (Eds.), *Teacher Development and Educational Change* (pp. 213–242). New York, NY: Falmer Press.

Webb, J., Corbett, H. D., & Wilson, B. L. (1993). Restructuring systematically for students: Can it be more than just talk? In J. Murphy & P. Hallinger (Eds.), *Restructuring Schools: Learning From Ongoing Efforts* (pp. 188–215). Thousuand Oaks, CA: Corwin Press.

Wideen, M. F. (1992). School-based teacher development. In M. Fullan & A. Hargreaves (Eds.), *Teacher Development and Educational Change* (pp. 123–155). New York, NY: Falmer Press.

Willis, G. (1991). Phenomenological inquiry: Life-world perceptions. In E. C. Short (Ed.), *Forms of Curriculum Inquiry* (pp. 173–186). Albany, NY: State University of New York Press.

Index